Writing Exercises

Building, Combining, and Revising

RICHARD F. NORDQUIST

ARMSTRONG STATE COLLEGE

Writing Exercises
Building, Combining, and Revising

MACMILLAN PUBLISHING COMPANY

NEW YORK

Collier Macmillan Publishers

LONDON

Macmillan Publishing Company
866 Third Avenue, New York, New York 10022

Collier Macmillan Canada, Inc.

Library of Congress Cataloging in Publication Data

Nordquist, Richard F.
  Writing exercises.

  Includes index.
  1. English language—Rhetoric—Problems, exercises, etc. 2. College readers. I. Title.
PE1408.N78 1985   808′.042   84-7842
ISBN 0-02-388220-4

Printing: 1 2 3 4 5 6 7 8 Year: 5 6 7 8 9 0 1 2 3

ISBN 0-02-388220-4

To the Instructor

Writing Exercises: Building, Combining, and Revising is a text for students in freshman composition courses. It offers a collection of sentence-combining exercises integrated with readings from the works of both student and professional writers. The aim of this book is to improve the overall quality of students' writing by giving them practice in building and revising sentences, paragraphs, and essays.

Over the past twenty years, sentence combining has come to be accepted as an effective way of improving students' ability to manipulate sentence structures. Thus, sentence combining has often been viewed as a friendly alternative to traditional grammar instruction, and such exercises have been associated primarily with the editing stage of the writing process. The premise of this book is that sentence combining can involve students in the *whole* writing process. The prominence of whole discourse exercises, the attention to prewriting, revising, and editing in the Discovery sections of Part I, and the numerous writing suggestions throughout the book all attempt to involve students in making rhetorical as well as grammatical decisions. In fact, many of the combining exercises themselves are presented as prewriting activities—warm-ups for the original compositions that are the true test of a writer's development.

The book's flexible structure and its wide range of exercises and essays allow for a variety of teaching approaches. For instance, Parts I and II may be treated in successive courses or may be combined in one course, with the exercises in Part II supplementing those in Part I. Likewise, the process-oriented Discovery sections may be studied without regard to context or sequence, perhaps together quite early in the course. And for instructors who prefer not to follow the traditional modes of discourse, an alternative table of contents in the Instructor's Guide groups the exercise and essays according to theme.

The Instructor's Guide is available from the publisher. In addition to providing the original sentences, paragraphs, and essays that served as models for the exercises in Part I, the guide suggests ways to use and evaluate these exercises in the classroom. It also contains discussion questions to accompany the essays in Part II.

I have been guided by the work of many specialists in the field of composition and sentence combining, but my greatest debt is to John Mellon of the University of Illinois at Chicago Circle, not only for his pioneering research (which has benefited us all), but also for his incisive reviews of this book in manuscript. I am grateful to Susan Didriksen, my editor at Macmillan, for securing John Mellon's assistance and for guiding this book from start to finish. I am also grateful to Kathleen E. Bell of the University of Miami, Jack Seltzer of Pennsylvania State University, John Clifford of the University of North Carolina at Wilmington, Miriam Chaplin of Rutgers University, James Berlin of the University of Cincinnati, Margaret P. Hassest of the University of Delaware, Frank Patterson of Central Missouri State University, and Douglas Salerno of Washtenaw Community College for their thoughtful reviews of the manuscript. Finally, I am grateful to Joel Brauser of Macmillan, and to Margaret B. Yamashita for a meticulous copyediting job.

I could not have written the book without the encouragement and assistance of my friends and colleagues at Armstrong State College. In particular, I want to thank Jackie Alwan, Lorie Roth, and Charles White for reviewing the manuscript and Denise Stahl for her help in the library. Special thanks also to Kent Brooks, Brad Crain, Jim Jones, and Bob Strozier for sharing their wisdom and wisecracks. I am particularly grateful to the tutors in the Writing Center: Margaret Brockland, Pat Conway-Polk, Debbie Haymans, Shyla Nambiar, Donna Nauschuetz, and Betty Reesor. Finally, I thank my students for sharing their discoveries and for teaching me so much about writing.

To the Student

Another English course, another textbook, another chance to scribble for another instructor: after all these years, you may be wondering, isn't it about time somebody recognized that you already know how to write? Just how much blue ink must you spill—and how much red ink must be spilled on your work—before you can be treated as a writer? Not as a dictating machine, or a grammarian, or a proofreader, but as a bona fide *writer.*

That is the premise of this book—that you are a writer, that you have been putting words on paper since you were quite young in order to share your ideas and experiences with others. You don't earn a living from your writing, as some professionals do, but writing is a part of your life. The exercises and readings in this book will give you many opportunities to write and will help you become a better writer.

What sort of exercises? There are several types, but essentially you will be building sentences, paragraphs, and essays by combining sets of short, choppy sentences into longer, more effective ones. This will give you greater control over your writing *style*—that is, the way you shape your ideas in writing. Chapter 1 will introduce you to some of the basic techniques of sentence combining.

What sort of readings? There are over fifty short essays in this book, some by student writers and others by professionals. They are here to be read, studied, and enjoyed. But more than that, they are linked with the exercises so that you can share in the experience of creating them. How you will be able to do that will also be explained in Chapter 1.

All of these exercises and readings would be of little benefit if you had no opportunity to apply your skills in original compositions. The many writing suggestions throughout the book will give you this opportunity. In addition, the Discovery sections at the end of each chapter will show you ways of finding topics and material for essays. They will also encourage you to examine your role as a writer and help you to recognize the needs of your readers.

Good writing takes work—and you will find much in this book that you can work with. But work does not have to be drudgery. Completing the exercises here can give you the pleasure of discovering what you can do with language and the satisfaction of seeing your writing improve.

Contents

CHAPTER 3   *Coordination*   43

CHAPTER 4   *Building with Adjective Clauses*   69

CHAPTER 8 *Building with Absolutes*   *159*

CHAPTER 9 *Building with Noun Clauses and Phrases*   *180*

PART I

Building Sentences, Paragraphs, and Essays

CHAPTER 1

An Introduction to Sentence Combining

If you skim through the first few chapters of this book, you will find several different types of exercises: Building, Revising, Expanding, and Recombining. Although the titles and the formats differ, most of the exercises will give you practice in combining sets of short, choppy sentences into longer, more effective ones. Such practice will help you become a more versatile writer, as you will see in this chapter. Here you will also learn some basic techniques of sentence combining and find out what distinguishes the various exercises.

Building Sentences

Each chapter after this in Part I will first introduce you to different sentence structures and then give you practice in using these structures. In some exercises (Sentence Building, Sentence Revising, Sentence Expanding) you will work with the structures to create individual sentences. In others (Building Paragraphs and Essays, Recombining) you will not only create sentences but also organize them into paragraphs and essays. The difference between the two types of exercises is more a matter of focus than of technique. Both require you to use combining strategies to build new sentences.

To find out what sentence combining involves, consider this short

Sentence Building exercise. See how many ways you can combine the three short sentences below into one longer sentence:

Walt Disney's Mickey Mouse was an influence.
He influenced the culture.
The culture was American.

By rearranging certain words, changing their forms, cutting out repetitious words and phrases, and adding new words to make clear connections, you should be able to create two or three different combinations, such as the following:

1. Walt Disney's Mickey Mouse was an influence on American culture.
2. Walt Disney's Mickey Mouse influenced American culture.
3. American culture was influenced by Walt Disney's Mickey Mouse.

There is no single correct answer to this short exercise, or indeed to any of the Sentence Building exercises. Good writing depends on a willingness to experiment, not merely on avoiding "mistakes."

But, you may be wondering, what is the point of combining sets of short sentences into longer ones? After all, you already know how to write sentences much longer than those that appear in the exercises. And why should long sentences be preferable to short ones? The answer is that they are not. Building effective sentences, not long ones, is the aim of sentence combining. In fact, you may now write sentences that are so long that your readers sometimes get tangled in them. Or you may have a habit of tacking sentences together with one *and* after another, without distinguishing between major points and minor details. Or you may write sentences that, again, are perfectly correct but that all sound the same and thus lull your readers when you would rather stimulate them. Then again, you may be satisfied with your ability to build sentences but feel that your paragraphs are choppy—that you need to make clearer transitions from one sentence to the next and from one paragraph to the next. All of these concerns are related to the skills practiced in sentence combining. Such practice will help you write sentences that are clear, coherent, emphatic, and varied in their sound and structure.

As a way of previewing some of the structures to be introduced in later chapters, try the following Sentence Building exercise—an expanded, more ambitious version of the one you have already done. Combine the following sentences in as many ways as you can, first, by creating six new sentences out of the original twelve and, then, by reducing the number of sentences to three, two, or even one. Don't be concerned about finding the "best" combination at this point; just create as many different versions as you can.

> Walt Disney's Mickey Mouse was an influence.
> He influenced the culture.
> The culture was American.
> He was one of the most disastrous influences ever to hit.
> Mickey Mouse was an idiot optimist.
> He marched forth every week.
> He marched forth in Technicolor.
> He marched forth against a battalion of cats.
> He humiliated them.
> He did this invariably.
> He did this with one trick after another.
> The tricks were clever.

Try combining these sentences on your own before you look at the sample combinations below.

There are countless ways of putting these sentences together, and so don't be surprised if your new sentences are not identical to any of the nine sample combinations that follow. Remember that sentence combining calls on you to experiment, not to seek "correct answers."

Our first version consists of six sentences instead of the original twelve:

1. Walt Disney's Mickey Mouse was an influence on American culture. He was one of the most disastrous influences ever to hit. Mickey Mouse was an idiot optimist. He marched forth each week in Technicolor against a batallion of cats. He invariably humiliated them. He did this with one clever trick after another.

A fairly simple way of combining sentences is to eliminate certain repeated words and phrases (such as *influenced, marched forth*) and to put related ideas next to each other in the same sentence. That's what has been done here. However, the fact that there still are several pronouns (*he* is repeated four times) referring to the same noun *(Mickey Mouse)* gives us a clue that more combinations are possible.

In this next version, the twelve original sentences have been combined into three new ones:

2. Walt Disney's Mickey Mouse was one of the most disastrous cultural influences ever to hit America. Each week that idiot optimist marched

5

forth in Technicolor against a battalion of cats. Invariably he humiliated them with one clever trick after another.

The sentences have been combined here by eliminating the pronoun
he in a number of places and by putting modifying words and phrases
closer to the words they refer to. This technique is discussed in
Chapter 2: Building with Simple Modifiers.

Adding the word and lets us make a different combination, one
with just two sentences:

3. One of America's most disastrous cultural influences was Walt Disney's Mickey Mouse. That idiot optimist marched forth each week
   in Technicolor against a battalion of cats, and he invariably humiliated them with one trick after another.

This technique (called *coordination*) is discussed in Chapter 3.

In the rest of our examples, the twelve original sentences have
been combined into just one sentence, each time according to a different method. Each method is discussed in a later chapter, as shown
in parentheses after the sample combination.

4. One of the most disastrous cultural influences ever to hit America
   was Walt Disney's Mickey Mouse, who each week would march
   forth in Technicolor against a battalion of cats, which invariably
   were humiliated by the idiot optimist's various tricks.
   (Chapter 4: Building with Adjective Clauses)
5. One of the most disastrous cultural influences ever to hit America
   was Walt Disney's Mickey Mouse, that idiot optimist who each week
   marched forth against a battalion of cats, invariably humiliating them
   with one clever trick after another.
   (Chapter 5: Building with Appositives)
6. Walt Disney's Mickey Mouse, one of the most disastrous cultural
   influences ever to hit America, each week would march forth in
   Technicolor against a battalion of cats so that he could humiliate
   them with one clever trick after another.
   (Chapter 6: Building with Adverb Clauses)
7. Each week marching forth against a battalion of cats, invariably humiliating them with one clever trick after another, Walt Disney's
   Mickey Mouse, that idiot optimist, was one of the most disastrous
   cultural influences ever to hit America.
   (Chapter 7: Building with Participle Phrases)
8. One of the most disastrous influences on American culture was Walt
   Disney's Mickey Mouse, that idiot optimist who each week marched

forth against a battalion of cats, his clever tricks invariably humiliating them.

(Chapter 8: Building with Absolutes)

9. The fact that each week Walt Disney's Mickey Mouse would march forth in Technicolor against a battalion of cats to humiliate them with one clever trick after another has made this idiot optimist one of the most disastrous influences on American culture.

(Chapter 9: Building with Noun Clauses and Phrases)

Although you have probably seen all of these structures before in your reading, you may have been reluctant to use them all in your own writing. But as you work your way through the exercises in this book you will gain the experience and confidence needed to use these structures effectively.

Evaluating Sentence Combinations

After you have combined a set of sentences in a variety of ways, you can then take time to evaluate your work and decide which combinations you like and which ones you don't. You may do this evaluation on your own or in a group in which you will have a chance to compare your sentences with those of others. In either case, read your sentences out loud when you evaluate them: how they *sound* to you can be just as revealing as how they look.

There are six qualities that you need to consider when you evaluate your new sentences. Each of these qualities, mentioned just briefly below, will be discussed in greater detail throughout the book.

1. *Meaning.* As far as you can determine, have you conveyed the idea intended by the original author?
2. *Clarity.* Is the sentence clear? Can it be understood on the first reading?
3. *Coherence.* Do the various parts parts of the sentence fit together logically and smoothly?
4. *Emphasis.* Are key words and phrases put in emphatic positions (usually at the very end or the very beginning of the sentence)?
5. *Conciseness.* Does the sentence clearly express an idea without wasting words?
6. *Rhythm.* Does the sentence flow, or is it marked by interruptions? Do the interruptions help emphasize key points (an effective technique), or do they merely distract (an ineffective technique)?

These six qualities are so closely related that one cannot be easily separated from another. The significance of the qualities—and their interrelationship—will become clearer to you as you do the exercises in the following chapters. In the meantime, either on your own or with the class, use these criteria to evaluate your combinations of the "Mickey Mouse" sentences.

Revising and Expanding Sentences

In addition to Sentence Building exercises, each chapter contains Sentence Revising exercises, which ask you to rewrite sentences according to specific instructions. These directed exercises will reinforce the skills you learned earlier in the chapter and prepare you for the undirected exercises later in the chapter.

Four of the chapters in Part 1 contain Sentence Expanding exercises, which give you an opportunity to create original sentences using the structures introduced in that particular chapter. The Sentence Expanding exercises will prepare you for the longer exercises that follow—Building Paragraphs and Essays.

Building Paragraphs and Essays

Each chapter after this in Part 1 contains three exercises in the Building Paragraphs and Essays section. You will again use combining techniques to build sentences, but here you will also put the sentences together in paragraphs and short essays.

Some of these exercises are based on the writings of students and others on essays written by professionals. In neither case are you expected to compete with the original author. Many combinations are possible besides the original ones; in fact, some of these other combinations may prove to be superior to the original sentences.

Often, however, you will have an opportunity to study the writer's style in a particular selection before you go on to complete the essay in the Building exercise. Many of the exercises are preceded by one or more paragraphs from the original essay. Read these carefully to acquaint yourself with the subject matter, the writer's attitude toward the subject, and the writer's way of expressing his or her ideas. In this way you will be guided by the original author but still have the freedom to experiment with different combinations.

Exercise: Building Paragraphs and Essays

The following is a typical exercise in Building Paragraphs and Essays. First you are given three paragraphs from the original essay, "New York Is a City of Things Unnoticed," by Gay Talese. Read these to get a sense of the author's subject and style. Then go on to complete the exercise, which consists of twenty-three sentences arranged in seven sets. Be guided by the sets (the sentences in each may be combined into a single sentence), but don't feel restricted by them. You are free to combine the sets or to make two or more sentences out of one set. You may rearrange the sentences in any fashion that seems suitable. Now, after reading the introductory paragraphs, do the exercise, combining the sets of short sentences into one clear paragraph. After you have done this, you can compare your paragraph with the four sample combinations.

New York Is a City of Things Unnoticed

New York is a city of things unnoticed. It is a city with cats sleeping under parked cars, two stone armadillos crawling up St. Patrick's Cathedral, and thousands of ants creeping on top of the Empire State Building. The ants probably were carried up there by wind or birds, but nobody is sure; nobody in New York knows any more about the ants than they do about the panhandler who takes taxis to the Bowery; or the dapper man who picks trash out of Sixth Avenue trash cans; or the medium in the West Seventies who claims, "I am clairvoyant, clairaudient, and clairsensuous."

New York is a city for eccentrics and a center for odd bits of information. New Yorkers blink twenty-eight times a minute, but forty when tense. Most popcorn chewers at Yankee Stadium stop chewing momentarily just before the pitch. Gumchewers on Macy's escalators stop chewing momentarily just before they get off—to concentrate on the last step. Coins, paper clips, ball-point pens, and little girls' pocketbooks are found by workmen when they clean the lion's pool at the Bronx Zoo.

A Park Avenue doorman has parts of three bullets in his head—there since World War I. Several young gypsy daughters, influenced by television and literacy, are running away from home because they don't want to grow up and become fortune tellers. Each month a hundred pounds of hair is delivered to Louis Feder on 545 Fifth Avenue, where blond hairpieces are made from German women's hair; brunette hair-pieces from Italian women's hair; but no hairpieces from American women's hair which, says Mr. Feder, is weak from too frequent rinses and permanents.

1. A saxophone player stands on the sidewalk.
   He stands there each afternoon.
   He is in New York.
   He is rather seedy.
   He plays *Danny Boy*.
2. He plays in a sad way.
   He plays in a sensitive way.
   He soon has half the neighborhood peeking out of windows.
   They toss nickles, dimes, and quarters at his feet.
3. Some of the coins roll under parked cars.
   Most of them are caught in his hand.
   His hand is outstretched.
4. The saxophone player is a street musician.
   He is named Joe Gabler.
5. He has serenaded every block in New York City.
   He has been serenading for the past fifty years.
   He has sometimes been tossed as much as $100 a day.
   This $100 is in coins.
6. He is also hit with buckets of water.
   He is hit with beer cans.
   The cans are empty.
   He is chased by wild dogs.
7. He is believed to be the last of New York's ancient street musicians.

Note that the seventh set contains just one sentence. Because most paragraphs are made up of both long and short sentences, you will sometimes find one-sentence sets in the exercises. You have the choice of either copying these sentences as they are or combining them with the sentences in another set.

Countless combinations are possible in these exercises. Read the four sample combinations below and compare them with your own.

Combination A

A rather seedy saxophone player stands on the sidewalk each afternoon in New York and plays *Danny Boy*. He plays in a sad, sensitive way and soon has half the neighborhood peeking out of windows and tossing nickels, dimes, and quarters at his feet. Some of the coins roll under parked cars, but most are caught in his outstretched hand. The saxo-

10

phone player, Joe Gabler, is a street musician. He has serenaded every block in New York for the past thirty years, and he has sometimes been tossed as much as $100 a day in coins. He is also hit with buckets of water and empty beer cans, and he is chased by wild dogs. He is believed to be the last of New York's ancient street musicians.

Combination B

Each afternoon in New York a rather seedy saxophone player stands on the sidewalk playing *Danny Boy* in such a sad, sensitive way that he soon has half the neighborhood peeking out of windows tossing nickels, dimes and quarters at his feet. Some of the coins roll under parked cars, but most of them are caught in his outstretched hand. The saxophone player is a street musician named Joe Gabler; for the past thirty years he has serenaded every block in New York and has sometimes been tossed as much as $100 a day in coins. He is also hit with buckets of water, empty beer cans and eggs, and chased by wild dogs. He is believed to be the last of New York's ancient street musicians.

Combination C

Each afternoon in New York a rather seedy saxophone player, Joe Gabler, stands on the sidewalk playing *Danny Boy* in a sad, sensitive way. For the past thirty years he has serenaded every block in New York and has sometimes been tossed as much as $100 a day in nickels, dimes, and quarters. Some of the coins roll under parked cars, but most of them are caught in his outstretched hand. He is also hit with buckets of water, empty beer cans, and eggs, and sometimes he is chased by wild dogs. Joe Gabler is believed to be the last of New York's ancient street musicians.

Combination D

In New York each afternoon a rather seedy saxophone player named Joe Gabler stands on the sidewalk and plays *Danny Boy* in a sad, sensitive way, so that soon half the neighborhood is peeking out of windows and tossing nickels, dimes, and quarters at his feet, some of which roll under parked cars but most of which are caught in his outstretched hand; sometimes he is tossed as much as $100 a day, although he is also hit with buckets of water, empty beer cans, and eggs, and he is chased by wild dogs. He has serenaded every block in New York for the past thirty years and is believed to be the last of New York's ancient street musicians.

Evaluating Paragraph and Essay Combinations

We can evaluate paragraphs and essays according to the same criteria used to judge individual sentences: meaning, clarity, coherence, emphasis, conciseness, and rhythm. Of course we must now consider these qualities in regard to how effectively the sentences work together. The following chapters will give you practice in making such evaluations, and Chapter 10 in particular will show you some techniques for making clear transitions from one sentence to the next. In the meantime, let us briefly consider the effectiveness of the four combinations just seen.

Most readers would agree that paragraphs A, B, and C are fairly clear, concise, and smooth. The seven sentences in paragraph A follow the order of the seven sets in the exercise. Although there are still opportunities to eliminate a few words and make further connections, the sentences are logically ordered and clearly related to one another. Paragraph B is similar to A, but here there are just five sentences as a result of joining sets 1 and 2 with the participle *playing* (discussed in Chapter 7) and sets 4 and 5 with a semicolon (discussed in Chapter 3). Paragraph C also contains five sentences, but the information has been rearranged, and a new structure (an appositive, discussed in Chapter 5) has been used in the first sentence. This new arrangement appears to be at least as clear and logical as that followed in the original sets.

Only paragraph D presents serious problems. The seven sets have been combined into just two sentences, and the reader may well feel overwhelmed by all the information packed into them. The structures used in this paragraph (several adjective and adverb clauses, discussed in Chapters 4 and 6) can be quite effective, but they are overworked here, and the paragraph's clarity, coherence, and rhythm suffer as a result.

It is worth repeating that the aim of sentence combining is not to make *long* sentences but to create *effective* sentences, paragraphs, and essays. Paragraph D needs to be broken down into shorter units that then can be recombined more effectively. In fact, five of the chapters in Unit 1 contain recombining exercises. The paragraphs in these exercises contain too many long sentences that are often awkward and unclear. You will be asked to untangle the sentences by first breaking them down into shorter sentences and then recombining them.

If you are interested in comparing your sentences with those created by the original writers, you will enjoy working out the Paragraph and Essay Building exercises in Part 2. The first part of each chapter consists of Building exercises like those we have just seen; the second part of the chapter contains the paragraphs and essays that served as models for the exercises. When you do these exercises, evaluate the original composition as well as your own, and keep in mind that your combinations, though sometimes different from the original ones, may be just as effective as they are or even superior to them. As an example, in the "New York City" exercise just seen, Combination B is the paragraph that appears in Gay Talese's original essay, but some readers may prefer Combination C to the original.

Summary

This chapter previewed the various types of exercises found throughout the book—Building, Revising, Expanding, and Recombining—and introduced some of the basic techniques of sentence combining. The next chapters will show how to build and arrange many different sentence structures and will offer many opportunities to use these structures in building sentences, paragraphs, and essays.

As a way of practicing what you have learned so far and preparing yourself for what lies ahead, try the Paragraph and Essay Building exercise below before moving on to the next chapter.

Exercise: Building Paragraphs and Essays

This exercise has been adapted from the final two paragraphs of an essay written by Sandy Klem, a student. Read the first four paragraphs of her essay, and then combine the sentences in each set. Feel free to rearrange the sentences, combine the sets, or make two or more sentences out of one set. Experiment with different combinations until you are satisfied that your two paragraphs are clear and concise.

13

Composing

Sandy is sitting at her desk, nervously tugging at her frizzy hair and worrying about the essay she should have written for her English class. Three days ago she was given the assignment, and now the paper is due in just one hour. She uncaps her Bic, carefully prints her name at the top of the page, and then squeezes her eyes shut as she waits for inspiration.

Writing about summer vacations, embarrassing moments, and the adventures of a quarter has never been one of her favorite pastimes. She would rather be outside missing a bus (it would be less frustrating) or catching a cold (it would be more enjoyable). Still, after burning hamburger patties all summer to pay for her tuition she is not about to throw in the towel—or the writing tablet—in this, the second week of the term.

Perhaps, she thinks, a few aerobic exercises will send the creative juices shooting up to her skull. She turns on the stereo, loud, and begins to gyrate across the room. Her souvenir spoons rattle on the dresser, posters unhinge themselves from the walls, and empty wine bottles shimmy off the book shelf and crash to the floor. Still, she receives no inspiration, just threats and curses from a few late-sleepers down the hall.

She squelches the stereo and trudges back to her desk. The blank sheet of paper stares at her, almost snickering it seems. She retaliates by defacing it with loops and squiggles and curlicues that puncture the paper. That accomplished, she glances at the clock: forty minutes to go.

1. She takes a fresh sheet of paper.
   She writes her name.
   She writes it once.
   She writes it twice.
   She writes it twenty times.
2. Then she crumples it into a ball.
   She tosses it at the alarm clock.
   The alarm clock is glowering.
3. She misses.
4. Her future flashes before her eyes.
5. She will be a failed writer.
   She will be a college drop-out.
6. She will become one of those bag ladies.
   Those ladies sleep in doorways.
   They drink sterno.

They argue with themselves.
They argue on buses.
7. Her life will be a summer vacation.
The vacation will be endless.
It will be a vacation with cold weather.
It will be a vacation with rainy weather.
8. Her life will be one embarrassing moment.
The moment will be long.
9. She will not have a quarter to her name.
She will never enjoy a single adventure.
10. Sandy picks up her pen.
She begins to write.
11. She writes quickly.
She writes with determination.
She writes with enthusiasm.
12. Here is how her essay begins: "Sandy is sitting at her desk, nervously tugging at her frizzy hair and worrying about the essay she should have written for her English class. . . ."

Writing Suggestion

Writing can sometimes be a pleasure and sometimes a pain. In a paragraph recall a writing experience that you found enjoyable. You may have been writing an assigned essay, a letter to a close friend, or perhaps a story or poem. Describe this particular "composing" experience and explain what made it so pleasurable. Then write another paragraph, this time describing a writing task that was particularly troublesome or nerve-racking. What made this writing experience so painful?

Discovery: Your Role As a Writer

You are a writer—but what sort of writer are you? How much and what kinds of writing have you done in your life? What is your attitude toward writing? Is it something you usually enjoy or dread? Answering questions like these in a letter to your instructor will help you discover your role as a writer.

This is not a composition assignment but a chance to write an informal letter of introduction to your instructor. You will tell that person something about your writing background, skills, and expectations and in so doing gain a clearer sense of what you hope to gain from your composition course and the exercises in this textbook.

Use the suggestions and questions below as a guide when you write your letter. Feel free, however, to provide additional information that you think will help define your role as a writer.

1. Describe your background as a writer. What kinds of writing were you most frequently asked to do in school— short reports, essays, journals, research papers, fiction? What sort of writing do you do outside school—letters, articles, fiction, poetry?

2. Describe what steps you follow during a typical writing project. How do you get started? Are you in the habit of writing several drafts, or do you attempt to write a perfect paper right from the start? Do you spend much time planning what you are going to say and how to organize it? Have you ever suffered from "writer's block," and if so how do you overcome it?

3. Identify your strengths and weaknesses as a writer. Perhaps you have no trouble connecting and organizing your ideas, but you feel it takes too long to discover those ideas in the first place. Or maybe you are satisfied that your writing is usually "correct," but not as interesting as it could be. Be as specific as you can in your self-evaluation.

4. Describe your attitude toward writing. Is writing something that you usually enjoy doing? Or is it just work? Are you interested in improving your writing skills? What connection do you see between good writing skills and success in college? How important do you expect writing will be in the career you are pursuing?

Be sure to make a copy of the letter before you give it to your instructor. At the end of the course you can read the letter again and reevaluate your role as a writer.

CHAPTER 2

Building with Simple Modifiers

Modifiers are words and phrases that add to the meaning of other words in a sentence. In this chapter you will be combining sentences that contain *simple modifiers:* adjectives, adverbs, and prepositional phrases. The simple modifiers themselves should be nothing new to you; in fact you have been using them since you first started to write. But the simple modifiers, like other structures, can be used either effectively or ineffectively. The exercises in this chapter will give you practice in arranging adjectives, adverbs, and prepositional phrases so that your sentences are clear, interesting, and forceful.

The Simple Modifiers

Sometimes the shortest sentences are the most effective. We might write the following sentence, for instance, and be satisfied that we have expressed an idea succinctly:

The pensioners wait.

But what if we wanted to tell our reader more than this—more about how the pensioners are feeling, perhaps? We then could add a few sentences containing adjectives that describe the pensioners:

> The pensioners are confused.
> The pensioners are afraid.
> The pensioners are destitute.

To describe how they are waiting, we could place an adverb after the verb:

> The pensioners wait submissively.

To explain where they are waiting, we could introduce a prepositional phrase:

> The pensioners are in the hallway.

Finally, we might want to describe the hallway, and so we use another adjective:

> The hallway is dreary.

Now we can combine all of these details in one sentence. Here is one way:

> Confused, afraid, and destitute, the pensioners wait submissively in the dreary hallway.

Our new sentence is certainly longer than the original one, but it is also more vivid because it uses simple modifiers to describe the feelings of the pensioners and to convey the mood of the scene. Used carelessly, the simple modifiers only make our writing longer, but used carefully, they can make our writing richer and more informative.

Arranging Adjectives

There are other ways to combine the short sentences given above. For example, instead of placing the three adjectives before the noun *pensioners*, we can put them after the noun:

> The pensioners, *confused*, *afraid*, and *destitute*, wait submissively in the dreary hallway.

Or we can break up the list of adjectives, putting one before the noun and two after it:

The *destitute* pensioners, *afraid* and *confused*, wait submissively in the dreary hallway.

Although adjectives more often come before the nouns they modify, they may also come after, particularly if we want to call attention to them in the sentence.

Practice 1

In the following sentence, the three underlined adjectives follow the noun they modify:

Mosquito larva, <u>tiny</u>, <u>white</u>, and <u>eyeless</u>, swam in puddles by the edge of the bridge.

Write two other versions of this sentence. In one, move the three adjectives to the beginning of the sentence, in front of the noun they modify. In the other version, move just one adjective to the beginning, and leave the other two after the noun.
(Sample answers to all Practice exercises are at the end of each chapter. Be sure to do the exercises before you check the answers.)

Arranging Adverbs

Adverbs usually follow the verbs they modify, as we have seen already:

The pensioners wait *submissively*.

However, adverbs that modify verbs may also appear before the verb or at the very beginning or end of a sentence, as shown below.

Arnold *carefully* picked up the vase.
Carefully, Arnold picked up the vase.
Arnold picked up the vase *carefully*.

Not all adverbs are this flexible in all sentences, and so you will need to try them out in different positions until you find an arrangement that sounds both smooth and clear.

Practice 2

Combine the three sentences below in three different ways. First, place the underlined adverb at the very beginning of the sentence. Next, place the adverb before the verb (pulled). Finally, place the adverb at the end of the sentence.

The man pulled out his wallet.
He did this slowly.
The man was old.

Prepositional Phrases

Like adjectives and adverbs, prepositional phrases are used to add meaning to the nouns and verbs in a sentence. A prepositional phrase has two parts—a preposition plus a noun or pronoun. A preposition is a word that shows how the noun or pronoun is related to another word in the sentence. Some of the words commonly used as prepositions are listed below.

about	behind	except	outside
above	below	for	over
across	beneath	from	past
after	beside	in	through
against	between	inside	to
along	beyond	into	under
among	by	near	until
around	despite	of	up
at	down	off	with
before	during	on	without

Prepositional phrases often do more than just add minor details to a sentence; they may, in fact, be needed for a sentence to make sense. Consider the vagueness of this sentence without prepositional phrases:

The workers gather a rich variety and distribute it.

Now observe how the sentence comes into focus when prepositional phrases are added:

> *From many sources,* the workers *at the Community Food Bank* gather a rich variety *of surplus and unsalable food* and distribute it *to soup kitchens, day-care centers, and homes for the elderly.*

Notice how these added prepositional phrases give us more information about certain nouns and verbs in the sentences:

Which workers?
  The workers <u>at the Community Food Bank</u>
What did they gather?
  A rich variety <u>of surplus and unsalable food</u>
Where did they gather the food?
  <u>From many sources</u>
Who did they distribute it to?
  <u>To soup kitchens, day-care centers, and homes for the elderly</u>

Prepositional phrases, like the other simple modifiers, should not be thought of merely as ornaments; rather, they can add details that are important to the meaning of a sentence.

Practice 3

Use simple modifiers to expand the sentence below. Add details that answer the questions in parentheses and make the sentence more interesting and informative.

> Jenny stood, raised her shotgun, aimed, and fired. *(Where did she stand? How did she aim? What did she fire at?)*

Note: There are, of course, no single correct answers to the questions in parentheses. Sentence-expanding exercises such as this one encourage you to use your imagination to build original sentences.

Arranging Prepositional Phrases

A prepositional phrase is frequently placed after the word it modifies, as in the sentence below.

He slipped <u>on the top rung of the ladder.</u>

In this sentence, the phrase <u>on the top rung</u> modifies and directly follows the verb <u>slipped</u>, and the phrase <u>of the ladder</u> modifies and directly follows the noun <u>rung</u>.

Like adverbs, prepositional phrases that modify verbs can often be shifted to either the beginning or the end of a sentence. This is worth keeping in mind when you want to break up a long string of prepositional phrases, as shown below.

> *Original:* We walked down <u>to a souvenir shop on the waterfront after breakfast in our hotel room</u>.
> *Revised:* <u>After breakfast in our hotel room</u> we walked down <u>to a souvenir shop on the waterfront</u>.

The best arrangement is one that is clear and uncluttered.

Practice 4

Break up the long string of prepositional phrases in the sentence below by shifting the underlined phrases to the beginning of the sentence.

Addiction to opiates frequently developed from the abuse of alcohol <u>in the United States during the nineteenth century and the early decades of the twentieth</u>.

Although several prepositional phrases may appear in the same sentence, avoid packing in so many phrases that you confuse the reader. The sentence below, for example, is awkward.

On a rickety stool in one corner of the crowded bar the folk singer sits playing lonesome songs on his battered old guitar about warm beer, cold women, and long nights on the road.

In this case the best way to break up the string of phrases is to make two sentences:

On a rickety stool in one corner of the crowded bar the folk singer sits hunched over his battered old guitar. He plays lonesome songs about warm beer, cold women, and long nights on the road.

Again, remember that a long sentence is not necessarily a good sentence.

22

Practice 5

Break up the long string of phrases in the sentence below by creating two sentences. Be sure to include all the details contained in the original sentence.

Up and down the coast the line of the forest is drawn sharp and clean in the brilliant colors of a wet blue morning in late spring on the edge of a seascape of surf and sky and rocks.

Eliminating Unnecessary Modifiers

We can improve our writing by using adjectives, adverbs, and prepositional phrases that add to the meaning of a sentence. We can also improve our writing by eliminating modifiers that add nothing to the meaning. A good writer does not waste words.

The following sentence is wordy because some of the modifiers are repetitious or insignificant:

Wordy: The steward was really a very friendly and agreeable man, quite round, rotund, and sleek, with a very costly set of dimples around his terribly pleasant smile.

We can make the sentence more concise—and thus more effective—by eliminating the repetitious and overworked modifiers:

Revised: The steward was an agreeable man, rotund and sleek, with a costly set of dimples around his smile.

(Lawrence Durrell, *Bitter Lemons*)

Practice 6

Make this sentence more concise by eliminating unnecessary modifiers:

It was a rainy morning, dull, wet, and gray, in the early part of the month of December.

Here are three other methods that can help make your writing more concise:

1. Try turning prepositional phrases into single adjectives or adverbs.
2. Try eliminating adjectives by using more specific nouns.
3. Try eliminating adverbs by using more specific verbs.

The following sentence can be improved by applying all three methods:

Wordy: The little child walked quietly on the tips of his toes past the very young dog.

By reducing or eliminating several modifiers and using more specific nouns and verbs, we can create a more effective sentence:

Revised: The toddler tiptoed past the puppy.

Revising sentences involves more than just cutting out words, but to revise effectively we need to eliminate words and phrases that add nothing to the sentence's meaning or forcefulness.

Practice 7

Make this sentence more concise by eliminating unnecessary modifiers:

Our boat was entirely surrounded on all sides by sharks in the water around us.

Summary

As we have seen in this chapter, simple modifiers are words and phrases that can make our sentences more interesting and informative. If selected and arranged carefully, these adjectives, adverbs, and prepositional phrases will add to the meaning and forcefulness of our writing.

The exercises that follow will give you more practice in selecting simple modifiers and arranging them in sentences, paragraphs, and essays.

Exercise: Sentence Revising

Rewrite each sentence below according to the instructions in parentheses.

1. The <u>hot, steamy</u> air reeked with the sweet stink of rotten fruit. *(Place the underlined adjectives* after *the word they modify.)*
2. We received a free complimentary copy of a book about the past history of education in America from the salesman. *(Eliminate the unnecessary modifiers and rearrange the details in the sentence to make it more clear.)*
3. The graduating class walked <u>over this rocky area relieved by a few shady tall persimmon trees</u>. *(Move the underlined phrases to the beginning of the sentence.)*
4. The architecture of farms in southern France is <u>squat</u> and <u>horizontal</u> and is dictated by the area's high winds and flat plateaus. *(Place the underlined adjectives before the word they modify and eliminate any unnecessary* ands.*)*
5. In the early part of the month of April we traveled in our car to the city of New Orleans. *(Make the sentence more concise by reducing phrases to single words and eliminating unnecessary modifiers.)*
6. Any listing of twentieth-century America's contribution to the world must surely include motels, <u>along with computers, rock music, and fast foods</u>. *(Move the underlined phrase to the beginning of the sentence.)*
7. With his inky fingers and with his bitten nails and with his cynical manner and with his nervous manner, anybody could tell he didn't belong—belong to the early summer sun, to the cool Whitsun wind off the sea, to the holiday crowd. *(Make this sentence more concise by eliminating any unnecessary prepositions.)*
8. I saw for the first time in my life the high grasslands of the Navajos, the fringes of the Painted Desert, the faraway buttes and mesas of the Hopi country, <u>through the wide open door of my sidedoor Pullman</u>. *(Move the underlined phrases to the beginning of the sentence.)*
9. Patients can regulate the dosage of their own pain medicine after major surgery <u>with a new experimental device</u>. *(Clarify this sentence by shifting the underlined phrase to the beginning.)*

10. Mr. Head's face <u>was</u> long <u>and</u> tubelike, <u>and he had</u> a long, rounded, open jaw, <u>and he had</u> a long, depressed nose. *(Make this sentence more concise by eliminating the underlined words. Begin your revised sentence in this way:* "Mr. Head had a long tubelike face with . . . .")

Exercise: Sentence Building

Combine the sentences in each set into a single, clear sentence with at least one simple modifier. Whenever possible, create a second combination by shifting the modifiers (adjectives, adverbs, prepositional phrases) to different positions in the sentence.

Example

She was our Latin teacher.
We were in high school.
She was tiny.
She was a birdlike woman.
She was swarthy.
She had dark eyes.
Her eyes were sparkling.
Her hair was graying.

Combination A

Our Latin teacher in high school was a birdlike woman, tiny and swarthy, with graying hair and dark sparkling eyes.

Combination B

Our high school Latin teacher was a tiny, birdlike woman, swarthy, with sparkling dark eyes, graying hair.
(Charles W. Morton, *It Has Its Charm*)

1. The boxer finally admitted defeat.
The boxer was weary.
The boxer was dejected.

2. Grandpa dropped his teeth.
His teeth were false.

His teeth dropped into a glass.
There was champagne in the glass.

3. Arthur stood in line.
Arthur stood patiently.
Arthur stood for two hours.
The line was at the soup kitchen.

4. Lucy played.
She was behind the sofa.
She was with her friend.
Her friend was imaginary.
They played for hours.

5. There was a man.
He wore a chicken costume.
He dashed across the field.
He did this before the ball game.
The ball game was on Sunday afternoon.

6. The horse danced about.
But the rider held the reins.
And the rider spoke.
The horse danced nervously.
The rider was young.
The reins were held firmly.
The rider spoke softly.

7. The judge delivered his verdict.
His delivery was brief.
His delivery was solemn.
His delivery was stern.
The verdict was awful.

8. A man stood, looking down.
He stood upon a railroad bridge.
The bridge was in northern Alabama.
He was looking down into the water.
The water was twenty feet below.
The water was swift.
   (Ambrose Bierce, "An Occurrence at Owl Creek Bridge")

9. The preacher preached a sermon, all moans and shouts and cries
   and pictures of hell.

The sermon was wonderful.
The sermon was rhythmical.
The cries were lonely.
The pictures of hell were dire.

(Langston Hughes, "Salvation")

10. The gray-flannel fog closed off the Salinas Valley.
The fog was high.
It was the fog of winter.
The Salinas Valley was closed off from the sky.
And the Salinas Valley was closed off from all the rest of the world.

(John Steinbeck, "The Chrysanthemums")

11. A man stood upon my office threshold.
The man was motionless.
The man was young.
The man was pallidly neat.
The man was pitiably respectable.
The man was incurably forlorn.

(Herman Melville, "Bartleby the Scrivener")

12. Her eyes were narrowed against the sun.
And her lips were still sulky.
Her lips were sulky like a child's.
Her eyes were dark blue.
Her lips were full.
Her lips were pink.
Her lips were slightly sulky.

(James Baldwin, "This Morning, This Evening, So Soon")

13. Reverend Dobson was a man.
He had dark eyes.
He had hands that fluttered like protesting doves when he preached.
He was a delicate man.
He was a young man.
His dark eyes were great.
His hands were small.
His hands were white.
His hands were shapely.

(John Updike, "Pigeon Feathers")

14. He was short, somewhat pockmarked.
He had red hair.
He had bleary eyes.

He had a bald patch.
He had wrinkles.
His eyes were rather dim.
His bald patch was small.
The wrinkles were deep.
The wrinkles were on both sides of his cheeks.

15. I climbed to my perch.
I did this one night.
The night was hot.
The night was in the summer.
The night was in 1949.
It was my usual perch.
My perch was in the press box.
The press box was cramped.
The press box was above the stands.
The stands were wooden.
These were the stands of the baseball park.
The baseball park was in Lumberton, North Carolina.

(Tom Wicker, "Baseball")

Exercise: Sentence Expanding

Use simple modifiers (adjectives, adverbs, prepositional phrases) to expand each of the simple sentences below. Add details that answer the question(s) in parentheses and make the sentence more interesting and informative. There is, of course, no single correct answer to each question in parentheses. Sentence-expanding exercises such as this encourage you to use your imagination to build original sentences.

Examples

1. The boy hid. *(Where did the boy hide?)*
Expanded Sentence: The frightened little boy hid in the clothes hamper.
2. The boy hid. *(Where did he hide? When did he hide? Whom or what was he with?)*
Expanded Sentence: During the thunderstorm the frightened little boy hid in the clothes hamper with his Raggedy Andy doll.

1. The children skated. *(Where did the children skate?)*
2. The cat jumped. *(What did the cat jump into?)*

29

3. The girl poured catsup. *(What did she pour the catsup over?)*
4. Jenny smashed the bottle. *(What did she smash the bottle against?)*
5. The man looked up in wonder. *(Where was the man from? What was he looking at?)*
6. Harry sat down and wrote a poem. *(Where did he sit? What did he write the poem about?)*
7. Silas danced. *(Where did he dance? Whom did he dance with?)*
8. Sandy rode her bicycle. *(Where did she start from? Where did she ride to?)*
9. The child fell asleep. *(When did the child fall asleep? Where was the child?)*
10. Gus waited. *(Who was Gus waiting for? How long did he wait? Where did he wait?)*

Exercise: Building Paragraphs and Essays

I. This exercise has been adapted from a paragraph written by Jesse Albright, a student. Combine the sentences into a paragraph that contains several adjectives, adverbs, and prepositional phrases. Practice rearranging the simple modifiers in each sentence until you find the combination that you think is most effective.

Nervous Norman

1. Mr. Elmo Norman was the principal.
   He was the principal of the school.
   It was my elementary school.
2. He was the most nervous man I have ever met.
3. He was a short man.
   He was a pudgy man.
   He was always overdressed.
4. In fact, he didn't just wear his clothes.
   He hid inside them.
5. His uniform consisted of a suit, a tie, a shirt, and shoes.
   The suit was pin-striped.
   The suit was neatly pressed.
   The tie was thin.
   The tie was black.
   The shirt was white.
   The shirt was starched.

His shoes were oxfords.
The oxfords were brown.
The oxfords were brightly polished.

6. He had gray hair.
His hair was receding.
His hair was always neat.
His hair was always trimmed.

7. His head was fat.
His head was wrinkled.
His head darted like a radar blip.
His head darted about on his neck.
His neck was flabby.

8. He paced the hallways.
The hallways were in the school.

9. He was in perpetual motion.
He was always twitching.
He was always fidgeting.
He was always twiddling.

10. In the space of a minute he would do several things.
He would wrinkle his nose.
His nose was little.
He would scratch his chin.
His chin was plump.
He would shrug his shoulders.
He would straighten his tie.
And he would glance at his watch.

11. He would never once look at the person he was with.

12. As he spoke, he would do several things.
He spoke in a drawl.
His drawl was lackadaisical.
He would glance at the ceiling.
He would inspect his knuckles.
And he would check the floorboards.
He checked for dust.

13. When the conversation was over, he would dash back.
He dashed like a bunny.
The bunny was frightened.
He dashed into his office.

14. He was probably praying.
He prayed that he could lock himself in his office forever.

15. For all I know he may be there today.
He may still be there.
He may be in his office.
He may be hiding.

Writing Suggestions

1. Notice how the writer identifies Norman's outstanding characteristic in the second sentence ("He was the most nervous man I have ever met.") and then goes on to give specific details that *show* why this is true. Try this in a paragraph of your own. Think of a person you know who has some notable trait (for example, the meanest, kindest, ugliest, most attractive, most boring, or most interesting person you know). At the beginning of the paragraph, identify the person and his or her outstanding trait. Then give specific details that illustrate your point.

2. The particular words we use to describe a subject can let our readers know how we feel toward that subject. For instance, "He was a short, pudgy man, always overdressed" is not a flattering description. The writer of "Nervous Norman" makes it clear that he did not hold his old school principal in very high esteem. On the other hand, he could have been much more severe; he did not, after all, describe Norman as a "fat little overdressed slob."

Careful writers choose words both for what they mean (that is, their *denotations*, or dictionary meanings) and for what they suggest (their *connotations*, or associations). For example, all of the following words refer to "a young person," but their connotations may be quite different, depending on the context in which they appear: youngster, child, kid, little one, small fry, brat, urchin, juvenile, minor. Some of the words tend to carry favorable connotations (little one), others unfavorable (brat), and still others fairly neutral connotations (child). Calling a young person a brat lets our readers know immediately how we feel about the rotten kid.

Working with the four passages below will help make you more aware of the importance of choosing words carefully for what they suggest as well as what they mean. In each case you will be given a fairly objective and colorless statement—one that uses words with neutral connotations. Here is an example:

Mary has six children and is expecting another.

You will be asked to write two new versions of each passage. In the first version you will use words with positive connotations that show the subject in an attractive light:

Mary has six kiddies, and another bundle of joy is on the way.

In the second version you will use words with negative connotations that show the same subject in an unfavorable way:

> Mary has six whelps and is still breeding.

The instructions following each passage will guide you in making your revisions.

> a. Sam cooked dinner for Harriet. He prepared some meat and vegetables and a special dessert.

1. Describe the meal that Sam prepared, making it sound appetizing by using words with favorable connotations.
2. Describe the meal again, this time using words with negative connotations to make it sound quite unappealing.

> b. The person did not weigh very much. The person had brown hair and a small nose. The person wore informal clothing.

1. Identify and describe this particularly attractive person.
2. Identify and describe this particularly unattractive person.

> c. Herman was careful with his money. He kept his money in a safe place. He bought only the necessities of life. He never borrowed or lent money.

1. Show that you are impressed by Herman's sense of thrift.
2. Make fun of Herman or pass scorn on him for being such a tightwad.

> d. There were many people at the dance. There was loud music. People were drinking. People were dancing. People were holding each other.

1. Make this sound as if you enjoyed the dance.
2. Show what a very unpleasant experience this was.

If you tried the first Writing Suggestion (description of a person and his or her outstanding characteristic), examine your paragraph now for its use of connotative words. Decide whether you have been consistent in your description—consistently favorable, unfavorable, or neutral toward your subject. You now may want to revise this paragraph to clarify your attitude.

II. This exercise has been adapted from a paragraph in *The Names: A Memoir,* by N. Scott Momaday. First you are given a paragraph that describes some of the activities on the day before the Feast of San Diego in Jemez, New Mexico. The exercise that follows describes a scene at the very end of that same day. Combine the sentences into a paragraph that contains several adjectives, adverbs, and prepositional phrases. Practice rearranging the simple modifiers in each sentence until you find the combination that you think is most effective.

Before the Feast of San Diego

The activity in the pueblo reached a peak on the day before the Feast of San Diego, November twelfth. It was on that day, an especially brilliant day in which the winter held off and the sun shone like a flare, that Jemez became one of the fabulous cities of the world. In the preceding days the women had plastered the houses, many of them, and they were clean and beautiful like bone in the high light; the strings of chilies at the vigas had darkened a little and taken on a deeper, softer sheen; ears of colored corn were strung at the doors, and fresh cedar boughs were laid about, setting a whole, wild fragrance on the air. The women were baking bread in the outdoor ovens. Here and there men and women were at the woodpiles, chopping, taking up loads of firewood for their kitchens, for the coming feast. Even the children were at work: the little boys looked after the stock, and the little girls carried babies about. There were gleaming antlers on the rooftops, and smoke arose from all the chimneys.

1. I walked later.
   I walked in the streets.
   The streets were dusky.
   I walked among the Navajo camps.
   I walked past the doorways of the town, from which came smells and sounds.
   The smells were good.
   They were smells of cooking.
   The sounds were festive.
   There were sounds of music.
   There were sounds of laughter.
   There were sounds of talk.
2. The campfires rippled in the wind.
   It was the wind that arose with evening.

34

The wind was crisp.
The campfires set a glow on the ground.
The glow was soft.
The glow was yellow.
The campfires set a glow low on the adobe walls.

3. Mutton sizzled above the fires.
   Mutton smoked above the fires.
4. Fat dripped into the flames.
5. There were great pots of coffee.
   The pots were black.
   The coffee was strong.
   And there were buckets.
   The buckets were full of fried bread.
6. Dogs crouched on the rim of the light.
   There were many circles of light.
7. Men sat hunched in their blankets.
   The men were old.
   The men sat upon the ground.
   The men sat in the shadows, smoking.
   The shadows were cold.
8. The fires cast a glare over the town.
   The fires cast a glare long into the night.
9. I could hear the singing.
   I heard it until it seemed that the voices fell away.
   One by one the voices fell away.
   One remained.
   And then there was none.
10. I was on the very edge of sleep.
    I heard coyotes.
    The coyotes were in the hills.

Writing Suggestion

The moments of anticipation in our lives often prove to be more memorable than the events we were anticipating. Following Momaday's lead, write a paragraph in which you recall a time just before some important, long-awaited event. For instance, you might describe the night before Christmas from a child's point of view. Or the moments before a wedding ceremony begins from the point of view of the bride- or groom-to-be. Use descriptive details to *show* what the person was doing at the time and how he or she felt.

III. This exercise has been adapted from paragraphs 3 and 4 of an essay by Steve Sipple, a student. The two opening paragraphs appear before the exercise, and the two closing paragraphs follow the exercise. Combine the sentences into two paragraphs that contain several adjectives, adverbs, and prepositional phrases. Practice rearranging the simple modifiers in each sentence until you find the combination that you think is most effective.

Antonino's

Step into Antonino's on any evening of the week and immediately you will be scorched by the heat of the pizza ovens and strafed by the noise of squealing electric guitars and exploding rocket ships. The air is thick with odors of pizza, beer, perfume, and sweat. Elbows jab you from every side, and a strange woman is laughing in your ear. Resist the impulse to flee this scene of bedlam: you have just entered the finest pizza joint in Pittsburgh.

Let the crowd jostle you a few yards across the room and you will find yourself squeezed between the Galaxy and the Outer Limits. Groups of eager warriors surround the video games, waiting for their chance to zap the evil invaders. Coin after coin is pushed into the slots; battle after battle is fought. The players are slack-jawed and hunch-backed after hours of shouting and button stabbing. But above their heads hang emblems of the only real game in Pittsburgh: the black-and-gold banners of the Pittsburgh Steelers.

1. Follow the banners.
   Follow them to your left.
   And you will reach the counter.
   The counter is greasy.
   The counter is made of formica.
   This is the counter where the pizzas are ordered.
   This is the counter where the pizzas are delivered.
   The pizzas are delivered eventually.
2. Don't take a number.
   Don't wait in line.
   Don't wait meekly.
3. Only those with the loudest voices get attention here.
   Only those with the brawniest arms get attention here.
   The attention is quick.
4. Bellow your order.
   Bellow to one of the two men.

36

The men are hairy.
The men are in T-shirts.
5. Each of the men has a cigarette.
The cigarette is in his mouth.
Each of the men has a pack of Salems.
The pack is folded up.
The pack is in his sleeve.
6. The oven doors are behind them.
The doors are big.
The doors are black.
The doors are ominous.
7. The oven doors stand guard.
They stand over trays.
The trays are made of aluminum.
The trays are overflowing.
Mozzarella is on the trays.
Canadian bacon is on the trays.
Sausage is on the trays.
Mushrooms are on the trays.
Olives are on the trays.
Peppers are on the trays.
Onions are on the trays.
Pepperoni is on the trays.
Anchovies are on the trays.
The anchovies are dreaded.
8. Medallions stud the wall.
The wall is above the ovens.
9. These medallions are black and gold.
They are the medallions of the Pittsburgh Steelers.
10. Once you have been served, take your carton.
Your carton is hot.
Your carton is leaking.
Your carton is white.
It is your carton of pizza.
Take the carton across the room.
Take the carton to the rows of booths.
The booths are cramped.
11. You will find the booths.
They are under a sign.
The sign is huge.
It is a sign that reads "You're in Steeler Country."
12. By now you've gotten the point.
13. There are people in here.
They are like a *kamikaze.*

37

14. These people would die for their football team.
15. They would kill anyone.
    Surely they would.
    Anyone who dared to make a remark would be killed.
    The remark would be about the Steelers.
    The remark would be derogatory.
16. If you don't believe me, try complaining.
    Complain when some fan plays a song.
    The fan is devoted.
    The song is the "Steeler Fight Song."
    The fan plays it twelve times in succession.
    He plays the song on the jukebox.

   Find, or fight for, a seat in one of the booths, and open your box of pizza. Be warned, however. The fumes are so enticing that more than one famished patron has passed out face first into his pizza after becoming instantly intoxicated by the heady aroma. Bite into the thick crust, let the steaming mozzarella dribble down your chin, and savor the rich sauces that trickle down your throat. Now that you have burned your mouth, douse the flame with a swig of draft beer. If you forgot to order a beer, borrow someone else's. The crowd at Antonino's is a friendly one, but just be sure to order a round of cream ales before you leave.

   Your belly full and your head throbbing, you decide at last to make your way out of Antonino's. As you pass through the crowd and take a last look around, you notice that Antonino's has no salad bar, no quiche dishes, no microwave oven, no waitresses in clog-dancer outfits. It does have a sign on the door that reads, "And on the eighth day God created the Pittsburgh Steelers." Antonino's is a joint—the finest pizza joint in Pittsburgh.

Writing Suggestion

In an essay, describe a place that you know quite well—a place rich in detail, a place that has a character all its own. You might follow this writer's lead and choose a restaurant or bar, but there are many other possibilities: a room in your house, your workplace, a recreation room, a church, a garage, a playing field. Study "Antonino's" carefully for its effective structure. Notice that details are organized both in space (that is, their actual physical arrangement in the pizza place) and in time (that is, chronologically from the point of entering Antonino's to the time of leaving it). Either one or both of these structural patterns should help you in organizing your own place description.

Exercise: Recombining

This exercise has been adapted from the first paragraph of Chapter 29 of *The Grapes of Wrath*, by John Steinbeck. The author's original eighteen sentences have been combined into seven sentences in the exercise. Untangle these seven sentences by breaking them down into short sentences and then recombining them, as shown in the example below.

Sentence

The gray clouds marched brokenly in from the ocean and over the high coast mountains and over the valleys, in puffs, in folds, in gray crags, and they piled in together and they settled low over the west.

Broken down

The clouds marched in from the ocean.
The clouds were gray.
The clouds marched over the high coast mountains.
The clouds marched over the valleys.
The clouds came in brokenly.
The clouds came in puffs.
The clouds came in folds.
The clouds came in gray crags.
They piled in together.
They settled low over the west.

Recombining

Over the high coast mountains and over the valleys the gray clouds marched in from the ocean. . . . They came in brokenly, in puffs, in folds, in gray crags; and they piled in together and settled low over the west.

Feel free to change the order of the sentences as you recombine them. Your aim is not to imagine what Steinbeck's original sentences might be, but to create a clear, effective paragraph. Many combinations are possible.

The Flood

1. The gray clouds marched brokenly in from the ocean and over the high coast mountains and over the valleys, in puffs, in folds, in gray crags, and they piled in together and they settled low over the west.
2. The wind blew fiercely and silently, high in the air, and it swished in the brush, and it roared in the forests, and then the wind stopped and left the clouds deep and solid.
3. The rain began with gusty showers, pauses and downpours, and then gradually it settled to a single tempo, small drops and a steady beat, rain that was gray to see through, rain that cut midday light to evening, and at first the dry earth sucked the moisture down and blackened.
4. For two days the earth drank the rain, until the earth was full, and then puddles formed, and in the low places muddy little lakes formed in the fields and rose higher, and the steady rain whipped the shining water until at last the mountains were full, and the hillsides spilled into the streams, built them to freshets, and sent them roaring down the canyons into the valleys.
5. The rain beat on steadily, and the streams and the little rivers edged up to the sides and worked at willows and tree roots, bent the willows deep in the current, cut out the roots of cottonwoods and brought down the trees.
6. Along the bank sides the muddy water whirled and crept up the banks until at last it spilled over, into the fields, into the orchards, into the cotton patches where the black stems stood, and level fields became lakes, broad and gray, where the rain whipped up the surfaces.
7. Then as the earth whispered under the beat of the rain and the streams thundered under the churning freshets, the water poured down the highways, and cars moved slowly, cutting the water ahead, and leaving a boiling muddy wake behind.

Discovery: Keeping a Journal

Writing is a more than just a record of our thoughts; it is also a *way of thinking.* In the words of author Henry Miller, "Writing, like life itself, is a journey of discovery." One way to practice making discoveries through writing is to keep a journal.

A journal is not a diary but a writer's private notebook. Your choice of stationery is unimportant: a spiral pad, a ring binder, or a loose-leaf folder all will serve equally well. What is important is that the journal be a place where you can hold conversations with yourself without fear of being locked up for madness or marked down for misspellings. In fact, the only rule about keeping a journal is that there are no rules. You are writing for yourself—to observe, plan, complain, remember, and daydream.

Keeping a journal can also help you become a better writer. As you make discoveries you will be practicing your writing skills and creating a file of ideas and observations, some of which may later be developed into formal essays.

Begin your journal by writing for at least ten minutes on any topic that comes to mind. If you have trouble getting started, consider the suggestions below.

1. Jot down any word or phrase that occurs to you—or select one from the following list. Write down anything (examples, definitions, personal experiences, and so on) that you associate with the word or phrase.

dead end	serendipity	running away
flying	peer pressure	thunder
blue	home	claustrophobia

2. Make a list of your goals, problems, chores, favorite foods, or whatever else comes to mind.
3. Write a letter that you will never send. Write to someone you haven't seen in a long time, to someone who is making life difficult for you, or to someone you have never met but would like to.
4. Copy the lyrics to a song that has special meaning to you. Then describe the thoughts and feelings aroused by this song.
5. Describe something that recently amused, interested, or troubled you.
6. Describe the person you would like to be ten years from now.

The Writing Suggestions thoughout the book will give you many other ideas for journal entries.

Keeping a journal should not take much of your time—perhaps ten or fifteen minutes each day. Soon you should find that keeping a journal is not a chore, but a chance to relax and make discoveries through writing.

Practice: Sample Combinations

Use the sentences below as a guide after you have completed the Practice exercises earlier in the chapter. Since in most cases more than one combination is possible, do not think that your sentences are "incorrect" just because they are not in exact agreement with the ones below.

1. a. Tiny, white, eyeless mosquito larva swam in puddles by the edge of the bridge.
   b. Tiny mosquito larva, white and eyeless, swam in puddles by the edge of the bridge.
2. a. Slowly the old man pulled out his wallet.
   b. The old man slowly pulled out his wallet.
   c. The old man pulled out his wallet slowly.
3. (There is no limit to the number of different sentences that can be constructed in this exercise.)
   Jenny stood ankle-deep in the swamp water, raised her shotgun to her shoulder, and, aiming carefully, fired at the eye of the fat declining moon.
4. In the United States during the nineteenth century and the early decades of the twentieth, addiction to opiates frequently developed from the abuse of alcohol.
5. The forest is brilliant with the colors of a wet blue morning in late spring. Up and down the coast the line of the forest is drawn sharp and clean on the edge of a seascape of surf and sky and rocks.
6. It was a gray, rainy morning in early December.
7. Our boat was surrounded by sharks.

CHAPTER 3

Coordination

A common way of building sentences is to link related ideas with a word such as <u>and</u> or <u>but</u>. When we connect words, phrases, and entire sentences in this way, we *coordinate* them. This chapter will introduce you to several methods of coordination that you can use to make your writing clear, balanced, and coherent.

The Coordinators

Coordinators are the small linking words <u>and</u>, <u>but</u>, <u>yet</u>, <u>or</u>, <u>nor</u>, <u>for</u>, <u>so</u>. We use coordinators often in our writing to join single words and phrases:

> Everything was fresh <u>and</u> cool <u>and</u> damp in the early morning. Nurses in uniforms <u>and</u> in peasant costume walked under the trees with children.
> (Ernest Hemingway, *The Sun Also Rises*)

We also use coordinators to join sentences:

> Dynamite was lavishly used, <u>and</u> many of San Francisco's proudest structures were crumbled by man himself into ruins, <u>but</u> there was no withstanding the onrush of the flames.
> (Jack London, "The San Francisco Earthquake")

43

Once a sentence has been coordinated with another, each of the original sentences is called a *main clause.* In London's sentence, for instance, there are three main clauses:

1. Dynamite was lavishly used.
2. Many of San Francisco's proudest structures were crumbled by man himself into ruins.
3. There was no withstanding the onrush of the flames.

Notice that a comma is used before each coordinator linking the main clauses in London's sentence. This method (comma plus coordinator) is the most common way of coordinating sentences.

Practice 1

a. Combine the sentences in each set below; then join the two new sentences with the coordinator <u>but</u>.

1. The sound of an automobile horn is far away.
   The sound is from the mainland.
   The sound is borne on the sea wind.
2. The sound is muffled.
   The sound is indistinct.
   The sound seems part of another world.

b. Combine the sentences in each set below; then join the three new sentences with the coordinators <u>and</u> and <u>for</u>.

1. There are shadows under the woman's eyes.
   The shadows are dark.
2. The flesh has fallen away.
   It has fallen from her neck.
3. She is like her fellow outcasts.
   She is at the end of a bitter struggle.

Paired Coordinators

Another, and sometimes more forceful, way of connecting related ideas is with *paired coordinators.* Consider the two sentences below.

1. Jenny <u>and</u> Gus have gone to Buffalo.
2. <u>Both</u> Jenny <u>and</u> Gus have gone to Buffalo.

In sentence 1, the two nouns are joined with the coordinator and, and in sentence 2, they are joined with a paired coordinator, both . . . and. The two versions carry the same meaning, but sentence 2 puts more emphasis on the two words being coordinated. The most common paired coordinators are both . . . and; either . . . or; neither . . . nor; not . . . but; not . . . nor; not only . . . but also; whether . . . or.

Practice 2

a. Replace the coordinator and with the paired coordinator not only . . . but also in the sentence below.

They went to Buffalo and Niagara Falls.

b. Replace the coordinator or with the paired coordinator either . . . or in the sentence below.

They will return on Sunday or Monday.

c. Replace the coordinator and with the paired coordinator neither . . . nor; you will also need to change are not to is.

Buffalo and Niagara Falls are not my favorite cities.

Paired coordinators can also be used to emphasize the connection between two main clauses. Compare the two sentences below.

1. The tides advance and retreat in their eternal rhythms, and the level of the sea itself is never at rest.
2. Not only do the tides advance and retreat in their eternal rhythms, but the level of the sea itself is never at rest.

(Rachel Carson, *The Edge of the Sea*)

Although both sentences contain the same information, the emphasis is not the same. The not only at the beginning of sentence 2 lets the reader know that a second main clause will eventually follow, and the but calls attention to this clause.

Practice 3

Replace the coordinator <u>and</u> with the paired coordinator <u>not only</u> . . . <u>but also</u> in the sentence below.

More Americans expect more out of life, and they are more sensitive to forces pronounced harmful to their newly discovered individuality.

The Semicolon

Using a coordinator or paired coordinator to connect two main clauses can help the reader see clearly how the two ideas relate to one another. However, there is a useful, though less common, method of coordination that does not rely on such coordinators. A semicolon (without a coordinator) can also link two main clauses that are roughly equal in importance. A semicolon is a particularly attractive option when one or both of the main clauses already contain a coordinator, as in the sentences below.

1. Levin wanted friendship and got friendliness; he wanted steak and they offered spam.

    (Bernard Malamud, *A New Life*)
2. Some players hit the golf ball and stand, dejected, waiting for it to land; others turn away and leave it up to the caddy.

    (Wright Morris, "Odd Balls")

Semicolons are frequently used when the second main clause rephrases the idea contained in the first (as in sentence 1) or when the second clause offers a contrast with the first (as in sentence 2). In each of these sentences, the two main clauses are *balanced:* that is, they are similar in form and approximately equal in length. Besides having a pleasing shape and sound, a balanced sentence can emphasize the relation between the two clauses without relying on a coordinator to identify that relation. But be careful not to overwork the semicolon. It should be used only when there is a close and obvious connection between the two main clauses.

Practice 4

Combine the sentences in each set below and then join the two main clauses with a semicolon to create a balanced sentence.

    a. She stood upright.
       She stood with the strength of an oak.
       She stood this way when strength was needed.
    b. She bent with grace.
       She bent with the ease of a willow.
       She bent this way when her help was needed.

Variations

In theory there is no limit to the number of items that can be joined with coordinators or semicolons. In the following sentence, for instance, the writer connects four verbs by using <u>and</u> three times.

> They lived <u>and</u> laughed <u>and</u> loved <u>and</u> left.
>
>   (James Joyce, *Finnegans Wake*)

A more common way of presenting a list of three or more items is to place commas between all items and to keep only the final coordinator (<u>and</u> or <u>or</u>). For example, Joyce's sentence could be rewritten this way:

> They lived, laughed, loved, <u>and</u> left.

Read the two versions aloud to notice the difference in sound, if not in sense. In the original sentence, the repetition of <u>and</u> makes us read the sentence more slowly; thus, we may pay more attention to each verb in the list. Most readers would agree that Joyce's sentence is more forceful and eloquent than the second version. Separating all the items in a list with coordinators can be an effective way of slowing the pace of your writing and emphasizing the individual items in the list. However, use this method sparingly: too many lists of words, phrases, or clauses strung together with coordinators will soon tire your readers rather than gain their attention.

Practice 5

The first four prepositional phrases in the sentence below are separated by commas. Replace each of these commas with <u>and</u> so that the sentence moves at a slower pace.

We came over the mountains, out of Spain, down the white roads, through the overfoliaged, wet, green Basque country, and finally into Bayonne.

A list of three or more words or phrases may be arranged in a variety of ways. For instance, to quicken the pace of a sentence we can leave out the coordinators altogether, as Mark Twain has done with this list of nouns:

Drays, carts, men, boys, all go hurrying from many quarters to a common center, the wharf.

(Mark Twain, *Life on the Mississippi*)

Yet another way of coordinating items in a list is to pair them off, as shown by this reworking of Twain's sentence:

Drays <u>and</u> carts, men <u>and</u> boys, all go hurrying from many quarters to a common center, the wharf.

This method of coordination allows you to emphasize logical connections within the list.

Practice 6

Using Twain's sentence above as a model, rewrite the following sentence, pairing off the four underlined nouns:

<u>Saints</u>, <u>sinners</u>, <u>princes</u>, <u>paupers</u>, all look forward to the same dusty death.

Another way to call attention to a list of items is to separate the list from the main clause. This is done with a colon, as in the sentence below.

48

There are three ingredients in the good life: learning, earning, and yearning.

(Christopher Morley, *Parnassus on Wheels*)

The colon introduces a list that explains or illustrates something that has just been mentioned. The colon should follow a complete sentence; it should not interrupt one. For example, there is no place for a colon in this version of Morley's sentence:

The three ingredients in the good life are learning, earning, and yearning.

Because the colon is not a particularly common mark of punctuation, it calls attention to itself and the list that follows it.

Practice 7

Combine the sentences below, using a colon to separate the list of items from the main clause.

The car can be divided into four main component systems.
This is the typical modern car.
There is the engine.
There is the transmission.
There is the electrical system.
There is the chassis.

Reducing Coordinated Constructions

You sometimes have a choice between coordinating main clauses or coordinating just parts of those clauses. Often, the more concise version is the more effective one. Consider these two sentences:

1. The universe is not hostile, and the universe is not friendly; the universe is indifferent.
2. The universe is neither hostile nor friendly; it is indifferent.

Sentence 1 consists of three main clauses, all of which have the same subject and verb: the universe is. Such repetition does give the sentence balance, but it may also distract the reader from the adjectives, which should probably be emphasized, not obscured. This emphasis is achieved in sentence 2, in which the first two adjectives are joined by a paired coordinator and the last (and most important) appears in a main clause set off by a semicolon.

Practice 8

Make the following sentence more concise by reducing the underlined clause to a phrase and inserting it between the words <u>effective</u> and <u>means</u>:

> Humor is a most effective means of handling the difficult situations in our lives; <u>yet it is a frequently neglected means.</u>

Another way to make your writing more concise is to omit certain words when you coordinate main clauses. The second sentence in the passage below demonstrates this technique, called *ellipsis* (in the plural, *ellipses*).

> Each noteworthy civilization has grappled with the great problem of its time. For the Greeks, it was the organization of society; for the Romans, the organization of empire; for the Medievalists, the spelling out of their relationship to God; for the Europeans of the 15th and 16th centuries, mastery of the oceans. And for the last two centuries, it has been the scientific understanding of nature and the creation of an industrial society.
>
> (Philip Handler, "In Praise of Science")

In the second sentence, only the first clause contains a subject and verb (<u>it was</u>). As we read the rest of this sentence, we complete each clause by assuming that <u>it was</u> is the subject and verb in each case:

> For the Greeks, it was the organization of society; for the Romans, [it was] the organization of empire; for the Medievalists, [it was] the spelling out of their relationship to God; for the Europeans of the 15th and 16th centuries, [it was] mastery of the oceans.

The writer has succeeded in repeating a sentence pattern without repeating words, and the result is a clear and concise sentence. The technique of ellipsis can be very effective for the compact expression of ideas when words can be omitted without sacrificing sense.

Practice 9

Make the following sentence more concise by eliminating the under-lined verbs:

The nave was dimly lit, the congregation <u>was</u> small, the sermon <u>was</u> short, and the wind howled a nihilistic counterpoint beyond the black windows blotted with garbled apostles.

Summary

In this chapter we have seen that there are many ways to coordinate words, phrases, and clauses. No one method is automatically superior to another. The method you choose should depend on just how you want to emphasize, pace, and organize the words, phrases, or clauses to be connected in each sentence.

The exercises that follow will give you practice in making such decisions.

Exercise: Sentence Revising

Rewrite each sentence below according to the instructions in parentheses.

1. Little Sylvester plays the piano loudly, but <u>he does</u> not <u>play the piano</u> well. (*Make this sentence more concise by omitting the underlined words.*)
2. The beer at the ballpark was warm and refreshing. (*Replace* and *with a coordinator that suggests a contrast between* warm *and* refreshing.)
3. The incredible nimbleness of flies is no secret to anyone who has attempted to catch one in his cupped hand, <u>and</u> their astronomical power of reproduction is no secret to anyone who has tried to eradicate them. (*Substitute* nor *for* and, *and make any other changes necessary in the second main clause.*)
4. The teacher undertakes to instruct her charges in all subjects of the first three grades, <u>and</u> she manages to function quietly and effectively

51

as a guardian of their health, their clothes, their habits, their mothers, and their snowball engagements. *(Replace the coordinator* and *with the paired coordinator* not only . . . but.)

5. Writing is not a way of escaping from life; <u>writing is</u> another way of experiencing it. *(Omit the semicolon and the underlined words; add an appropriate coordinator.)*

6. The porcupine looks like an uncombed head; he has a grumpy personality; he fights with his tail; he hides his head when he's in trouble; he floats like a cork; he attacks backing up; he retreats going ahead; he eats toilet seats as if they were Post Toasties. *(Make this sentence more concise and faster moving by eliminating all semicolons and the pronoun* he *wherever it appears; coordinate the verb phrases instead of the main clauses.)*

7. By barge, keelboat and raft, the early settlers freighted southward flour, millstones and tobacco, pelts, iron and Monongahela whiskey. *(To slow the pace of this sentence, eliminate commas wherever possible and substitute* and.)

8. Down the streams the first Americans who had pushed past the Appalachians brought the products of <u>Kentucky</u>, Indiana, <u>Tennessee</u>, Pennsylvania, and of the forests and clearings along the Cumberland, the Ohio, the Wabash, and even such a little stream as the Sangamon. *(Pair off the items in the first list by omitting the commas after the underlined words and substituting* and.)*

9. Our local drunk was <u>not</u> poetic like some <u>or</u> ambitious like others; his drinking bouts were truly awe inspiring; he was not without his sensitivity. *(Replace the underlined words with a paired coordinator; replace the semicolons with coordinators.)*

10. His hands are mittened, his ears <u>are</u> muffed, and his body <u>is</u> cased with thermal underwear; the damp sock chilling his right foot is really uncomfortable. *(Omit the underlined verbs to make the sentence more concise; replace the semicolon with an appropriate coordinator.)*

Exercise: Sentence Building

By coordinating words, phrases, or main clauses, combine the sentences in each set into a single, clear sentence. Whenever possible, create a second combination by using a different method of coordination.

Example

All ball games feature hitting.
All ball games feature socking.
All ball games feature chopping.
All ball games feature slicing.
All ball games feature smashing.
All ball games feature slamming.
All ball games feature stroking.
All ball games feature whacking.
Only in football are these blows diverted from the ball to the opponent.

Combination A

All ball games feature hitting, socking, chopping, slicing, smashing, slamming, stroking, and whacking; only in football are these blows diverted from the ball to the opponent.

Combination B

All ball games feature hitting and socking, chopping and slicing, smashing, slamming, stroking, and whacking, but only in football are these blows diverted from the ball to the opponent.

(Wright Morris, "Odd Balls")

1. Cigarettes are harmful to the health of the smoker.
   Cigarettes are also harmful to the health of those who live with the smoker.

2. A few of the strikers obeyed the court order.
   They returned to work.
   Most of the strikers remained on the picket line.

3. Omar may be down at the Rainbow Bar.
   Omar may be over at Sammy's Lounge.
   Omar is at one of these two places.

4. The girl was little.
   She pressed her nose against the window.
   The window was icy.
   She giggled with delight.
   She had never seen snow before.

5. There is a stream that passes my house.
   The stream is broad.
   The stream is shallow.
   Every year thousands of salmon run up through the stream.
   I have scarcely ever seen one on its way.

6. He was afraid of rats.
   The fear was horrible.
   He did not try to sleep.
   He sat looking at the dark.
   He looked distrustfully.

7. Miss Lockhart played golf well.
   Miss Lockhart drove a car.
   She could also blow up the school.
   She could blow it up with her jar of gunpowder.
   She would never dream of doing so.
                    (Muriel Spark, *The Prime of Miss Jean Brodie*)

8. The waitress tugged the pencil out of her hair.
   Her hair was lacquered.
   She licked the pencil point.
   She flicked over her bill pad.
   She asked if she could take our order.

9. He turned.
   He pushed the bottom strand of the wire.
   He pushed it down to the ground.
   He pushed it with his foot.
   He held the middle strand up.
   He held it up with his hands.
   He did this so Ed and I could walk through.
                    (Anne Moody, "Coming of Age in Mississippi")

10. A tree grew on our side of the trench.
    It was a pecan tree.
    The tree was big.
    We made our playhouse under it.
    We did this so we could sit in the trench.
    We could watch the white children.
    We could watch them without their knowing we were actually out
       there staring at them.
                    (Anne Moody, "Coming of Age in Mississippi")

11. Papa would sit on the front porch.
    Papa would sit after supper.
    Papa would sit on summer nights.
    The nights were warm.
    Papa would tell us stories.
    The stories were about witches.
    The stories were about ghosts.
    At other times Papa would sing songs.
    The songs were about lovers.
    The songs were about thieves.

12. She got out of the car.
    She walked around a little.
    Then she sat down on the front bumper.
    She sat down to wait.
    She sat down to rest.
    She was very tired.
    She lay her head back.
    She lay her head against the hood.
    She closed her eyes.

13. The sun would dry the dew.
    The dew was on the grass of the park.
    The sun would soften the tar.
    The sun would bake the rooftops.
    The sun would brown us on the beaches.
    The sun would make us sweat.
    The sun would keep us from the flats.
    These were the flats of the tenements.
    The flats were tight.
    The flats were small.

                         (Pete Hamill, "Spaldeen Summer")

14. I took the aisle seat.
    The seat was in the second row.
    I watched the bus fill up.
    It filled up rapidly.
    It filled up with all kinds of people.
    The people were young.
    The people were old.
    There were mothers.
    The mothers were with cranky children.
    There were children.

The children were with cranky mothers.
There were people who were obviously ill.
(Dorothy Rodgers, "Waiting and Waiting, but Not for Naught")

15. I fought migraine then.
I ignored the warnings it sent.
I went to school in spite of it.
I sat through lectures in Middle English.
I sat through presentations to advertisers.
I sat with tears running down the right side of my face.
The tears were involuntary.
I threw up in washrooms.
I stumbled home by instinct.
I emptied ice trays.
I emptied them onto my bed.
I tried to freeze the pain.
The pain was in my right temple.
I wished only for a neurosurgeon who would do a lobotomy on house call.
I cursed my imagination.

(Joan Didion, "In Bed")*

Exercise: Building Paragraphs and Essays

I. This exercise has been adapted from the third paragraph of John Steinbeck's essay "Paradox and Dream." The first two paragraphs of the essay appear below. Use different methods of coordination as you combine the sentences in each set of the exercise.

Paradox and Dream

One of the generalities most often noted about Americans is that we are a restless, a dissatisfied, a searching people. We bridle and buck under failure, and we go mad with dissatisfaction in the face of success. We spend our time searching for security, and hate it when we get it.

---

* Didion's extraordinary sentence suggests by its very length the seemingly endless agony of a migraine headache. First combine the sixteen sentences into one sentence; then recombine the sentences into three or four. Which combination do you prefer?

For the most part we are an intemperate people: we eat too much when we can, drink too much, indulge our senses too much. Even in our so-called virtues we are intemperate: a teetotaler is not content not to drink—he must stop all the drinking in the world; a vegetarian among us would outlaw the eating of meat. We work too hard, and many die under the strain; and then to make up for that we play with a violence as suicidal.

The result is that we seem to be in a state of turmoil all the time, both physically and mentally. We are able to believe that our government is weak, stupid, overbearing, dishonest, and inefficient, and at the same time we are deeply convinced that it is the best government in the world, and we would like to impose it upon everyone else. We speak of the American Way of Life as though it involved the ground rules for the governance of heaven. A man hungry and unemployed through his own stupidity and that of others, a man beaten by a brutal policeman, a woman forced into prostitution by her own laziness, high prices, availability, and despair—all bow with reverence toward the American Way of Life, although each one would look puzzled and angry if he were asked to define it. We scramble and scrabble up the stony path toward the pot of gold we have taken to mean security. We trample friends, relatives, and strangers who get in the way of our achieving it; and once we get it we shower it on psychoanalysts to try to find out why we are unhappy, and finally—if we have enough of the gold—we contribute it back to the nation in the form of foundations and charities.

1. We fight out way in.
   We try to buy our way out.
2. We are alert.
   We are curious.
   We are hopeful.
   We take more drugs than any other people.
   These drugs are designed to make us unaware.
3. We are self-reliant.
   At the same time we are completely dependent.
4. We are aggressive.
   We are defenseless.
5. Americans overindulge their chidren.
   Americans do not like their children.
   The children in turn are overly dependent.
   The children are full of hate for their parents.
6. We are complacent in our possessions.
   We are complacent in our houses.
   We are complacent in our education.

It is hard to find a man or woman who does not want something better for the next generation.
7. Americans are remarkably kind and hospitable and open with guests.
Americans are remarkably kind and hospitable and open with strangers.
They will make a wide circle around the man dying on the pavement.
8. Fortunes are spent getting cats out of trees.
Fortunes are spent getting dogs out of sewer pipes.
A girl screaming in the street draws only slammed doors.
A girl screaming in the street draws only silence.
A girl screaming in the street draws only closed windows.

Writing Suggestions

1. In a paragraph, identify some of your personal paradoxes—apparent contradictions in your attitudes, habits, values, and tastes. Use specific examples.
2. As Steinbeck himself says later in "Paradox and Dream," "Now there is a set of generalities for you." Just about any one of the sentences in his essay could be the starting point for a lengthy, detailed study. In an essay, discuss one of the paradoxes that Steinbeck observes. State whether you agree or disagree with Steinbeck's observation, and then support your view by drawing on your own experiences and observations. Where Steinbeck is very general, you want to be very specific, and where Steinbeck speaks broadly of "Americans," you want to speak of individuals you have known.

II. This exercise has been adapted from Jack London's eyewitness account of the San Francisco earthquake of 1906. Paragraphs 1 through 3 and 6 and 7 are given as they originally appeared in *Collier's* (May 5, 1906). Reconstruct paragraphs 4 and 5 by combining the sentences in each set. Several of the sets, though not all, require the coordination of words, phrases, and clauses.

The San Francisco Earthquake

The earthquake shook down in San Francisco hundreds of thousands of dollars worth of walls and chimneys. But the conflagration that followed burned up hundreds of millions of dollars worth of property. There is no estimating within hundreds of millions the actual damage wrought.

Not in history has a modern imperial city been so completely destroyed. San Francisco is gone. Nothing remains of it but memories and a fringe of dwelling houses on its outskirts. Its industrial section is wiped out. Its business section is wiped out. Its social and residential section is wiped out. The factories and warehouses, the great stores and newspaper buildings, the hotels and the palaces of the nabobs, all are gone. There remains only the fringe of dwelling houses on the outskirts of what was once San Francisco.

Within an hour after the earthquake shock, the smoke of San Francisco's burning was a lurid tower visible a hundred miles away. And for three days and nights this lurid tower swayed in the sky, reddening the sun, darkening the day, and filling the land with smoke.

1. The earthquake came on Wednesday morning.
   It came at quarter past five.
2. The flames were leaping upward.
   This happened a minute later.
3. Fires started in a dozen different quarters south of Market Street.
   Fires started in the working class ghetto.
   Fires started in the factory.
4. There was no opposing the flames.
5. There was no organization.
   There was no communication.
6. This was a twentieth-century city.
   All the cunning adjustments of this city had been smashed.
   The earthquake had smashed those adjustments.
7. The streets were humped into ridges.
   The streets were humped into depressions.
   The streets were piled with debris.
   The debris was the result of fallen walls.
8. The rails were twisted into angles.
   The rails were made of steel.
   The angles were perpendicular.
   The angles were horizontal.
9. The telephone system was disrupted.
   The telegraph system was disrupted.
10. And the great water mains had burst.
11. There were shrewd contrivances of man.
    There were shrewd safeguards of man.
    All of the contrivances had been thrown out of gear.
    All of the safeguards had been thrown out of gear.
    Thirty seconds' twitching of the earth-crust had thrown them out of gear.

12. Half the heart of the city was gone.
    It was gone by Wednesday afternoon.
    It was gone inside of twelve hours.

13. I watched the conflagration.
    The conflagration was vast.
    I watched at that time.
    I watched from out on the bay.

14. It was dead calm.

15. Not a flicker of wind stirred.

16. Yet wind was pouring in.
    It poured in from every side.
    It poured in upon the city.

17. There were winds from the east.
    There were winds from the west.
    There were winds from the north.
    There were winds from the south.
    The winds were strong.
    The winds were blowing upon the city.
    The city was doomed.

18. The heated air rising made an enormous suck.

19. Thus did the fire of itself build a chimney.
    The fire built its own chimney.
    The chimney was colossal.
    The chimney was built through the atmosphere.

20. This dead calm continued all day.
    This dead calm continued all night.
    Near to the flames, the wind was often half a gale, so mighty was
    the suck.

Wednesday night saw the destruction of the very heart of the city. Dynamite was lavishly used, and many of San Francisco's proudest structures were crumbled by man himself into ruins, but there was no withstanding the onrush of the flames. Time and again successful stands were made by the firefighters, and every time the flames flanked around on either side, or came up from the rear, and turned to defeat the hard won victory.

An enumeration of the buildings destroyed would be a directory of San Francisco. An enumeration of the buildings undestroyed would be a line and several addresses. An enumeration of the deeds of heroism would stock a library and bankrupt the Carnegie medal fund. An enumeration of the dead—will never be made. All vestiges of them were destroyed by the flames. The number of the victims of the earthquake will never be known.

Writing Suggestions

1. In a paragraph or short essay, describe the effects of some act of nature you have witnessed. You may, like London, choose a dramatic subject, such as a hurricane or a blizzard, or you may choose something as common as an April shower or a midwinter thaw.

2. To add excitement and color to a report, a writer may occasionally relate a past event as if it were happening right now. Rewrite your two paragraphs on "The San Francisco Earthquake," changing them from the past to the present. For instance, your new opening sentences might read as follows:

   > It is quarter past five on Wednesday morning when the earthquake comes. A minute later the flames are leaping upwards. . . .

   Make any changes necessary to keep your new sentences clear and consistent.

III. This exercise has been adapted from the last two paragraphs of an essay by Mark Hulme, a student. The first five paragraphs appear below. Complete the essay by combining the sentences in each set of the exercise. Several of the sets, though not all, require the coordination of words, phrases, and clauses.

Note: Two early drafts of this essay appear in the Discovery sections at the end of Chapters 9 and 10.

Growing Up at the Victory Drive-In

Located on Highway 16 between a cow pasture and a junk yard, the Victory is a typical American drive-in. By day it's just a gravel lot with a few white shacks and a towering blank screen. But on hot summer nights, it's a place where children dream, teenagers prowl, and young adults check their watches and wonder if time is passing them by. The Victory has changed only a little in my lifetime, but my perceptions of it have changed greatly since my first visit almost fifteen years ago.

To an eight-year-old boy who rarely ventured more than a block away from his apartment in the city, a trip to the Victory was a genuine adventure. We would head out of the city just before sundown, with mom and dad in the front seat of the station wagon and the back loaded with pillows, blankets, a shopping bag full of homemade popcorn, and us four pajama-clad kids. As we entered the lot, the howling of the junk yard dogs and the smell of manure from the neighboring pasture only added to the sense that we were entering a magical world.

After collecting our root beers from the refreshment stand and bundling up under blankets in the back seat, we would shriek with delight at the antics of Mickey, Minnie, and Pluto. The cartoons seemed so much funnier than those on TV simply because they were so much bigger. During the first feature we munched popcorn greedily and sat spellbound before the monsters, spacemen, or cowboys on the screen. As the night wore on past our bedtime, we grew restless and cranky, shifting our attention from the flickering screen to the twinkling stars out the back window, stars that carried us to sleep. We rode home and were carried to bed, still dreaming drive-in dreams: spaceships on the roof, Godzilla under the bed.

A few years later I was back at the drive-in, not with my family but with my tenth-grade buddies. Charley took us in his father's old Camaro—a half-dozen guys packed into the seats and another one or two of us stowed in the trunk, trying not to giggle as Charlie paid for the tickets. We watched a movie now and then—if it was sexy enough—but more often we hung out at the refreshment stand or cruised the lot, always on the lookout for parties of girls.

Horror movies were the most fun. Just when the crazed murderer was about to pounce on the innocent maiden, we would scream on cue and hurl ourselves on a Mustang filled with not-quite-so-innocent maidens. Then we'd hide in our car for the rest of the night, heroically guzzling beers and exchanging lies about our lives. We'd go home sick as dogs, but next day boast, "Drank a case of beer at the drive-in—didn't feel a thing."

1. I returned to the Victory.
   I returned a few months ago.
   I was accompanied by my girlfriend.
   I returned for the first time in a few years.
2. The twin bill—*Valley of the Sabine Women* and *The Man with the Golden Eyesocket*—was not very promising.
   The movies did seem appropriate to their surroundings.
   The surroundings were seedy.
3. The screen itself had deteriorated over the years.
   Or hadn't I noticed before how wrinkled it really was?
   It was really stained.
   It was really torn.
4. Perhaps I'm just spoiled by my home stereo system.
   I found listening to the sound track a painful experience.
5. Sounds came through my car radio speaker.

Sounds of the Sabine women came through.
Sounds of every airplane in the area came through.
Sounds of every ham radio in the area came through.
Sounds of every CB in the area came through.

6. There was competition from drag racers.
There was competition from beer-swilling punks.
There was competition from kiddies.
The kiddies were shrieking.
The kiddies were in nearby station wagons.
All this competition was noisy.
With all this competition, the movies didn't stand a chance.

7. Turning from film to food, we visited the refreshment stand.
It was a grease pit.
It was filthy.
It was ominously close to the lavatories.

8. We savored ten dollars worth of "piping hot pizza."
It was pizza that tasted like frozen styrofoam.
We washed it down with cokes.
The cokes were warm.
The cokes were flat.
These were cokes that leaked out of their containers.

9. We left the drive-in early.
We left in time to catch a Woody Allen movie.
The movie was on Home Box Office.

10. The drive-in itself has changed over the past fifteen years.
I'm not sure how much it has changed.
I know that I have changed a good deal.

11. Now I'm just bored by things.
I'm annoyed by things.
I'm disgusted by things.
These are things that enchanted me not so long ago.
These are things that amused me not so long ago.
These are things that titillated me not so long ago.

12. Perhaps at twenty-two I'm already an old bore.

13. Or maybe I've just grown up.

14. I'll probably be back at the drive-in.
I'll probably be back a few years from now.

15. I'll be a different man.

16. I'll sip a coke.
I'll do this behind the steering wheel.
I'll do this contentedly.
I'll do this while my kids shriek.
The kids will shriek in my ear.
The kids will spill popcorn down my back.

63

Writing Suggestions.

1. In an essay, identify three distinct periods or stages in your own life, and show to what extent your interests and attitudes have changed over the years.
2. In an essay, identify the basic types of people one may find at a particular place, such as a cafeteria, a classroom, a church, or a football stadium. Describe a typical member of each group.

Exercise: Recombining

This exercise has been adapted from four paragraphs in Chapter 2 of *New York City Baseball*, by Harvey Frommer. The author's original thirteen sentences have been combined into six sentences in the exercise. Untangle these six sentences by breaking them down into short sentences and recombining them, as shown in the example below.

Sentence

The deeds and personalities of the Dodgers and the Giants and the Yankees transformed the huge metropolis into a small town of neighborhood rooting through the long and steamy summer nights and in the blaze of its days, from early spring to the winds of autumn: baseball dominated New York City.

Broken down

The Dodgers, the Giants, and the Yankees performed deeds.
The Dodgers, the Giants, and the Yankees had personalities.
These deeds and personalities transformed the huge metropolis into a small town.
This happened through the summer nights.
The nights were long.
The nights were steamy.
This happened in the blaze of its days.
This happened from early spring to the winds of autumn.
Baseball dominated New York City.

Recombining

Through the long and steamy summer nights and in the blaze of its days, from early spring to the winds of autumn, baseball dominated New York City. The deeds and personalities of the Dodgers, the Giants, and the Yankees transformed the huge metropolis into a small town of neighborhood rooting.

Feel free to change the order of the sentences as you recombine them. Your aim is not to imagine what Frommer's original sentences might be, but to create four clear, effective paragraphs. Many combinations are possible.

New York City Baseball

1. The deeds and personalities of the Dodgers and the Giants and the Yankees transformed the huge metropolis into a small town of neighborhood rooting through the long and steamy summer nights and in the blaze of its days, from early spring to the winds of autumn: baseball dominated New York City.
2. Baseball was a sport played and viewed from childhood on, and for a nation as well as a city at a crossroads after the death and disruption of a world at war, baseball brought reunion with normalcy, constancy, controlled and familiar excitement.
3. It was fidgety anticipation during the playing of our national anthem, the camaraderie of the seventh-inning stretch, the familiar taste of hot dogs, mustard, the record of the program, the yearbook, the box score, the scorecard, the crack of wood against ball and the smack of ball against leather and the fraction of the plate shaved close and the fielder magically in position for the leap, the stab, the catch.
4. Baseball was the ceremonious regularity of the set lineup and the fixed positions, four men in the outfield, three outfielders, the pitcher throwing the ball on a white line from the mound to the plate to the catcher, and it was the flawless geometry of the diamond and the green outfield pastureland, and each team was allowed its four balls, three strikes, three outs.
5. Baseball was the comforting regularity of one dugout along the third base line and the other facing it along the first base line, alternately filling up and spilling out between innings as the sides changed from offense to defense, and it was the individual battles of pitcher against batter and the varying degrees of intensity of time used up and shadings and nuances and tempo set by players and not the clock.

6. The season—April and May and June and July and August and September—gave plenty of time for personalities to emerge and for fans to learn the names and styles and strategies of the players and the teams, and there was the appealingly symmetric major league tradition of eight teams in each league facing each other twenty-two times, half the time at home, half the time at the other club's park; most schoolboys could recite by heart the names of the teams in both leagues, and the sport's familiarity was underscored by the uniforms—white for the home team, dusty gray for the visitors.

Discovery: Freewriting

If the prospect of having to write makes you uneasy, consider how one student copes with the problem:

> When I hear the term *compose*, I go berserk. How can I make something out of nothing? That's not to imply that I have nothing upstairs, just no special talent for organizing thoughts and putting them down on paper. Instead of "composing," I simply jot, jot, jot and scribble, scribble, scribble—and then I try to make sense of it all.
>
> (Mary White)

Mary's practice of jotting and scribbling is sometimes called *freewriting*—that is, writing without rules. It is a practice many writers follow to discover what is on their minds and to overcome the dread of beginning a writing project.

Freewriting can help you find a topic to write about or develop your thoughts on a subject that has been assigned to you. If you are searching for a topic, start by jotting down the first thoughts that come to mind, no matter how trivial or unrelated to one another they may appear. If you already have at least a general idea of what you will be writing about, put down your first thoughts on that subject. Then, for at least ten minutes, continue writing—about anything. Don't stop to ponder or make corrections or cross out anything you have written: just keep writing.

While you are freewriting, forget the "rules" of formal English. Because you are writing for only yourself, don't worry about awkward or incomplete sentences, spelling or punctuation, organization or clear connections. If you get stuck for something to say, just keep repeating the last word you have written, or write "I'm stuck, I'm stuck" until a new idea emerges. Your hand will get tired, your paper will probably be a mess, but you will have started writing.

What will you do with your freewriting? Well, eventually you will just toss it away—nobody else will ever look at it. But first read it over carefully to see if you can find a key word, phrase, maybe even a sentence or two that can be developed in a longer piece of writing. Whether or not freewriting gives you specific material for a future essay, it will help get you into the frame of mind for writing.

Most people need to practice freewriting several times before they are able to make it work as a means of discovery. So try freewriting as a regular exercise, perhaps three or four times a week, until you find you can write without rules comfortably and productively.

Practice: Sample Combinations

Use the sentences below a a guide after you have completed the Practice exercises in the first part of this chapter. Since in most cases more than one combination is possible, do not think that your sentences are "incorrect" just because they may not be in exact agreement with the ones below.

1. a. Far away, from the mainland, the sound of an automobile horn is borne on the sea wind, but it is muffled and indistinct and seems part of another world.

    (Caskie Stinnett, "Of Men and Islands")

   b. There are dark shadows under the woman's eyes and the flesh has fallen away from her neck, for she, like her fellow outcasts, is at the end of a bitter struggle.

2. a. They went not only to Buffalo but also to Niagara Falls.

   b. They will return on either Sunday or Monday.

   c. Neither Buffalo nor Niagara Falls is my favorite city.

3. Not only do more Americans expect more out of life, but they are also more sensitive to forces pronounced harmful to their newly discovered individuality.

    (Andrew Hacker, *The End of the American Era*)

4. She stood upright with the strength of an oak when strength was needed; she bent with grace and the ease of a willow when her help was needed.

    (Wilma Dykeman, *Look to This Day*)

5. We came over the mountains and out of Spain and down the white roads and through the overfoliaged, wet, green Basque country, and finally into Bayonne.

    (Ernest Hemingway, *The Sun Also Rises*)

67

6. Saints and sinners, princes and paupers, all look forward to the same dusty death.

7. The typical modern car can be divided into four main component systems: the engine, the transmission, the electrical system, and the chassis.

8. Humor is a most effective, yet frequently neglected, means of handling the difficult situations in our lives.

9. The nave was dimly lit, the congregation small, the sermon short, and the wind howled a nihilistic counterpoint beyond the black windows blotted with garbled apostles.

(John Updike, "Packed Dirt, Churchgoing, a Dying Cat, a Traded Car")

CHAPTER 4

Building with Adjective Clauses

As we saw in Chapter 3, coordination is a useful technique for connecting ideas that are roughly equal in importance. Often in our writing, however, we need to show that one idea is more or less important than another. On these occasions we use *subordination* to show that one part of a sentence is secondary (or subordinate) to another part. The simplest kind of subordination involves the adjectives, adverbs, and prepositional phrases discussed in Chapter 2. Other forms of subordination involve whole clauses (containing their own subjects and verbs) that are attached to main clauses. In this chapter you will practice building sentences with *adjective clauses*—subordinate clauses that modify nouns.

From Coordination to Subordination

Consider how we might combine the two sentences below:

> Lila lives in a trailer with a parakeet and some scrappy dogs and cats. Lila has been the town fire warden for nearly thirty years.

We have the option of coordinating the two sentences, as follows:

1. Lila lives in a trailer with a parakeet and some scrappy dogs and cats, <u>and</u> she has been the town fire warden for nearly thirty years.

We have connected the two main clauses with <u>and</u>, but we have not demonstrated that one idea is more significant than the other. What if we wanted to show that where Lila lives is more important than what she does for a living? We could reduce the second main clause to an adjective clause:

2. Lila, <u>who has been the town fire warden for nearly thirty years</u>, lives in a trailer with some scrappy dogs and cats.

To emphasize Lila's job, on the other hand, we need to subordinate the information concerning her home:

3. Lila, <u>who lives in a trailer with a parakeet and some scrappy dogs and cats</u>, has been the town fire warden for nearly thirty years.
   (Mary and Charles Bolte, "News and Politics at the Texaco Station")

The point is not that subordination is inherently superior to coordination—it's not. The point is that subordination with adjective clauses lets us add details that *support* nouns in a main clause rather than compete with them for the reader's attention.

Practice 1

The following sentence consists of two main clauses joined by <u>and</u>:

The manager was wearing a scruffy sort of undertaker's suit, <u>and</u> he was wandering around jangling his keys.

To emphasize what the manager was wearing, we can turn the second main clause into an adjective clause, as follows:

The manager, <u>who was wandering around jangling his keys</u>, was wearing a scruffy sort of undertaker's suit.

Now, to emphasize what the manager was doing, turn the adjective clause into the main clause, and vice versa.

An adjective clause, like a main clause, contains a subject and a verb. In the following sentence, for instance, which is the subject of the adjective clause, and lives is the verb.

The never silent CB radio, which serves as a central information exchange on fires, supplies a lot of other information as well.
(Mary and Charles Bolte, "News and Politics at the Texaco Station")

However, unlike a main clause, an adjective clause cannot stand alone; it must be attached (that is, *subordinated*) to a main clause.

The Relative Pronouns

An adjective clause often begins with a *relative pronoun:* a word that *relates* the information in the adjective clause to a word or phrase in the main clause. The relative pronouns are that, which, and who (with its forms whom and whose). That may refer to either people or things. Which refers exclusively to things or ideas, not people, and who and whom refer to people, not things. Whose usually refers to people and occasionally to things.

Practice 2

a. Combine the two sentences below by turning the first sentence into an adjective clause. Use John Wayne as the subject of the sentence and who as the subject of the adjective clause.

1. John Wayne appeared in over two hundred films.
2. John Wayne was the biggest box-office attraction of his time.

b. Combine the two sentences below by turning the second sentence into an adjective clause. Use The sea as the subject of the sentence and which as the subject of the adjective clause.

1. The sea is often difficult to reach.
2. The sea looks so near and so tempting.

Nonrestrictive Adjective Clauses

In the examples so far, the adjective clause has been set off from the main clause by a pair of commas. Here is another example:

Old Dr. Bones, <u>who tries to act and dress like a teenager</u>, is going through his second childhood.

An adjective clause set off by commas is *nonrestrictive:* in other words, the information in the clause does not restrict or limit the noun it modifies (for example, <u>Old Dr. Bones</u> in the sentence above). The commas signify that the adjective clause provides added, not essential, information. An adjective clause that can be omitted from a sentence without affecting the basic meaning of the sentence should be set off by a pair of commas.

Restrictive Adjective Clauses

On the other hand, an adjective clause that is *restrictive* should not be set off by commas. Here is an example:

An older person <u>who tries to act and dress like a teenager</u> is often an object of ridicule or pity.

In this sentence, the adjective clause restricts or limits the meaning of the noun it modifies (<u>An older person</u>). An adjective clause that cannot be omitted from a sentence without affecting the basic meaning of the sentence should *not* be set off by a pair of commas. The relative pronoun <u>that</u> begins restrictive clauses only. <u>Which</u> and <u>who</u> begin both restrictive and nonrestrictive clauses, although some writers prefer to use <u>that</u> instead of <u>which</u> in restrictive clauses.

Practice 3

a. Combine the two sentences below by turning the first sentence into a nonrestrictive adjective clause.

1. Uncle Fred says that his dull job is unendurable.
2. Uncle Fred does not know what to do with his leisure time.

b. Combine the two sentences below by turning the first sentence into a restrictive adjective clause. Omit the word <u>certain</u>.

1. Certain people find their dull jobs unendurable.
2. These people often do not know what to do with their leisure time.

Arranging Adjective Clauses

Whether an adjective clause is restrictive or nonrestrictive, it usually appears closely after the noun it modifies. Often the adjective clause *immediately* follows the noun, as in the sentence below:

A lightning flash is born as a leader stroke <u>which works its way across the cloud and downward in a jerky path</u>.

However, as long as there is no chance of confusing the reader, one or more phrases may separate an adjective clause from the word it modifies:

Television's most overwhelming characteristic is the size of its audience, always measured in millions, <u>which makes it the greatest shared popular experience in the world</u>.

Be careful not to place the adjective clause so far from the noun it modifies that your sentence becomes awkward or confusing.

Practice 4

Combine the sentences below by turning the third sentence into an adjective clause.

a. The world is full of people.
b. These people are in positions of responsibility.
c. These people are ignorant of their own business.

Using Whom

Whom is a word that sounds old fashioned and excessively formal to many contemporary writers, and so they do their best to avoid using it. Nevertheless, the <u>whom</u> construction (as well as its alternatives) is a useful one.

We have seen that *who* can serve as the subject of an adjective clause. Here is another example:

Anne Sullivan was the teacher <u>who</u> helped Helen Keller overcome her severe handicaps.

<u>Whom</u> serves as the object of an adjective clause: in other words, <u>whom</u> represents a noun that receives the action of the verb in the adjective clause. Consider this example:

Anne Sullivan was the teacher <u>whom</u> Helen Keller met in 1887.

In this sentence, <u>Helen Keller</u> is the subject of the adjective clause, and <u>whom</u> is the object. Stated another way, <u>who</u> is equivalent to <u>he</u>, <u>she</u>, or <u>they</u> in a main clause; <u>whom</u> is equivalent to <u>him</u>, <u>her</u>, or <u>them</u> in a main clause.

Some writers avoid <u>whom</u> by using <u>that</u> in its place:

Anne Sullivan was the teacher <u>that</u> Helen Keller met in 1887.

An alternative is to omit the relative pronoun altogether:

Anne Sullivan was the teacher Helen Keller met in 1887.

These two constructions, particularly the second one, are less formal (and, to some ears, less stilted) than is the construction with <u>whom</u>.

Practice 5

Write two versions of the following sentence without the relative pronoun <u>whom</u>:

Andy Warhol is the artist whom one critic dubbed the "King of Kitsch."

Using Whose

Whose, the possessive form of who, begins adjective clauses that de-scribe something that belongs to or is a part of someone or something mentioned in the main clause. An adjective clause beginning with whose may be either restrictive (as in sentence 1 below) or nonres-trictive (as in sentence 2).

1. The star baseball pitcher whose arm is sore because of a torn muscle or tissue damage may need sustained rest more than anything else.
2. The ostrich, whose wings are useless for flight, can run faster than the swiftest horse.

Practice 6

Combine the sentences below by turning the second sentence into a whose clause and the third into a which clause.

a. The popular image of a scientist is a scrawny runt.
b. The sole purpose in life of this runt is to synthesize a compound.
c. The compound when injected into beautiful blondes turns them into gorillas.

Prepositions plus Relative Pronouns

The relative pronouns which, whom, and whose often follow prep-ositions, as the following sentences demonstrate:

Old Nat Burge was chewing on a splinter of wood and watching the moon come up lazily out of the cemetery in which nine of his daughters were lying, and only two of them were dead.

(James Thurber, "Bateman Comes Home")

Often students who are most in trouble with the police over drugs are those for whom the need for crime and punishment was more significant than the need for drugs.

(Herbert Hendlin, *The Age of Sensation*)

The children went to visit Mr. Singer, <u>in whose</u> house they played all summer long.

Practice 7

Combine the sentences below by turning the first sentence into an adjective clause beginning with <u>by which</u> and the third sentence into an adjective clause beginning with <u>in which</u>.

    a. A man can become a writer.
    b. There is no formula.
    c. A man can be one.
    d. There is no end to the number of ways.

Reducing Adjective Clauses

Adjective clauses can often be shortened by omitting the relative pronoun. Some clauses (particularly those with a form of the verb <u>to be</u>: <u>is</u>, <u>are</u>, <u>was</u>, <u>were</u>) can be reduced to phrases, as shown below.

1. Dr. Witless, <u>who is my philosophy instructor</u>, was arrested last week for stealing ideas.
2. Dr. Witless, <u>my philosophy instructor</u>, was arrested last week for stealing ideas.

The adjective clause in sentence 1 has been reduced to an *appositive* in sentence 2. Appositive constructions will be discussed in detail in the next chapter.

Another way of shortening certain adjective clauses is to omit the relative pronoun <u>that</u>, as the next sentence demonstrates.

> One of the more detestable euphemisms [<u>that</u>] I have come across in recent years is the name "Operation Sunshine," which is the name the U.S. Government gave to some experiments [<u>that</u>] it conducted with the hydrogen bomb in the South Pacific.
> (Neil Postman, *Crazy Talk, Stupid Talk*)

Do not omit the relative pronoun if the reader will be confused without it. In many cases, though, dropping the relative pronoun will make the sentence sound less cluttered as well as less formal.

Practice 8

Make two of the sentences below more concise by eliminating the relative pronouns. One of the three sentences needs the relative pronoun for the sentence to make sense, and so make no changes.

a. One of the finest stories that I have ever read is Isaac Bashevis Singer's "Gimpel the Fool."

b. The woman is wearing golden stretch pants, green eyelids, and a hiveshaped head of hair that looks both in color and texture exactly like 25¢ worth of cotton candy.

(Edward Abbey, *Desert Solitaire*)

c. Hurling, which has been the national sport of Ireland since legendary times, is to American eyes like a soccer game played at ice-hockey speed.

Summary

Subordination with adjective clauses is a useful way of combining two sentences that refer to the same person or thing. Later chapters will introduce you to other methods of subordination—structures that help show the relative importance of different ideas in a sentence. Now, however, you can practice building with adjective clauses in the exercises that follow.

Exercise: Sentence Revising

Rewrite each sentence according to the instructions in parentheses.

1. Gus took a correspondence course in taxidermy; he is stuffing the Christmas turkey with cement. (*Eliminate the semicolon, and turn the first main clause into an adjective clause.*)

2. Tutankhamen was an Egyptian pharaoh of the eighteenth dynasty, and his tomb was discovered in 1922. (*Eliminate* and; *turn the second main clause into an adjective clause.*)

3. Buffy, who has taken a part-time job at Bargain World, is saving her money for a trip to Izod, Connecticut. (*Turn the underlined adjective clause into the main clause, and vice versa.*)

4. There is a difference between going somewhere by walking, which <u>is</u> a matter of transportation, and going for a walk, which <u>is</u> a matter of recreation. (*Make this sentence more concise by eliminating the relative pronouns and the underlined verbs.*)

5. <u>We bought</u> a sailboat <u>from your uncle in Nantucket</u> that has a hole in the bottom and rats nesting in the bow. (*Begin the sentence with* The sailboat *as subject, and turn the underlined word group into an adjective clause.*)

6. The TV and radio field <u>used to be rich ground for swindlers</u> but has been notably cleaned up in recent years. (*Eliminate* but, *and turn the underlined word group into an adjective clause.*)

7. <u>This beer made Milwaukee famous</u>; this beer has made a loser out of me. (*Eliminate the semicolon, and turn the first main clause into an adjective clause.*)

8. There was a tile stove in Shosha's apartment, and <u>a cricket lived there behind</u> the stove. (*Eliminate* and; *turn the underlined word group into an adjective clause.*)

9. One day a window was blown right out of its sashes by a strong gust of wind; the window <u>frame had rotted</u>. (*Eliminate the semicolon, and turn the underlined word group into a* whose *clause.*)

10. Willie Sarkis, <u>who now plays for drunks at the Rainbow Bar & Grill</u>, once gave a piano concert at Carnegie Hall. (*Turn the underlined adjective clause into the main clause, and vice versa.*)

Exercise: Sentence Building

Combine the sentences in each set into a single, clear sentence with at least one adjective clause. Subordinate the information that *you* think is of secondary importance. Then create a second combination whenever possible.

1. The first alarm clock woke the sleeper by gently rubbing his feet.
   The first alarm clock was invented by Leonardo da Vinci.

2. Some children have not received flu shots.
   These children must visit the school doctor.

3. Success encourages the repetition of old behavior.
   Success is not nearly as good a teacher as failure.

4. I showed the arrowhead to Rachel.
   Rachel's father is an archaeologist.

5. Jenny was born in a boxcar.
   Jenny was born somewhere in Arkansas.
   Jenny gets hysterical every time she hears the shriek of a train whis-
   tle.

6. A drunk lived up on the corner.
   He was a true phenomenon.
   He could surely have qualified as the king of all the world's winos.
   This does not exclude the French.

   (Ralph Ellison, "Living with Music")

7. Future generations can look forward to a burden of work.
   The burden will be increasingly lighter.
   Future generations can look forward to an increasing share of free
   time.
   Future generations require a liberal education.

8. The space shuttle is a rocket.
   The rocket is manned.
   This rocket can be flown back to earth.
   This rocket can be reused.

9. Henry Aaron played baseball.
   Henry Aaron played with the Braves.
   Henry Aaron played for twenty years.
   Henry Aaron was voted into the Hall of Fame.
   The vote was taken in 1982.

10. Oxygen is colorless.
    Oxygen is tasteless.
    Oxygen is odorless.
    Oxygen is the chief life-supporting element of all plant life.
    Oxygen is the chief life-supporting element of all animal life.

11. *Bushidō* is the traditional code of honor of the *samurai*.
    Bushidō is based on the principal of simplicity.
    Bushidō is based on the principal of honesty.
    Bushidō is based on the principle of courage.
    Bushidō is based on the principle of justice.

12. Jenny danced on the roof.
    It was the roof of her trailer.
    Jenny danced during the thunderstorm.
    The thunderstorm flooded the county.
    The thunderstorm was last night.

13. Men have grown inconceivably lonely.
    They have grown lonely in a universe.
    The size of the universe is beyond imagining.
    Our world floats in this universe.
    Our world floats like a dust mote.
    Our world floats in the void of night.

    > (Loren Eiseley, "Little Men and Flying Saucers")

14. There are fish.
    These fish breathe air.
    They do not breathe through a lung.
    They breathe through their stomachs.
    Or they breathe through chambers.
    The chambers are where their gills should be.

15. The cat watches solemnly.
    The cat watches these two-legged creatures.
    These creatures are great.
    These creatures are hulking.
    The cat has unaccountably been born into the strange tribe of these creatures.
    These creatures are so clumsy.
    These creatures are so noisy.
    These creatures are so vexing to the spirit.
    His spirit is quiet.
    Love is not in his feline heart.
    Gratitude is not in his feline heart.

    > (Alan Devoe, "Our Enemy, the Cat")

Exercise: Building Paragraphs and Essays

I. This exercise has been adapted from two paragraphs in *Farewell to Manzanar*, by Jeanne Wakatsuki Houston and James D. Houston. The five paragraphs preceding the exercise describe the arrival, in 1942, of Mrs. Houston's family at an internment camp in Manzanar, California. Complete the selection by combining the sentences in each set. Several of the sets, though not all, require one or more adjective clauses.

First Night at Block 16, Manzanar

The name Manzanar meant nothing to us when we left Boyle Heights. We didn't know where it was or what it was. We went because the government ordered us to. And, in the case of my older brothers and sisters, we went with a certain amount of relief. They had all heard stories of Japanese homes being attacked, of beatings in the streets of California towns. They were as frightened of the Caucasians as Caucasians were of us. Moving, under what appeared to be government protection, to an area less directly threatened by the war seemed not such a bad idea at all. For some it actually sounded like a fine adventure. . . .

We had pulled up just in time for dinner. The mess halls weren't completed yet. An outdoor chow line snaked around a half-finished building that broke a good part of the wind. They issued us army mess kits, the round metal kind that fold over, and plopped in scoops of canned Vienna sausage, canned string beans, steamed rice that had been cooked too long, and on top of the rice a serving of canned apricots. The Caucasian servers were thinking the fruit poured over rice would make a good dessert. Among the Japanese, of course, rice is never eaten with sweet foods, only with salty or savory foods. Few of us could eat such a mixture. But at this point no one dared protest. It would have been impolite. I was horrified when I saw the apricot syrup seeping through my little mound of rice. I opened my mouth to complain. My mother jabbed me in the back to keep quiet. We moved on through the line and joined the others squatting in the lee of half-raised walls, dabbing courteously at what was, for almost everyone there, an inedible concoction.

After dinner we were taken to Block 16, a cluster of fifteen barracks that had just been finished a day or so earlier—although finished was hardly the word for it. The shacks were built of one thickness of pine planking covered with tarpaper. They sat on concrete footings, with about two feet of open space between the floorboards and the ground. Gaps showed between the planks, and as the weeks passed and the green wood dried out, the gaps widened. Knotholes gaped in the uncovered floor.

Each barracks was divided into six units, sixteen by twenty feet, about the size of a living room, with one bare bulb hanging from the ceiling and an oil stove for heat. We were assigned two of these for the twelve people in our family group; and our official family "number" was enlarged by three digits—16 plus the number of this barracks. We were issued steel army cots, two brown army blankets each, and some mattress covers, which my brothers stuffed with straw.

The first task was to divide up what space we had for sleeping. Bill and Woody contributed a blanket each and partitioned off the first room: one side for Bill and Tomi, one side for Woody and Chizu and their baby girl. Woody also got the stove, for heating formulas.

1. Young couples like these had it hardest.
   It was hardest during the first few months.
   Many of these people had married just before the evacuation began.
   They married in order not to be separated and sent to different camps.
2. Our two rooms were crowded.
   At least it was all in the family.
3. Some of the compartments were sixteen-by-twenty feet.
   My oldest sister was shoved into one of those compartments.
   Her husband was with her.
   They were shoved in with six people.
   They had never seen these people before.
4. Partitioning off a room like that wasn't easy.
5. It was bitter cold when we arrived.
   The wind did not abate.
6. They used those army blankets for room dividers.
   These were all they had to use.
   Two of the blankets were barely enough to keep one person warm.
7. They argued over whose blanket should be sacrificed.
   They later argued about noise at night.
   They continued arguing over matters like that for months.
   They continued arguing until my sister and her husband left.
   They left to harvest sugar beets in Idaho.
8. A call came through the camp.
   The call was for workers to alleviate the wartime labor shortage.
   It was grueling work up there.
   Wages were pitiful.
   It sounded better than their life at Manzanar.
9. They knew they'd have, if nothing else, a room.
   Perhaps they'd have a cabin of their own.
10. The rest of us squeezed into the second room.
    We squeezed into the room that first night in Block 16.
    These were the rest of us—Granny, Lillian, age fourteen, Ray, thirteen, May, eleven, Kiyo, ten, Mama, and me.
11. I didn't mind this at all at the time.
12. I was youngest.
    That meant I got to sleep with Mama.
13. I had a great time jumping up and down on the mattress.
    I had a great time before we went to bed.

14. The boys had stuffed straw into her mattress.
    There was so much straw we had to flatten it some.
    We flattened it so we wouldn't slide off.
15. I slept with her every night after that.
    I did this until Papa came back.

Writing Suggestion

Recall a particular time in your life when you were discriminated against or treated unfairly. In an essay, describe the circumstances and how you coped with them. Explain if your perception of the incident is any different now from what it was at the time.

II. This exercise has been adapted from two paragraphs in "The Dream Animal," an essay by Loren Eiseley. After discussing the remarkable development of the human brain in the first year of life (it triples in size), Eiseley continues in the paragraphs below to consider an analogy between the brain's development and the development of the human species. Combine the sentences in each set of the exercise, using adjective clauses when appropriate. The final two paragraphs of Eiseley's essay follow the exercise.

Out of the Ice Age

We can . . . weigh, measure and dissect the brains of any number of existing monkeys. We may learn much in the process, but the key to our human brain clock is not among them. It arose in the germ plasm of the human group alone and we are the last living representatives of that family. As we contemplate, however, the old biological law that, to a certain degree, the history of the individual tends to reproduce the evolutionary history of the group to which it belongs, we cannot help but wonder if this remarkable spurt in brain development may not represent something roughly akin to what happened in the geological past of man—a sudden or explosive increase which was achieved in a relatively short period, geologically speaking. . . .

In discussing the significance of the Piltdown hoax and its bearing upon the Darwin-Wallace controversy, I used the accepted orthodox geological estimate of the time involved in that series of fluctuating events which we speak of popularly as the "Ice Age." I pointed out that almost all of what we know about human evolution is confined to this period. Long though one million years may seem compared with our few millennia of written history, it is, in geological terms, in evolutionary terms, a mere minute's tick of the astronomical clock.

1. Among other forms of life than man, few marked transformations occurred.
2. Rather, the Ice Age was a time of great extinctions.
   This was true particularly toward its close.
3. Some of the huge beasts vanished totally.
   The huge beasts vanished from the earth.
   The intercontinental migrations of the huge beasts had laid down the first paths.
   Man had traveled along the first paths.*
4. Mammoths were the Temperate Zone elephants.
   Mammoths dropped the last of their tusks.
   Their tusks were heavy.
   The tusks were dropped along the fringes of the ice.
   The fringes were receding.
5. The bisons faded back into the past.
   The bisons were long horned.
   Man had nourished himself upon the herds of the bisons.
   Man had nourished himself for many a century.
   It had been many a long century of wanderings.
   The wanderings were illiterate.
6. There are cultural remnants of the ape at the beginning of the first glaciation.
   These remnants can scarcely be distinguished from chance bits of stone.
   By the ending of the fourth ice, the ape has become an artist.
   By the ending of the fourth ice, the ape has become a world rover.
   By the ending of the fourth ice, the ape has become the penetrator of the five continents.
7. There is nothing quite like this event in all the time that went before.
   There had been brute animal dominance on earth.
   The end of this dominance had come at last.
8. The growth of forests would lie more and more at the whim of that creature.
   The destruction of forests would lie more and more at the whim of that creature.
   The spread of deserts would lie more and more at the whim of that creature.
   For good or ill, these things would lie at the whim of that creature.
   That creature was cunning.

* Create two adjective clauses, one beginning with <u>whose</u>, the other with <u>along which</u>.

That creature was insatiable.
That creature slipped out of the twilight of nature's laboratory.
That creature slipped so mysteriously.
The twilight was green.
That creature slipped out a short million years ago.

It is unlikely . . . in our present comfortable circumstances that the pace of human change will ever again speed at the accelerated rate it knew when man strove against extinction. The story of Eden is a greater allegory than man has ever guessed. For it was truly man who, walking memoryless through bars of sunlight and shade in the morning of the world, sat down and passed a wondering hand across his heavy forehead. Time and darkness, knowledge of good and evil, have walked with him ever since. It is the destiny struck by the clock in the body in that brief space between the beginning of the first ice and that of the second. In just that interval a new world of terror and loneliness appears to have been created in the soul of man.

For the first time in four billion years a living creature had contemplated himself and heard with a sudden, unaccountable loneliness, the whisper of the wind in the night reeds. Perhaps he knew, there in the grass by the chill waters, that he had before him an immense journey. Perhaps the same foreboding still troubles the hearts of those who walk out of a crowded room and stare with relief into the abyss of space so long as there is a star to be seen twinkling across those miles of emptiness.

Writing Suggestions

1. Reread the last paragraph of Eiseley's essay, and then, in a paragraph, describe some experience you have had looking at the night sky. Describe what you saw, what you felt, and what you thought about.
2. Elsewhere in his essay, Eiseley describes man as a

   . . . dream animal—living partially within a secret universe of his own creation and sharing that secret universe in his head with other, similar heads. Symbolic communication had begun. Man had escaped out of the eternal present of the animal world into a knowledge of past and future.

   In an essay, compare and contrast human beings with other animals. There are many different approaches you can take to this subject. Consider some of these approaches in a brainstorming session (see the Discovery section at the end of this chapter).

III. This exercise has been adapted from paragraphs 2 through 6 of an essay by Heidi Becker, a student. Read the introductory paragraph below, and then complete the essay by combining the sentences in each set of the exercise, using adjective clauses where appropriate.

Diets: An American Obsession

The fastest growing industry in America today is the diet industry. Every week there are new diet, exercise, or health-and-beauty books, all promising to make us thin forever. Few of them offer anything very new or effective, and not one of them can provide us with self-discipline, which, after all, is the one thing we must have to stay in shape. After making a thorough study of American diets I have found a few that offer positive proof that dieting is a form of madness, one often involving much expense and suffering.

1. One diet amuses me.
   This is the Hollywood Diet.
2. The creator of this diet promises something.
   "Eat all you want," he promises.
   "Eat as often as you want," he promises.
3. There is a trick.
   You must spend two months at a health spa.
   Machines pummel you at the health spa.
   Machines squeeze you at the health spa.
   Machines slap you at the health spa.
4. The machines do this at a moderate cost.
   The cost is $1,000 per week.
5. Doctors can remove pouches from the face.
   Doctors can remove wrinkles from the eyes.
   Doctors can remove wattles from the neck.
   Doctors do this surgically.
   Doctors do this for another ten grand.
6. The superrich often graduate from the Hollywood Diet.
   They graduate to the Cocaine Diet.
7. You inhale the cocaine.
   You do this simply.
   You inhale through your nose.
   You inhale with a straw.
   You wait for your face to turn numb.
   You then forget about eating.
   You forget for days at a time.

8. The Cocaine Diet will set you back a few hundred dollars a day.
   You are guaranteed to lose weight on the Cocaine Diet.
   You are guaranteed to lose various parts of your anatomy as well.
9. Some people can't afford either of these California diets.
   For these people I recommend the Starvation Diet.
10. You avoid all food.
    You drink nothing but water.
    You lose a pound a day.
11. Eventually your stomach begins to grumble a lot.
    You are likely to feel depressed.
    You are likely to feel tired.
12. Nausea follows.
    Dizziness follows.
    Sleepless nights follow.
    Soon your blood pressure drops.
    Your vision blurs.
    Your brain shrivels up.
    It shrivels like desiccated tapioca.
13. Of course you lose weight.
14. The Starvation Diet produces results.
    The Cocaine Diet produces results.
    The results of both are similar.
    The Starvation Diet is far more economical.
15. There is the Partnership Diet.
    This one is more romantic than most.
16. You sign a diet pact.
    Your chubby chum signs a diet pact.
    This pact is similar to a suicide pact.
17. You both agree to support each other.
    You are supporting your efforts to lose weight.
18. You enjoy the same meals.
    The meals consist of carrot juice, celery, and prunes.
    You encourage each other.
    You may catch your partner cheating.
    Then you go crazy.
19. In the end, you are alone.
    You try to assuage your loneliness.
    You try desperately.
    You do this with pepperoni pizzas.
    You do this with schooners of ale.
20. I suggest you avoid all diets.
    This is my opinion.
21. Diets only make you fat—or dead.
22. Sure, Big Macs may not be ideal.

French fries may not be ideal.
They may not be ideal for rapid weight loss.
You can maintain a steady weight.
You can do this with exercise.
23. Dieters are dreamers.
24. One may feel deprived of his or her favorite dishes.
Then one is more likely to lapse into binges.
These binges are uncontrolled.
25. Forget the fad diets.
Enjoy your favorite foods.
Run for your life.

Writing Suggestions

1. If you have ever attempted to diet, describe your experience in an essay.
2. In "Diets: An American Obsession," Heidi Becker uses examples to demonstrate that "Diets only make you fat—or dead." In an essay of your own, use examples to point out the advantages or disadvantages of one of the following subjects: Exercise, Working Your Way Through College, Cable Television, The Telephone, Computers.

Exercise: Recombining

This exercise has been adapted from four paragraphs in Neil Postman's *Crazy Talk, Stupid Talk: How We Defeat Ourselves by the Way We Talk and What to Do About It.* The author's twenty-seven original sentences have been combined into eleven in the exercise. Untangle these eleven sentences by breaking them down into short sentences and recombining them, as shown in the example below.

Sentence

People who are partial to euphemisms—which are commonly defined as an auspicious or exalted term (like "sanitation engineer") that is used in place of more down-to-earth terms (like "garbage man")—stand accused of being "phony" or of trying to hide what it is they are really talking about, and there is no doubt that in some situations the accusation is entirely proper.

Broken down

There are people who are partial to euphemisms.

Euphemisms are commonly defined as an auspicious or exalted term (like "sanitation engineer") that is used in place of a more down-to-earth term (like "garbage man").

These people stand accused of being phony.

These people stand accused of trying to hide what it is they are really talking about.

There is no doubt that in some situations the accusation is entirely proper.

Recombining

A euphemism is commonly defined as an auspicious or exalted term (like "sanitation engineer") that is used in place of a more down-to-earth term (like "garbage man"). People who are partial to euphemisms stand accused of being "phony" or of trying to hide what it is they are really talking about. And there is no doubt that in some situations the accusation is entirely proper.

Feel free to change the order of the sentences as you recombine them. Your aim is not to imagine what Postman's original sentences might be, but to create four clear, effective paragraphs. Many combinations are possible.

1. People who are partial to euphemisms—which are commonly defined as an auspicious or exalted term (like "sanitation engineer") that is used in place of a more down-to-earth term (like "garbage man")—stand accused of being "phony" or of trying to hide what it is they are really talking about, and there is no doubt that in some situations the accusation is entirely proper.

2. For example, it is obvious that the government, in choosing the term "Operation Sunshine," which is the name it gave to some experiments it conducted with the hydrogen bomb in the South Pacific, was trying to expunge the hideous imagery that the bomb evokes and in so doing committed, as I see it, an immoral act.

3. This sort of process of giving pretty names to essentially ugly realities is what has given euphemizing such a bad name, and people like George Orwell have done valuable work for all of us in calling attention to how the process works, but there is another side to euphemizing that is worth mentioning, and a few words here in its defense will not be amiss.

4. To begin with, we must keep in mind that things do not have "real" names (although many people believe that they do), which is to say that a garbage man is not "really" a "garbage man," any more than he is really a "sanitation engineer."

5. There are things and then there are the names of things, and it is considered a fundamental error in all branches of semantics to assume that a name and a thing are one and the same, though it is true, of course, that a name is usually so firmly associated with the thing it denotes that it is extremely difficult to separate one from the other.

6. It would appear that human beings almost naturally come to *identify* names with things, which is one of our more fascinating illusions, for if you change the names of things, you change how people will regard them, and that is as good as changing the nature of the thing itself.

7. Now all sorts of scoundrels who know this perfectly well can make us love almost anything by getting us to transfer the charm of a name to whatever worthless thing that they are promoting, but at the same time and in the same vein, euphemizing is a perfectly intelligent method of generating new and useful ways of perceiving things.

8. The man who wants us to call him a "sanitation engineer" instead of a "garbage man" is hoping that we will treat him with more respect than we presently do; he, whose euphemism is laughable only if we think that he is not deserving of such notice or respect, wants us to see that he is of some importance to society, just as the teacher who prefers to use the term "culturally different children" instead of "slum children" is euphemizing, all right, but is doing it to encourage us to see aspects of a situation that might otherwise not be attended to.

9. The point I am making is that there is nothing in the process of euphemizing itself that is contemptible, but euphemizing is contemptible when a name makes us see something that is not true or diverts our attention from something that is.

10. To call an experiment "Operation Sunshine" is to suggest a purpose for the bomb that simply does not exist, for the hydrogen bomb kills, there is nothing else that it does, and when you experiment with it, you are trying to find out how widely and well it kills.

11. But to call "slum children" "culturally different," which calls attention, for example, to legitimate reasons why such children might feel alienated from what goes on at school, is something else.

Discovery: Brainstorming

Most of the writing you do is probably solitary. You must discover ideas, compose rough drafts, revise your writing, and finally proofread—all with little or no assistance from others. However, writing does not always have to be such a lonesome activity. In fact, working with others can help you become a better writer. *Brainstorming* is a group project that is particularly useful for generating, focusing, and organizing ideas for an essay.

A brainstorming group may be small (three or four people) or large (an entire class). Begin a session by introducing a subject to the group. This subject may be one that has been assigned by an instructor or one you have chosen on your own. Invite the participants to contribute *any* ideas they may have concerning your subject. No idea should be criticized or rejected out of hand. As in freewriting, the oddest notions may be just the ones that stimulate original approaches to a subject. If the participants feel free to express themselves, one idea will very likely inspire many more.

Take brief notes during the brainstorming session, but don't be so busy taking notes that you cut yourself off from the exchange of ideas. After the session—which may last from ten minutes to half an hour or more—you can evaluate the suggestions and reflect on them privately.

Effective brainstorming, like freewriting, takes practice, and so don't be disappointed if your first session is not very productive. Many people find it difficult at first to exchange ideas without stopping to criticize. Just remember that your aim is to stimulate thinking, not inhibit it.

Here is a project that will introduce you to brainstorming and give you some practice in group writing. Join with three or four other writers to compose a letter of complaint. You may write to an instructor to complain about his or her grading policies, to the cafeteria supervisor to complain about the food, to the governor to complain about cuts in the education budget—whatever the members of your writing group find interesting and worthwhile. Begin by suggesting topics, and have one member of the group write them down as they are given. Don't stop at this point to discuss or evaluate the topics; simply prepare a long list of possibilities.

Once you have filled a page with topics, you can decide among yourselves which one you would like to write about. Then discuss the points you think should be raised in the letter. Again, have one member of the group keep track of these suggestions. Your letter will need to explain the problem clearly and show why your complaint should be taken seriously.

After collecting sufficient material for your letter, elect one member of the group to prepare a rough draft. When this has been completed, the draft should be read out loud so that all members of the group can recommend ways to improve the draft through revision. Each member should have the opportunity to revise the letter according to the suggestions made by the others. Finally, proofread the letter, and to test its effectiveness, mail it.

You can use any of the Writing Suggestions in this book as the starting point for a brainstorming session. Present the suggestion to the group, and together decide on what to say, who to say it to, and a purpose for saying it at all. Group writing such as this will not only help you become a better writer, it will also give you a clearer understanding of the writing process itself.

Practice: Sample Combinations

Use the sentences below as a guide after you have completed the Practice exercises in the first part of this chapter. Since in most cases more than one combination is possible, do not think that your sentences are "incorrect" just because they may not be in exact agreement with the ones below.

1. The manager, who was wearing a scruffy sort of undertaker's suit, was wandering around jangling his keys.
2. a. John Wayne, who appeared in over two hundred films, was the biggest box-office attraction of his time.
   b. The sea, which looks so near and so tempting, is often difficult to reach.
3. a. Uncle Fred, who says that his dull job is unendurable, does not know what to do with his leisure time.
   b. People who find dull jobs unendurable often do not know what to do with their leisure time.
4. The world is full of people in positions of responsibility who are ignorant of their own business.
5. a. Andy Warhol is the artist that one critic dubbed the "King of Kitsch."
   b. Andy Warhol is the artist one critic dubbed the "King of Kitsch."
   c. Andy Warhol, the artist, was dubbed the "King of Kitsch" by one critic.
   d. One critic dubbed artist Andy Warhol the "King of Kitsch."

6. The popular image of a scientist is a scrawny runt whose sole purpose in life is to synthesize a compound which when injected into beautiful blondes turns them into gorillas.

(Paul Saltman, "The Science Jungle")

7. There is no formula by which a man can become a writer, and there is no end to the number of ways in which a man can be one.

(John Ciardi, "Of Writing and Writers")

8. a. One of the finest stories I have ever read is Isaac Bashevis Singer's "Gimpel the Fool."

   b. (No change.)

   c. Hurling, the national sport of Ireland since legendary times, is to American eyes like a soccer game played at ice-hockey speed.

CHAPTER 5

Building with Appositives

An *appositive* is a word or group of words that renames another word in a sentence. Appositive constructions offer concise ways of describing or defining a person, place, or thing. In this chapter you will practice building sentences with these economical constructions.

From Adjective Clauses to Appositives

Consider how the sentences below might be combined:

> Willie Sarkis was a concert pianist in his youth.
> He now plays at the Rainbow Bar & Grill.
> He plays for tips.
> He plays for drunks.

One way to combine these sentences is to convert the first sentence into an adjective clause:

> 1. Willie Sarkis, <u>who was a concert pianist in his youth</u>, now plays for tips and drunks at the Rainbow Bar & Grill.

As we saw in Chapter 4, adjective clauses containing a form of the verb <u>to be</u> (<u>is</u>, <u>are</u>, <u>was</u>, <u>were</u>) can often be shortened to phrases by omitting the relative pronoun and the verb:

2. Willie Sarkis, <u>a concert pianist in his youth</u>, now plays for tips and drunks at the Rainbow Bar & Grill.

This shorter construction—an appositive—clearly and concisely serves to identify or rename the subject of the sentence.

Practice 1

Convert the underlined adjective clause into an appositive by eliminating the relative pronoun and the verb <u>is</u>.

My sister, <u>who is a supervisor at Union Camp</u>, has just been given a company car.

Arranging Appositives

The simplest appositives are those that immediately follow a noun and offer a title or another name for that noun, as in the sentence below.

Arizona Bill, "<u>The Great Benefactor of Mankind</u>," arrayed in buckskins like a dime-novel Indian scout, toured Oklahoma with herbal cures and a liniment of peculiar and powerful properties.

(Sisley Barnes, "The Voyage of Life")

Note that this appositive, like most, could be omitted without changing the basic meaning of the sentence. In other words, it is nonrestrictive and needs to be set off with a pair of commas.

Practice 2

Combine the two sentences below by treating <u>an American journalist</u> as an appositive. Set off the appositive with a pair of commas.

a. Sydney J. Harris is an American journalist.
b. Sydney J. Harris once observed, "Few men ever drop dead from overwork, but many quietly curl up and die because of undersatisfaction."

An appositive may also appear in front of a word it identifies, as this sentence demonstrates:

A dark wedge, the eagle hurtled earthward at nearly two hundred miles per hour.

An appositive at the beginning of a sentence is usually followed by a comma.

Practice 3

Combine the sentences below into a single clear sentence. Arrange the underlined words as an appositive at the beginning of the sentence.

a. Mr. Arnold is a sneaky man.
b. Mr. Arnold is a sinister man.
c. Mr. Arnold lingers in the back alley at dawn.
d. Mr. Arnold creeps along the front walk every evening.

In the examples seen so far, the appositive has always referred to the subject of the sentence. However, an appositive may precede or follow any noun in the sentence. In the following example the appositive refers to *roles*, the object of a preposition:

People are summed up largely by the roles they fill in society—wife or husband, soldier or salesperson, student or scientist—and by the qualities others ascribe to them.

This sentence demonstrates another way to punctuate appositives—with dashes. When the appositive itself contains commas, setting off the construction with dashes helps prevent confusion. Using dashes rather than commas also serves to emphasize the appositive.

Practice 4

Combine the sentences below by turning the first sentence into an appositive. Place the appositive after Hawaii in the middle of the sentence, and set it off with dashes.

a. Hawaii is an island far distant from the major sources of pollution.
b. The amount of junk in the air over Hawaii has increased 35 percent in the past decade.

Placing the appositive at the very end of a sentence is another way to give it special emphasis. Compare the two sentences below.

1. At the far end of the pasture, the most magnificent animal I had ever seen—a white-tailed deer—was cautiously edging toward a salt-lick block.
2. At the far end of the pasture, cautiously edging toward a salt-lick block, was the most magnificent animal I had ever seen—a white-tailed deer.

Whereas the appositive merely interrupts sentence 1, it marks the climax of sentence 2.

Practice 5

Rewrite the sentence below so that the appositive appears at the end.

The final gift—hope—lay at the bottom of Pandora's box.

Variations

Although an appositive usually renames a noun in a sentence, it may, in fact, repeat a noun for the sake of clarity and emphasis.

In America, as in anywhere else in the world, we must find a focus in our lives at an early age, a focus that is beyond the mechanics of earning a living or coping with a household.

(Santha Rama Rau, "An Invitation to Serenity")

Notice that the appositive in this sentence is modified by an adjective clause. Adjectives, prepositional phrases, and adjective clauses (in other words, all the structures that can modify any noun) are frequently used to add details to an appositive.

Practice 6

Combine the two sentences below by turning the second sentence into an appositive. Repeat the word <u>laws</u>, and place the appositive at the end of the sentence.

  a. The puritans are pressing now, and sometimes achieving, various laws designed to restrict hunting.
  b. These are laws that have nothing to do with game protection or safety.

Most appositives identify what something <u>is</u>, but there are also negative appositives that identify what something <u>is not</u>.

Japanese line managers and production employees, <u>rather than staff specialists</u>, are primarily responsible for quality assurance.

Negative appositives begin with a word such as <u>not</u>, <u>never</u>, or <u>rather than</u>.

Practice 7

Combine the sentences below by turning the first sentence into a negative appositive.

  a. Marcus Aurelius was not a political innovator.
  b. Marcus Aurelius strove diligently to sustain and preserve the civilization and social order that he had inherited.

Two, three, or even more appositives may appear alongside the same noun, as the following sentence shows:

Leningrad, <u>presently a city of four million, the Soviet Union's second largest and northernmost metropolis</u>, was built to the taste of the czars.

So long as we do not overwhelm the reader with too much information at one time, the double or triple appositive can be a very effective way of adding supplementary details to a sentence.

Practice 8

Combine the sentences below into one clear sentence, and turn sentences d and e into two appositives, both referring to <u>snow</u>.

   a. The sky was sunless.
   b. The sky was grey.
   c. There was snow in the air.
   d. The snow was buoyant motes.
   e. The snow was playthings that floated like the toy flakes inside a crystal.

A final variation is the list appositive that precedes a pronoun such as <u>all</u> or <u>these</u> or <u>everyone</u>. Here is an example:

<u>Streets of yellow row houses, the ochre plaster walls of old churches, the crumbling sea-green mansions now occupied by government offices— all</u> seem in sharper focus, with their defects hidden by the snow.

(Leona P. Schecter, "Moscow")

In fact, the word <u>all</u> is not essential to the meaning of the sentence: the list at the beginning of the sentence could serve alone as the subject. However, the pronoun contributes to the sentence's clarity by drawing together the items before the sentence goes on to make a point about them.

Practice 9

Combine the sentences below into one clear sentence, and arrange sentences a through f as a list appositive at the beginning of the sentence.

   a. There is birth.
   b. There is the emergence into manhood.
   c. There is graduation from school at various levels.
   d. There are birthdays.
   e. There is marriage.
   f. There is death.
   g. Each of these outstanding steps is acknowledged by a ceremony of some sort.

Summary

We have seen that the appositive can be viewed, first of all, as a simplified adjective clause. But the appositive is a useful and versatile structure in its own right—one that adds information to nouns without lengthening a sentence with connecting words.

The exercises that follow will give you practice in building sentences with appositives.

Exercise: Sentence Revising

Rewrite each of the following sentences according to the instructions in parentheses.

1. My wife, who is a peculiar woman, put ground glass in my spinach salad last night. (*Reduce the underlined adjective clause to an appositive.*)
2. The house we lived in, a barracks with single plank walls and rough wooden floors, was nothing more than a shack, like the cheapest kind of migrant workers' housing. (*Place the underlined appositive after the noun* shack.)
3. Poppa was a good quiet man who spent the last hours before our parting moving aimlessly about the yard, keeping to himself and avoiding me. (*Eliminate* who *and use the underlined word group as an appositive.*)
4. The horses, the powerful electrical system, and the deep-tread tires go for nothing in a snowstorm. (*Use the underlined word group as a list appositive before the subject* all.)
5. Jim Thorpe, who was born on May 28, 1888, in a two-room farmhouse near Prague, Oklahoma, was the greatest American athlete of modern times. (*Eliminate* who *and treat the underlined word group as an appositive.*)
6. Success may be too costly if the end result is fear of not repeating the success. (*Make this more emphatic by repeating the word* fear *and treating the underlined word group as an appositive.*)
7. The new moon floats above the mountains and the ragged black clouds, a pale fragment of what is to come. (*Shift the underlined prepositional phrase to the beginning of the sentence so that the appositive immediately follows* the new moon.)

8. The little crowd of mourners <u>was made up of</u> all men and boys, no women, <u>and they</u> threaded their way across the market place between the piles of pomegranates and the taxis and the camels. *(Create an appositive by eliminating the underlined words.)*

9. The road began to curve and houses <u>with lawns, driveways, and hedges</u> appeared on either side. *(Create an appositive at the end of the sentence by repeating* houses *and following it with the underlined prepositional phrase.)*

10. The gardener <u>was</u> a shortish fellow, <u>and he had</u> a little brown moustache and sharp little brown eyes; <u>he</u> tiptoed into the room, touched his imaginary cap to Paul's mother, and stole to the bedside. *(Eliminate the semicolon and the underlined words to create an appositive.)*

Exercise: Sentence Building

Combine the sentences in each set into a single, clear sentence with at least one appositive. Create a second combination whenever possible.

1. We were waiting outside the prison cells.
   The cells were a row of sheds fronted with double bars.
   The cells were like small animal cages.

   (George Orwell, "A Hanging")

2. Joan Rivers cracked a few jokes.
   The jokes were about Heidi Bromowitz.
   Heidi Bromowitz was her easy-living chum in high school.

3. My father was outside.
   My father was beneath the window.
   My father whistled for Queen.
   Queen was our English setter.

4. We saw the stream in the valley.
   The stream was black.
   The stream was halted.
   The stream was a tarred path through the wilderness.

   (Laurie Lee, "Winter and Summer")

5. The prisoner was a Hindu.
   The prisoner was a puny wisp of a man.
   The prisoner had a shaven head.
   The prisoner had vague liquid eyes.

   (George Orwell, "A Hanging")

6. We arrived at a group of peasant houses.
   The group was small.
   The houses were low yellow constructions.
   The houses had dried-mud walls.
   The houses had straw roofs.

   (Alberto Moravia, *Lobster Land: A Traveler in China*)

7. A great many old people came.
   They knelt around us.
   They prayed.
   They included old women with jet-black faces.
   The women had braided hair.
   They included old men with work-gnarled hands.

   (Langston Hughes, "Salvation")

8. When you live in a country place you learn to endure the constant
   company of deaths around you.
   The deaths mean the rip and twist of the knife in hogs' throats in
   December.
   The deaths mean the snap of the chipmunk's spine between the
   weasel's teeth.
   But I have not learned to look without a flinch when the hawks
   are at their work.

   (Alan Devoe, "The Hawks")

9. One of the Cratchet girls had borrowed the books.
   She was a hatchet-faced girl.
   She was thin.
   She was eager.
   She was a transplanted Cockney.
   She had a frenzy for reading.

   (Wallace Stegner, *Wolf Willow*)

10. The woman is an untouchable.
    She is a "sweeper" in Indian parlance.
    She is a scavenger of the village.
    She cleans latrines.

She disposes of dead animals.
She washes drains.
> (Peggy and Pierre Streit, "The Well: Drama of India")

11. The teacher was a shaky old fellow.
    He wore gold-framed bifocals.
    The teacher started off by informing us that there was no secret to
    doing well on College Boards.
    The teacher went on to talk a little about a sister of his.
    His sister was about to undergo surgery.
    The teacher then had us spend the rest of the time taking mock
    College Boards in exercise books.
    We bought the exercise books from the school for five dollars apiece.
    > (Andrew Ward, *Fits and Starts: The Premature Memoirs of
    > Andrew Ward*)

12. It was the kind of home that gathers memories like dust.
    It was a place filled with laughter.
    It was filled with play.
    It was filled with pain.
    It was filled with hurt.
    It was filled with ghosts.
    It was filled with games.
    > (Lillian Smith, *Killers of the Dream*)

13. A light breaks through.
    The light is fresh.
    The light is golden.
    Now the rainbow sign appears in the east.
    The double rainbow has one foot in the canyon of the Colorado.
    The double rainbow has the other far north in Salt Wash Valley.
    > (Edward Abbey, *Desert Solitaire*)

14. Connie Chaser was tall.
    Connie Chaser was blond.
    Connie Chaser was high-cheekboned.
    Connie Chaser was an actress.
    Connie Chaser was a scholar.
    Connie Chaser was irrevocably alienated.
    Connie Chaser had a hostile and perceptive wit.
    Connie Chaser was the unrivaled desideratum of each young man
    at the party.
    > (Woody Allen, "Retribution")

15. I led a raid on the grocery.
    It was the grocery of Barba Nikos.
    The grocery was small.
    The grocery was shabby.
    Barba Nikos was old.
    Barba Nikos was short.
    Barba Nikos was sinewy.
    Barba Nikos was a Greek.
    Barba Nikos walked with a slight limp.
    Barba Nikos sported a flaring handlebar moustache.
            (Harry Mark Petrakis, *Stelmark: A Family Recollection*)

Exercise: Sentence Expanding

Some of the word groups below are sentences. Expand each one by adding an appositive according to the instructions in parentheses.

Example

For two years I lived in a one-room basement apartment. (*Add an appositive that further describes this apartment.*)

For two years I lived in a one-room basement apartment, a rat's nest that offered a view of shoes, paws, and dog poop.

The other word groups below can be used as appositives. Attach each to a sentence according to the instructions in parentheses.

Example

a congealed mass of soy protein, sawdust, and monosodium glutamate (*Use this word group as an appositive in a sentence that identifies some food you were once served.*)

Dick's idea of a "big date" was a trip to the cafeteria for a deluxe cheeseburger—a congealed mass of soy protein, sawdust, and monosodium glutamate.

There are, of course, no single "correct" answers. Sentence-expanding exercises encourage you to use your imagination to build original sentences.

1. We had lunch today at Harry's Grease Pit. (*Add an appositive that tells something more about either the lunch or the restaurant.*)

2. the finest movie I have ever seen *(Use this word group as an appositive in a sentence that identifies the movie.)*
3. I have difficulty communicating with my boss. *(Add an appositive that describes the boss and suggests why communication with him is difficult.)*
4. the saddest sound I have ever heard *(Use this word group as an appositive in a sentence that identifies the sound.)*
5. I lay back on the grass and gazed up in wonder at the sky. *(Add an appositive that describes the sky.)*
6. the most peculiar man I have ever known *(Use this word group as an appositive in a sentence that identifies the person and gives an example of his peculiar behavior.)*
7. Last Saturday at the shopping mall I was introduced to Miss America. *(Add an appositive that tells us something about Miss America—or your perception of her.)*
8. a wall-shuddering, brain-damaging noise that broke every pane of glass on the block *(Use this word group as an appositive in a sentence that identifies the source of this sound.)*
9. Last night I sat home with Henry and watched a rerun of "Dallas." *(Add an appositive that lets us know what you think of this television program.)*
10. a sarcastic and insensitive person *(Use this word group as an appositive in a sentence that identifies this person and illustrates his or her behavior.)*

Exercise: Building Paragraphs and Essays

I. This exercise has been adapted from the four paragraphs of "Goodbye Yellow Brick Road," by Debbie Meador, a student. Combine the sentences into a short essay containing several appositives.

Goodbye Yellow Brick Road

1. My childhood came to an end.
   I know when this happened.
   I know the exact moment.
2. It was on a July morning.
   It was two years ago.
   It was when I attempted to return to the Land of Oz.

3. I had convinced my boyfriend to take me to Beach Mountain.
   Beach Mountain is in North Carolina.
   Beach Mountain is a place.
   I had visited this place many years earlier.
   I had visited Beach Mountain with my parents.

4. I told him about my earlier visit.
   I had ridden a ski lift.
   I had ridden to the top of the mountain.
   I discovered a farmyard.
   The farmyard was at the top of the mountain.
   The farmyard was a replica of Dorothy's farmyard.
   Dorothy's farmyard was in *The Wizard of Oz*.
   The Wizard of Oz is a classic film.

5. The farmhouse was open.
   People could walk inside.
   People could feel the effect of the house flying through the air.
   The house flew when the tornado hit.

6. Munchkin Land was behind the house.
   A winding yellow brick road was also behind the house.
   The road led to Oz.
   The road was really a row of snack shops and souvenir stands.
   The road was still a marvelous sight.
   It was marvelous for any child to behold.

7. Now it was several years later.
   I rode up the ski lift.
   I rode up with my boyfriend.
   I was bubbling with enthusiasm.
   I felt I was taking a journey.
   The journey was back to my early childhood.

8. We reached the top of the mountain.
   Then my bubble burst.

9. The farmyard was in ruins.
   It was as if a real tornado had struck.

10. The yellow brick road had turned brown.
    It was overrun with weeds.

11. The shops were shut down.
    The rides were shut down.
    The small stage was rotting away.
    Dorothy and Toto had danced on that stage.
    They had danced with the Scarecrow, the Tin Woodman, and the
       Cowardly Lion.
    The small stage was a haven for squirrels now.

12. It was as if all of the people had been killed off.
    Then the place had been left to decay.

13. We rode back down the ski lift.
    We rode back down in silence.
14. I felt as if my entire childhood was another country.
    The country was far, far away.
    I could never return to that country.
15. "There's no place like home."
    Dorothy said that.
16. Now there's no place at all.
17. Goodbye yellow brick road.

Writing Suggestions

1. Can you pinpoint a time when you felt *your* childhood had come to an end? Describe this experience in a paragraph or short essay.
2. A return to a place we knew in the past can reveal changes in ourselves as well as in the place visited. Describe some return visit you have made and all the changes you observed while you were there.

II. This exercise has been adapted from two paragraphs of "Tom Wolfe's Seventies," by Tom Wolfe, the writer who labeled the Seventies as the "Me Decade." Wolfe's "essay" is actually a collection of separate paragraphs, each describing some fad, fashion, product, character, or event associated with the 1970s. Four of these paragraphs precede the exercise. Combine the sentences in the exercise into two paragraphs containing several appositives.

Summing Up the Seventies

Disco

The press was never very candid about Studio 54, which was Disco Fever's chronically inflamed viral center. We were told only that Studio 54 was the hot ticket at night for every sort of celebrity in New York, from Vitas Gerulaitas and Dolly Parton to Laurance Rockefeller, and a Land of Cockaigne for the high and the groovy. But you only had to spend an evening there yourself to see that it was much stranger than that: Of the thousand-or-so souls on the dance floor at any one time, 750 were men, young and old, wearing strap undershirts, string vests, leather wristlets, and other Under the Expressway gear and dancing with one another to seamless music and exploding lights in a homoerotic frenzy. Ever since the Second World War, the reigning styles in popular music, dress, and dance have tended to be created by marginal or outcast groups. Negroes (the term then) and poor whites (some of them from Liverpool) created rock. New Jersey teenage juvies brought about the drastic change in dance styles that began with the twist at the old Peppermint Lounge. And the male-homosexual netherworld created disco. The discotheque is the 1970s' quotidian and commercial ritualization of what used to be known as a homosexual rout, a fact that generally has not been laid on Mom & Dad & Buddy & Sis as they drive the Bonneville over to the mall to take disco lessons so they'll be ready for the Vesper Disco nights at the church in Lubbock, De Kalb, Grand Forks, Riverhead, or wherever.

Designer Jeans

As every student of the history of fashion knows, clothing styles since the French Revolution have been a classic example of the trickle-down concept. The rich had clothes made by couturiers, tailors, or designers, and the masses wore knockoffs of the same. That held true until the 1970s, when certain staples of High Bohemia began to be hauled up the scale from the land of the proles. Tops on the list—and the greatest testament to how credulity and wealth (i.e., fools and money) walk tall in our time—were designer jeans. I once indulged in a little (I thought) hyperbole about "prewashed prefaded two-tone tie-dyed patched-and-welted velvet-hand elephant-bell hip-hugging blue jeans with a procession of aluminum studs down the outseams and around the pockets in back bought for $29.95 at the New Groovissimo boutique." Well, that merely illustrates Philip Roth's (and Malcolm Muggeridge's) crack about the paucity of the writer's imagination in the face of the true stories of the twentieth century. Designer jeans at $29.95 are cheap, and they have nothing added except a few inches of cotton thread stitched to form the we-believe-in-magic autograph.

People

The most successful new mass-circulation magazine, in a decade that was not always kind to mass-circulation magazines, was *People,* Time, Inc.'s Pantagruelian offspring of *Time* magazine's one-or-two page back-of-the-book section called People. The success of *People* was due to three things: (1) It always showed you other people's living rooms (e.g., Mo Dean's as John headed off to jail); (2) it always showed you where other people's libidos were plugged in (e.g., there might be an article about a brain surgeon, but if he were polymorphous-perversely involved with a melon or a squash, *People* always ran a photograph of that sweetmeat); (3) it was a print annex to the TV set. Instead of ignoring television, *People* assumed that television was its audience's main interest, and people and *People* had to fit into the picture where they could. . . .

The Pocket Calculator

This marvelous machine was the 1970s' most notable contribution to the impressive list of time-&-labor-saving devices that have made it possible for Americans, since the Second World War, to waste time in jobs lots and get less and less done—but with sleekness and precision of style. The time you can waste (I speak from experience) going chuk, chuk, chuk, chuk, chuk on your calculator and watching the little numbers go dancing across the black window—all the while feeling that you are living life at top speed—is breathtaking. Earlier additions to the list: the direct-dial long-distance telephone, the Xerox machine, the in-office computer, the jet airliner (not to mention the Concorde). The jet airliner, for example, encourages you to drop everything, hop on a plane, and go to Los Angeles, or wherever, at a moment's notice. Later on you can't understand how the better part of a week got shot. In light of my own not exactly staggering literary output, I have become interested in the life of Balzac. I am convinced that the reason this genius was so productive—he published at least *sixty* books between ages thirty and fifty-one—was that he enjoyed no time- or labor-saving aids whatsoever, not even a typewriter. He dropped nothing and went nowhere on a moment's notice, not even to Maison-Lafitte, which was twelve miles from Paris. He didn't ring up anybody in Brittany, much less London. He either wrote a note by hand or said the hell with it. Now, friends, *there* is a time-&-labor-saving device.

Punk

1. John Simon Ritchie was the protagonist of Punk in America.
   He was the greatest protagonist.
   He was the most luridly putrid protagonist.
   He was an Englishman.
   He renamed himself Sid Vicious.
2. Punk had no American roots at all.
3. It was a concept.
   The concept had vitality.
   It had vitality only as a gob of spit.
   The spit was a sopping lunger.
   The spit was in the face of the British class system.
4. American children read about it in *People.*
   American children read about it in *Vogue.*
   They had to read about it to know what to wear.
   They had to read about it to know how to act.

5. The 1960s became known as an era of "pseudoevents."
   Pseudoevents were events.
   The events took place only because the press set them up.

6. The 1970s did that one better.
   The 1970s became the era of Knockoff Pseud.
   Knockoff Pseud refers to forms of life.
   These forms of life existed *nowhere* but in the press.
   Then they were acted out by people.
   The people thought the forms of life were real.

7. Sid Vicious had a great misfortune.
   His misfortune was in believing that Punk in America was real.
   He thought it was real just because he was its star.

8. He really believed that the Dead Kennedys meant every minute of it.
   The Dead Kennedys played at Harrah's.

9. He really *did* have a girlfriend.
   Her name was Nancy Spungen.

10. He really did slice his wrists.
    He really did overdose on heroin.
    He really did die young.
    He died to make a good-looking corpse.

11. Incredible.

Woody Allen

12. Woody Allen is the archetypal Hollywood figure.
    He is a figure of the 1970s.
    He is the New Yorker.
    He affects an Upper Bohemian aloofness.
    It is an amused aloofness.
    He is aloof from Hollywood.
    He goes to the Polo Lounge.
    He wears nightwatchman pants.
    He wears Keds basketball shoes.

13. There is a man.
    He is any man.
    He wears a suit, shirt, and tie.
    He is on the premises.
    He is presumed to be a representative of Wells Fargo.
    He is presumed to be the representative of some other burglar alarm company.
    This presumption is made in movie circles.
    This presumption is made today.

14. Allen is the archetype.
    Allen wears the funkiest raiment of all.

He is in an era of Funky Chic.
He wears a cheap plaid cotton shirt.
The shirt was seen on math and chem majors at CCNY in the 1950s.

15. Elaine's was the reigning Hollywood restaurant of the 1970s.
Allen was on view regularly there.
Elaine's is not in Los Angeles.
It is in New York—of course.

16. In the old days of café society the greatest treat was to see Bruce Cabot.
One looked across the velvet rope and saw Bruce Cabot.
The velvet rope was at El Morocco.
Cabot was sitting at table number one.
Cabot had a tuxedo on.
His teeth were boiling.
His irises were lit up like flashlight bulbs.
His hair was plastered back like the Patent Leather Kid's.

17. Today it's Woody Allen.
Allen is sitting in Elaine's
He is sitting at *his* table.
He has his math-major outfit on.
His head is down.
He is looking neither left nor right.
It is as if *being noticed* were the last fate in the world.
It is the last fate he would want to encourage.

Writing Suggestion

Write several paragraphs in which you sum up the 1980s. In each paragraph describe some fad, fashion, product, character, or event that has gained wide attention sometime over the past few years. Analyze each of your subjects briefly, considering the source of its appeal and the effect it has had on people.

III. This exercise has been adapted from five paragraphs in "How Curious the Camel," by Alexander Theroux. Combine the sentences into a short essay containing several appositives.

How Curious the Camel

1. The camel is a beast of mystery.
The mystery is great.
The camel is an enigma.

The enigma is ancient.
The camel alone knows the hundredth name of Allah.
This is according to legend.

2. It is the ultimate paradox of whole parts.
It is a mode of transportation.
It is a mode of exchange.
It is a mode of sustenance.
Indeed, it is a mode of survival itself.

3. The Arabs eat them.
The Arabs beat them.
The Arabs ride them.
The Arabs race them.
The Arabs bet on them.
The Arabs sleep in their shadows.

4. They do everything but marry them.

5. They drink their milk.
They wash in their urine.
They cut them open for water.

6. Camel hair is used for everything from clothes to tents.

7. Their droppings provide fuel.

8. Arabian camels have one hump.

9. This is the famed dromedary.
This is the runner.

10. There is the two-humped Bactrian variety of central Asia.
Many nomads might be astonished to see this variety.
This variety is a beast of burden.
This variety is slow.
This variety is plodding.

11. The distinction has confused schoolboys for generations.
The distinction is like that between stalactites and stalagmites.

12. A camel has been described as a horse planned by a committee.

13. It has a comic munch of a face.
The face is loony.
The face is serene.
The face is disgusted.
The face is all these things at once.
It has liquid eyes.
The eyes shine bottle-green at night.

14. Its eyelashes are as long as Ann Sheridan's.

15. Its nostrils are large.
Its nostrils can close against blowing sand.

16. It is a ruminant.
It chews its cud.
Cud is the slop.

The slop is half-chewed.
The animal sucks this slop back up to its mouth.
It sucks with a slobbering sound.
It sucks as it plods along.

17. The camel is called the Ship of the Desert.
The desert is its habitat.

18. It survives on guddha.
Guddha consists of leaves.
Guddha consists of dried plants.
Guddha consists of grass.
Guddha consists of withered tribulus.

19. It relies on its humpfat as well.
The humpfat is stiff and upright when in top condition.
The humpfat decreases in size when the camel is overworked.

20. The camel is indeed an intricate equation.
The camel is a beast of binaries.
It is wild but domesticated.
It is savage.
It is submissive.
It is vile.
It is vulnerable.
It is patient.
It is perverse.

21. One thing can be said of the camel.
It can be said proudly.
The camel bears its load.

Writing Suggestion

Write a humorous essay, modeled after Theroux's, in which you identify the essential characteristics of some professional person. Your essay might carry a title such as "How Curious the Professor" or "How Curious the Campus Cop."

Discovery: Probing

Probing is a technique for exploring a subject to discover different ways of looking at it and thinking about it. When you probe a subject, you ask questions about it. Your answers to these questions can help you narrow down your subject to a specific topic and find effective ways of approaching that topic and organizing your ideas.

Begin by asking the following questions about your subject: <u>who</u>, <u>what</u>, <u>where</u>, <u>when</u>, <u>why</u>, and <u>how</u>. Your first questions—and responses—will likely be quite general, but by letting one question lead to another, you should find that both the questions and answers will become more specific. As with freewriting and brainstorming, write down all the ideas that come to you.

If you have difficulty coming up with questions of your own, use the ones below to probe your subject. Not all the questions are relevant to all subjects, and so if you are unable to answer one question, skip to the next.

I. DESCRIPTION (What does your subject look like?)

What does your subject look, sound, feel, taste, and smell like?
What size is it?
Where is it?
What is it next to, above, below, in front of, behind?
What are its outstanding characteristics?
What color is it?
What other thing does it resemble?
What shape is it?
How heavy is it?

II. NARRATION (What happened?)

What happened first?
  Where did it happen?
  When did it happen?
  Why did it happen?
  How did it happen?
  Who was involved?
What happened next?
What happened in the end?

III. EXPLANATION (What is it?)

What are its parts?
What larger group does it belong to?
What are some examples of it?
What is something similar to it?
What is something different from it?
What makes it work?
How does it work?
What causes it?
What are the results of it?
What is the purpose of it?

IV. ARGUMENT (What do you want to prove?)

Why is it necessary?
What are the advantages of it?
What are the disadvantages of it?
When should it be done?
How should it be done?
Where should it be done?
Has it been done before?
    If so, what happened?
    If not, why not?
What effects will it produce?

V. EVALUATION (How good or bad is it?)

What does it aim to do?
Does it succeed?
What parts are successful? Why?
What parts are not successful? Why not?
What should be done with it?

The following assignment will give you practice in probing a subject. Write a full report of an accident you were once involved in, explaining such things as where, how, and when it occurred. You will find the Narration questions most useful in exploring this subject, but try other questions as well.

Practice: Sample Combinations

Use the sentences below as a guide after you have completed the Practice exercises in the first part of the chapter. Since in most cases more than one combination is possible, do not think that your sentences are "incorrect" just because they may not be in exact agreement with the ones below.

1. My sister, a supervisor at Union Camp, has just been given a company car.
2. Sydney J. Harris, an American journalist, once observed, "Few men ever drop dead from overwork, but many quietly curl up and die because of undersatisfaction."
3. A sneaky, sinister man, Mr. Arnold lingers in the back alley at dawn and creeps along the front walk every evening.

115

4. The amount of junk in the air over Hawaii—an island far from the major sources of pollution—has increased 35 percent in the past decade.
5. At the bottom of Pandora's box lay the final gift—hope.
6. The puritans are pressing now, and sometimes achieving, various laws designed to restrict hunting—laws that have nothing to do with game protection or safety.
7. Not a political innovator, Marcus Aurelius strove diligently to sustain and preserve the civilization and social order that he had inherited.
8. The sky was sunless and grey, and there was snow in the air, buoyant motes, playthings that seethed and floated like the toy flakes inside a crystal.

(Truman Capote, *The Muses Are Heard*)

9. Birth, the emergence into manhood, graduation from school at various levels, birthdays, marriage, death—each of these outstanding steps is acknowledged by a ceremony of some sort.

(Marcia Seligson, *The Eternal Bliss Machine*)

CHAPTER 6

Building with Adverb Clauses

In this chapter you will practice building sentences with *adverb clauses*. Like an adjective clause, an adverb clause is always subordinate to a main clause. Like an ordinary adverb, an adverb clause usually modifies a verb, though it can also modify an adjective, an adverb, or even the rest of the sentence in which it appears. Adverb clauses show the relationship and relative importance of ideas in our sentences.

From Coordination to Subordination

Consider how we might combine the two sentences below:

> The national speed limit was reduced to fifty-five miles per hour.
> Road accidents decreased sharply.

One option is to coordinate the two sentences, as follows:

> 1. The national speed limit was reduced to fifty-five miles per hour, <u>and</u> road accidents decreased sharply.

Coordination with <u>and</u> allows us to connect the two main clauses, but it does not clearly identify the relationship between the ideas in those clauses. To clarify that relationship, we may choose to change the first main clause to an adverb clause:

2. <u>When the national speed limit was reduced to fifty-five miles per hour,</u> road accidents decreased sharply.

In this version the time relationship is emphasized. By changing the first word in the adverb clause, we can establish a different relationship—one of cause:

3. <u>Because the national speed limit was reduced to fifty-five miles per hour,</u> road accidents decreased sharply.

Notice that an adverb clause, like an adjective clause, contains its own subject and verb, but it must be subordinated to a main clause in order to make sense.

Practice 1

The following sentence consists of two main clauses joined by <u>but:</u>

The police questioned Sam for over an hour, <u>but</u> he was released without being charged.

Emphasize the time relationship between the two clauses by eliminating <u>but</u> and turning the first main clause into an adverb clause beginning with <u>after.</u>

Adverb Connectives

An adverb clause begins with an *adverb connective*—an adverb that connects the subordinate clause to the main clause. The adverb connective may indicate a relationship of time, place, comparison, concession, condition, or cause. The common adverb connectives are listed below.

TIME

after	once	when
as soon as	since	whenever
as long as	till	while
before	until	

EXAMPLE

<u>When she got up</u> her legs twinkled through the dining room like swords.
(Anthony Carson, *A Rose by Any Other Name*)

PLACE

where   wherever

EXAMPLE

Put your money <u>where your mouth is.</u>

CONCESSION and COMPARISON

although	even though	whereas
as	just as	while
as though	though	

EXAMPLE

When I looked down from the roof, I could see my corpse splattered on the driveway beneath me and mused about clowns rushing out with large firemen's nets for me to jump into, <u>as I had seen trapeze artists do in the circus.</u>
(Francis Blessington, "Roots")

CONDITION

even if	in case	unless
if	provided that	

EXAMPLE

<u>If you have ever lain awake at night and repeated one word over and over, thousands and millions and hundreds of thousands of millions of times,</u> you know the disturbing mental state you can get into.
(James Thurber, "More Alarms at Night")

CAUSE

as	in order that	so that
because	since	

119

EXAMPLE

So much of what passes for education in the United States deadens the desire for learning <u>because it fails to awaken the student to the value of his own mind.</u>

(Lewis H. Lapham)

Practice 2

a. Combine the two sentences below by turning the second sentence into an adverb clause beginning with an appropriate *time* connective.

(1) In a Junction City diner, a sunburned young farmer comforts his squirming son.
(2) His wife sips coffee and recalls the high school prom.

b. Combine the two sentences below by turning the second sentence into an adverb clause beginning with an appropriate *place* connective.

(1) Diane wants to live somewhere.
(2) The sun shines every day there.

c. Combine the two sentences below by turning the second sentence into an adverb clause beginning with an appropriate *concession* or *comparison* connective.

(1) The teacher is supported by what he teaches.
(2) The writer faces a daily battle with self-questioning, self-doubt, and conflict about his own work.

d. Combine the two sentences below by turning the first sentence into an adverb clause beginning with an appropriate *condition* connective.

(1) The nineteenth century was the age of the editorial chair.
(2) Ours is the century of the psychiatrist's couch.

e. Combine the two sentences below by turning the first sentence into an adverb clause beginning with an appropriate *cause* connective.

(1) Satchel Paige was black.
(2) He was not allowed to pitch in the major leagues until he was in his forties.

Although some of these adverb connectives can be used inter-changeably, be alert to the fine distinctions that exist among many of them. Consider, for instance, what distinguishes the first sentence below from the second.

1. <u>As soon as</u> Linda moved into my apartment, the landlord doubled the rent.
2. The landlord doubled the rent <u>because</u> Linda had moved into my apartment.

A cause is only implied in sentence 1, but a cause is stated in sentence 2. The exercises in this chapter will help you make such distinctions.

Arranging Adverb Clauses

An adverb clause, like an ordinary adverb, can be shifted to different positions in a sentence. The most natural and straightforward position is usually after the main clause:

We waited inside the diner <u>until the rain stopped.</u>

However, if the action described in the adverb clause precedes the action in the main clause, it is logical to begin with the adverb clause:

<u>When Gus asked Jenny for a light,</u> she set fire to his toupee.

Placing an adverb clause at the beginning helps create suspense as the sentence builds up to a main point:

<u>As I shuffled humbly out the door and down the front steps,</u> my eyes to the ground, I felt that my pants were baggy, my shoes several sizes too large, and the tears were coursing down either side of a huge putty nose.

(Peter DeVries, *Let Me Count the Ways*)

When working with two adverb clauses, you may want to place one in front of the main clause and one behind it, as shown below.

<u>When a bus skidded into a river just outside of New Delhi,</u> all seventy-eight passengers drowned <u>because they belonged to two separate castes and refused to share the same rope to climb to safety.</u>

121

An adverb clause at the beginning of a sentence is usually separated from the main clause with a comma. When the adverb clause follows the main clause, a comma is usually not necessary.

Practice 3

a. Shift the underlined adverb clause to the beginning of the sentence. Make it the subject of the adverb clause.

The forest supports incessant warfare, most of which is hidden and silent, <u>although the forest looks peaceful.</u>

b. Shift the underlined adverb clause to the end of the sentence.

<u>When chipmunks carry their tails high and squirrels have heavier fur and mice come into country houses early in the fall,</u> the superstitious gird themselves for a long, hard winter.

(Edwin Way Teale, *Country Superstitions*)

An adverb clause can also be placed inside a main clause, usually between the subject and verb:

The best thing to do, <u>when you've got a dead body on the kitchen floor and you don't know what to do about it,</u> is to make yourself a good strong cup of tea.

(Anthony Burgess, *One Hand Clapping*)

This middle position, though not a particularly common one, can be effective as long as the reader does not lose track of the idea in the main clause. When an adverb clause interrupts a main clause, as in the example above, it is usually set off by a pair of commas.

Practice 4

Shift the underlined adverb clause to a position between the subject and verb in the main clause and set it off with a pair of commas.

<u>While he was on maneuvers in South Carolina,</u> Billy Pilgrim played hymns he knew from childhood.

Reducing Adverb Clauses

Adverb clauses, like adjective clauses, can sometimes be shortened to phrases, as shown below:

1. <u>If your suitcase is smashed or torn,</u> it will be replaced by the airline.
2. <u>If smashed or torn,</u> your suitcase will be replaced by the airline.

Sentence 2 is just as clear as sentence 1 and more concise. Sentence 2 has been shortened by omitting the subject and the verb *is* from the adverb clause. Adverb clauses can be shortened in this fashion only when the subject of the adverb clause is the same as the subject of the main clause.

Practice 5

Reduce the underlined adverb clause to a phrase by dropping the subject and verb from the adverb clause.

<u>While he was on maneuvers in South Carolina,</u> Billy Pilgrim played hymns he knew from childhood.

Summary

Adverb clauses, like adjective clauses, show the relationship and relative importance of ideas in our sentences. Adverb clauses are more flexible than adjective clauses: they may be placed at the beginning, in the middle, or at the end of a sentence.

The exercises that follow will give you practice in building and arranging adverb clauses.

Exercise: Sentence Revising

Rewrite each sentence below according to the instructions in parentheses.

1. One scarcely ever sees a sailboat or a hardy swimmer in these icy waters, <u>but</u> one does occasionally spot a seal, an otter, or a sperm

123

whale. (Replace the coordinator but with an adverb connective that shows concession or comparison.)

2. Studies have shown that divorced women often have better working records, with less absenteeism, than men do, and the reason for this is that they have a responsibility to support their families. (Make this sentence more concise by replacing the underlined word group with an adverb connective that shows cause.)

3. The sea builds a new coast, and waves of living creatures surge against it. (Turn the underlined main clause into an adverb clause beginning with whenever.)

4. We had just tied off six loads at the Joliet landing, one afternoon a few weeks before Christmas when the wind from Lake Michigan was slicing down through the frame houses and factories, and the shore watchman came hunting me up where I was having coffee in the gallery. (Shift the underlined phrases and adverb clause to the beginning of the sentence.)

5. Although she was exhausted after the long drive home, Paula insisted on going to work. (Make this sentence more concise by dropping the subject and the verb was from the underlined adverb clause.)

6. The storm has passed, and the flash floods dump their loads of silt into the Colorado River; water still remains in certain places on rimrock, canyon beach, and mesa top. (Omit the semicolon and convert the underlined main clause into an adverb clause beginning with after.)

7. The fox heard the click of a tree squirrel's claws and raced toward the oak, barking, although he must have known he could not reach the squirrel. (Shift the underlined adverb clause to the middle of the sentence, following and.)

8. Teachers who contend with blank or hostile minds deserve our sympathy, and those who teach without sensitivity and imagination deserve our criticism. (Emphasize the contrast in this sentence by converting the underlined main clause to an adverb clause beginning with although.)

9. Blood pressure may be raised sufficiently high to burst a blood vessel in the brain, thus causing a stroke, when large amounts of amphetamines are used. (Shift the underlined adverb clause to the beginning of the sentence.)

10. Because he was frightened by the thunder and lightning, the boy hid under the bed, clutching his teddy bear. (Make the sentence more concise by omitting the underlined words.)

124

Exercise: Sentence Building

Combine the sentences in each set into a single, clear sentence with at least one adverb clause. In each case, choose what you think is an appropriate adverb connective, and subordinate the information that you think is of secondary importance. Create a second combination whenever possible.

1. Many people have attempted to climb Mount Soddoff.
   Only Granny Hamner has succeeded.

2. You can still be disappointed.
   You are still young.

3. The boy hid the gerbil.
   No one would ever find it.

4. Our neighbors installed a swimming pool.
   The pool is in their backyard.
   They have gained many new friends.

5. Chris played the violin.
   The dog hid in the bedroom.
   The dog whimpered.

6. The salaries in rural schools were kept low.
   The low salaries kept the profession from being attractive to men.
   The teacher was invariably a woman.

7. Women are more frequently ill than men.
   Women recover from illnesses more easily than men.
   Women recover from illnesses more frequently than men.
   (Ashley Montagu, *The Natural Superiority of Women*)

8. Argentina invaded the Falkland Islands.
   Argentina invaded in 1982.
   Few people had ever heard of this British outpost.
   This outpost is remote.

9. Credit cards are dangerous.
   They encourage people to buy things.

125

Often these are things people are unable to afford.
Often these are things people do not really need.

10. I kissed her once.
    I kissed her by the pigsty.
    She wasn't looking.
    I never kissed her again.
    She was looking all the time.

    (Dylan Thomas, *Under Milk Wood*)

11. Elisa looked toward the river road.
    The willow-line was yellow there.
    It was yellow with leaves.
    The leaves were frosted.
    The leaves seemed to be a thin band of sunshine.
    That is how they seemed under the high gray fog.

    (John Steinbeck, "The Chrysanthemums")

12. People have been using various kinds of cleansing agents.
    They have been doing this for thousands of years.
    They have been doing this for a reason.
    Water alone does not readily get rid of dirt.
    Water alone does not readily get rid of grease.
    Our ancestors discovered this long ago.

13. Someday I shall take my glasses off.
    Someday I shall go wandering.
    I shall go out into the streets, never to be heard from again.
    I shall do this deliberately.
    I shall do this when the clouds are heavy.
    I shall do this when the rain is coming down.
    I shall do this when the pressure of realities is too great.

    (James Thurber, "The Admiral on the Wheel")

14. Wing Biddlebaum continued to walk up and down.
    He walked upon the veranda.
    It was the veranda of his house.
    His house was by the ravine.
    He walked until the sun had disappeared.
    He walked until the road was lost.
    It was lost in the grey shadows.
    The road was beyond the field.

    (Sherwood Anderson, *Winesburg, Ohio*)

15. The December dusk was swift.
The dusk had come tumbling.
The tumbling was clownish.
The dusk had come after its day.
The day was dull.
Stephen felt his belly crave.
His belly craved for its food.
Stephen stared through the dull square of the window of the classroom and felt this.

(James Joyce, *A Portrait of the Artist As a Young Man*)

Exercise: Sentence Expanding

Some of the word groups below are sentences. Expand each one by adding information in an adverb clause that answers the question in parentheses.

Example

Sam installed a burglar alarm. *(When or why did Sam install the alarm?)*
Sam installed a burglar alarm after his house had been broken into on three successive nights.

The other word groups below are adverb clauses. Attach each adverb clause to a sentence that answers the question in parentheses.

Example

Before he roasted the turkey *(What did Charles do or forget to do before he roasted the turkey?)*
Charles forgot to remove the giblets before he roasted the turkey.

There is, of course, no single correct answer to each question in parentheses. Sentence-expanding exercises encourage you to use your imagination to build original sentences.

1. Although tarantulas pose no threat to human beings *(How do many people respond to these large hairy spiders?)*
2. It is unwise to strike a match. *(When is it unwise to strike a match?)*
3. Once you have tasted calves' liver smothered with onions *(How will you be affected or what will be your response once you have tasted the liver?)*

4. We were having a good time at the party. *(You were having a good time until what happened?)*
5. Whenever you begin to feel sorry for yourself *(What should you do whenever this happens?)*
6. Because our television set has been broken for the past week *(How has your family coped with this misfortune?)*
7. The baby cried loudly. *(What was going on while the baby cried?)*
8. After the storm blew over *(What happened after the storm blew over?)*
9. Classes were canceled today. *(Why were classes canceled?)*
10. As long as the Republicans are in office *(What is likely to happen or not happen as long as the Republicans are in office?)*

Exercise: Building Paragraphs and Essays

I. This exercise is adapted from the final three paragraphs of "I'll Meet You at the Y," a chapter in John Craig's *How Far Back Can You Get?* The book recounts Craig's experiences growing up in Peterborough, Ontario, during the Great Depression. Read the paragraph preceding the exercise, and then combine the sentences in each set, using adverb clauses when appropriate.

I'll Meet You at the Y

The Y was like a home away from home. You could play table tennis there, shoot pool, bowl, have a swim, play volleyball or basketball, read the papers and magazines in the reading room, go to the dances on Saturday nights. Even on Sunday nights, when it was officially closed, there was a way to get in and make use of some of the facilities. The Y had a few boarders, more or less impoverished bachelors, who used to come and go by a side door to which each of them had a key. You could hide in the shadows in the lane, slip out after a boarder entered, and quickly insert a foot so that the door wouldn't close. Then you waited until the boarder's footsteps receded up the stairs, opened the door and went in.

1. There was an atmosphere about the place.
   There was an atmosphere on Sunday nights.
   The atmosphere was ghostly.

2. You couldn't turn on any lights, of course.
   There was a glow from the streetlights.
   The glow was faint.
   The streetlights were outside the windows.
   The glow would transform the familiar shapes.
   They would be transformed in subtle ways.
   They would be transformed in mysterious ways.

3. Sometimes the snooker balls had been left out.
   You could shoot a game of pool.
   You could play in the pale, bluish light.

4. You winced with each click of the ivory balls.
   You were afraid somebody might hear.

5. We didn't dare bowl.
   This was because of the noise.

6. There were always some lights left on in the gym.
   Sometimes we would go in.
   We shot some baskets.
   Dribbling was strictly forbidden.

7. There was a cafeteria on the second floor.
   They served meals there.
   They served meals to the boarders.
   They provided occasional banquets.
   The banquets were for various Y groups.

8. There was a door to the kitchen.
   The door led off a back hall.
   The bolt could be slipped quite easily.
   The bolt could be slipped with a piece of cardboard.

9. Once inside, it was often possible to pilfer.
   A pie could be pilfered.
   A plate of doughnuts could be pilfered.
   These could do a lot to brighten up a night.
   It was a winter night.
   The night was cold.
   The night was dark.

10. The caretaker might happen to come by.
    You were there in the kitchen.
    Then there was trouble.
    There was only one way out.
    It was through a window and onto a ledge.
    The ledge ran around one of the corner towers.

11. It was a perch.
    It was pretty precarious.
    You had to outwait the caretaker.
    You might have to outwait him any length of time.

129

You might have to outwait him on a Sunday night.
You might have to outwait him in January.
A Sunday night in January was bitter cold.

12. Gus Gunsolus was out there once.
He was there for almost an hour.
We finally got him in.
He looked like a survivor from a seal-hunting disaster.
The disaster occurred on the Labrador ice floes.

13. Icicles were hanging from his hair.
Icicles were hanging from his eyebrows.
Icicles were hanging from his nose.
He was shaking like the last maple leaf.
The leaf was in a November gale.
The leaf was dried.

14. He came around to talk.
He talked coherently.
It was a long time before this happened.

15. Here is the worst part of it.
There was a pot of carrots.
The pot was big.
The carrots were tired.
The carrots were old.
The carrots were soaking in water.
The kitchen staff had left out that pot.
The pot was left out on Sunday night.
Nothing else was left out by the kitchen staff.

Writing Suggestions

1. Have you, like Gus Gunsolus, ever gone through a lot of trouble over something that proved to be insignificant? Describe your experience in a paragraph or short essay.

2. In an essay, recall some of the "crimes" you committed as a child—trespassing, perhaps, or stealing. Describe particular incidents and your feelings at the time.

II. There are no sets in this exercise. First group the sentences logically, and then combine them into a short essay with several adverb clauses.

Workaholics

1. Workaholics are people.
2. These people are addicted to their jobs.
3. These people love their work so much.
4. They find it hard to stop working.
5. They find it hard even in extreme circumstances.
6. The office building may be on fire.
7. The city may be paralyzed by a snowstorm.
8. The workaholics stay on the job.
9. Workaholics get satisfaction from their jobs.
10. They can't get this satisfaction from their families.
11. They can't get this satisfaction from their friends.
12. A job provides a pay check.
13. But a job also provides much more.
14. A job offers a person a sense of identity.
15. A job offers a person self-respect.
16. Workaholics are sometimes pitied.
17. Workaholics are sometimes scorned.
18. They are pitied and scorned for reasons.
19. Workaholics are sometimes considered to be miserable.
20. Workaholics are sometimes considered to be overanxious.
21. Workaholics are sometimes considered to be antisocial.
22. Most workaholics are not dismal.
23. Most workaholics are not timid.
24. Most workaholics enjoy what they do.
25. Most people complain.
26. They complain about having to work hard.
27. Workaholics are happiest when they are hard at work.
28. All workaholics work hard.
29. Not all hard workers are workaholics.
30. Some people work hard to please a boss.
31. Some people work hard to make money.
32. Workaholics work hard to satisfy themselves.
33. People in the medical field are often associated with workaholism.
34. People in business are often associated with workaholism.
35. People in politics are often associated with workaholism.
36. Other people may be workaholics.
37. Assembly line workers may be workaholics.
38. Janitors may be workaholics.
39. Truckers may be workaholics.
40. Some men are workaholics.

41. Some women are workaholics.
42. Some work in an office.
43. Some work in a factory.
44. Some work at home.
45. Not all workaholics are effective workers.
46. All are busy workers.
47. Most are productive.
48. Most are satisfied with their lives.

Writing Suggestions

1. In a paragraph or short essay, describe your own attitude toward work (either class work or a particular job you have held). Does your work give you satisfaction? Does it give you a sense of identity and self-respect?
2. In a paragraph or short essay, describe the characteristics of someone just the opposite of a workaholic—a person who loathes work and does whatever he or she can to get out of it.

III. This exercise has been adapted from the final chapter of *Mrs. Bridge*, a novel by Evan Connell. An earlier chapter precedes the exercise. Mrs. Bridge has material comforts, but she is not satisfied emotionally, socially, or intellectually, and the final chapter offers an appropriate image of her entrapment. Combine the sentences in each set of the exercise, using adverb clauses when appropriate.

Mrs. Bridge

Quo Vadis, Madame?

That evening, while preparing for bed, Mrs. Bridge suddenly paused with the fingertips of one hand just touching her cheek. She was seated before her dressing table in her robe and slippers and had begun spreading cold cream on her face. The touch of the cream, the unexpectedness of it—for she had been thinking deeply about how to occupy tomorrow—the swift cool touch demoralized her so completely that she almost screamed.

She continued spreading the cream over her features, steadily observing herself in the mirror, and wondered who she was, and how she happened to be at the dressing table, and who the man was who sat on the edge of the bed taking off his shoes. She considered her fingers, which dipped into the jar of their own accord. Rapidly, soundlessly, she was disappearing into white, sweetly scented anonymity. Gratified by this she smiled, and perceived a few seconds later that beneath the mask she was not smiling. All the same, being committed, there was nothing to do but proceed.

Hello?

1. It was one December morning.
   It was near the end of the year.
   Snow was falling moist.
   Snow was falling heavy.
   Snow was falling for miles all around.
   The earth and the sky were indivisible.
   Mrs. Bridge emerged from her home.
   Mrs. Bridge spread her umbrella.

2. She proceeded with small steps.
   The steps were cautious.
   She proceeded to the garage.
   She pressed the button.
   She waited for the door to lift.
   She waited impatiently.

3. She was in a hurry to drive downtown.
   She intended to buy some Irish lace antimacassars there.
   These were advertised in the newspaper.
   She would browse through the stores.
   She intended to spend the remainder of the day in this fashion.
   She had a reason for this.
   It was Harriet's day off.
   The house was empty—so empty.

4. She had backed just halfway out of the garage.
   The engine died.

5. She touched the starter.
   She listened without concern.
   She had experienced difficulties with the Lincoln.
   Despite this, she had grown to feel secure in it.

6. The Lincoln was a number of years old.
   It was recalcitrant.
   She could not bear the thought of parting with it.
   In the past she had resisted this suggestion of her husband.
   She was attached to the car.
   Her husband had been mildly puzzled by this.
   Her husband had allowed her to keep it.

7. She thought she might have flooded the engine.
   This was often true.
   Mrs. Bridge decided to wait a minute or so.

8. Presently she tried again.
   She tried again.
   Then she tried again.
9. She was deeply disappointed.
   She opened the door to get out.
   She discovered something.
   She had stopped in a position.
   In this position the car doors were prevented from opening.
   The doors could not open more than a few inches.
   The doors were prevented on one side by the garage partition.
   The doors were prevented on the other side by the wall.
10. She tried all four doors.
    She began to understand something.
    Perhaps she could attract someone's attention.
    In the meantime she was trapped.
11. She pressed the horn.
    There was not a sound.
12. She remained half inside.
    She remained half outside.
13. She sat there not knowing what to do.
    She sat there for a long time.
    She sat there with her gloved hands folded in her lap.
14. She looked in the mirror.
    She looked at herself.
    She looked once.
15. She took the keys finally.
    She took them from the ignition.
    She began tapping on the window.
    She called to anyone.
    Anyone might be listening.
    She called, "Hello? Hello out there?"
16. But no one answered, unless it was the falling snow.

Writing Suggestions

1. In a paragraph, describe Mrs. Bridge. Use the information in the exercise to guide you, but use your imagination to describe what she looks like, how she relates to her husband, and how she behaves in the company of others.
2. In an essay, describe a time when you felt trapped. You may have been physically trapped, like Mrs. Bridge, or you may have been caught in a dilemma that seemed impossible to re-

solve without hurting yourself or someone else. Perhaps you felt trapped by a job, by your parents or a mate, by certain responsibilities, or even by a decision that you made yourself.

Discovery: Discovering Your Readers

You are a writer, but who are your readers? Well, *you* are, first of all. You are the reader who counts the most when you are first working out your ideas and preparing an early draft. But as you begin revising your work, you should begin to consider readers other than yourself. These readers are your instructors, your fellow students, anyone with whom you are trying to communicate. In fact, for each new writing project you need to discover just who your readers are and what they expect from your writing.

Whoever your readers may be, you can begin to understand their needs by considering these questions:

1. What do my readers already know about this subject?
2. What do my readers need to know?
3. What will interest my readers?

The answers to these questions are important, though not always easy to find out. You don't want to bore your readers by telling them what they already know. On the other hand, you don't want to confuse them by presuming they know more than they actually do. Similarly, you want to find out if your readers already recognize that your subject is important and interesting or if you need to convince them that this is so. And of course, if your readers are expecting particular information in your writing, you want to make sure that you deliver that information.

One way to find out what your readers expect from you is to ask them. Sit down with one of your instructors or another student, and ask that person some questions about his or her background, interests, and reading and writing habits. Here are some questions that you might ask, but the best questions will be those that you make up yourself: What do *you* want to know about *your* readers?

What subjects do you enjoy reading about?
What subjects don't interest you at all?
What subjects disturb or irritate you?

Which professional writers do you most enjoy reading?

How do you define "good writing"?

Are there certain expressions or writing errors that particularly annoy you?

Do you associate unclear writing with unclear thinking?

Are you more interested in what a writer says or in how he or she says it?

Are you impressed by a writer who has a large vocabulary?

Are you impressed by a writer who keeps his or her language short and simple?

How do you react when you discover that a writer has misspelled a word?

What is the highest compliment you could pay a writer?

Jot down notes as you carry out your interview; later, organize these notes into a "reader profile": that is, a short report in which you identify your reader and discuss that person's reading tastes and habits, likes and dislikes. You can use this profile as a guide when you revise your writing.

In many cases, however, you will not have the opportunity to interview your readers; you may not even know who they are. At these times you will have to imagine what your readers are like: their personal and educational backgrounds, their tastes, interests, viewpoints, and needs. In effect, you will have to *invent* your readers. Defining who your readers are will help you define your purpose for writing.

Here is a writing project that will help you become sensitive to the needs of your readers. Imagine that friends of yours from out of town are thinking of moving to your neighborhood (this might be a city block, a college dormitory, an apartment complex, a trailer park, or several square miles of countryside—whatever you call "home"). Write them a letter in which you identify some of the important characteristics of your neighborhood. Provide the sort of information that will help them make the decision to move or not. To do this effectively, you have to put yourself in the position of your readers, and so consider the three questions posed earlier: What do my friends already know about this neighborhood? What do they need to know about it? What sort of things will they be interested in?

The way you define your audience (in this writing project and others) affects not just what you write about but also how you write. The tone and style of your writing depend to a great extent on who you are writing to. To write effectively, you must discover your readers each time you sit down to write.

Practice: Sample Combinations

Use the sentences below as a guide after you have completed the Practice exercises in the first part of this chapter. Since in most cases more than one combination is possible, do not think that your sentences are "incorrect" just because they may not be in exact agreement with the ones below.

1. After the police questioned Sam for over an hour, he was released without being charged.
2. a. In a Junction City diner, a sunburned young farmer comforts his squirming son while his wife sips coffee and recalls the high school prom. (Or as)

      (Richard Rhodes, *The Inland Ground*)
   b. Diane wants to live where the sun shines every day. (Or wherever)
   c. The teacher is supported by what he teaches, whereas the writer faces a daily battle with self-questioning, self-doubt, and conflict about his own work.

      (Mary Sarton, *Plant Dreaming Deep*)
   d. If the nineteenth century was the age of the editorial chair, ours is the century of the psychiatrist's couch.

      (Marshall McLuhan, *Understanding Media*)
   e. Because he was black, Satchel Paige was not allowed to play in the major leagues until he was in his forties.
3. a. Although it looks peaceful, the forest supports incessant warfare, most of which is hidden and silent.
   b. The superstitious gird themselves for a long, hard winter when chipmunks carry their tails high and squirrels have heavier fur and mice come into country houses early in the fall.
4. Billy Pilgrim, while he was on maneuvers in South Carolina, played hymns he knew from childhood.
5. While on maneuvers in South Carolina, Billy Pilgrim played hymns he knew from childhood.

CHAPTER 7

Building with Participle Phrases

As we have seen, both main clauses and subordinate clauses contain *verbs*—words that usually tell what a subject does. However, certain verb forms can also be used in phrases that modify other words in a sentence, usually nouns or pronouns. These verb forms, called *participles,* can add vigor to our writing as they add information to our sentences. In this chapter you will practice building sentences with participle phrases.

Present and Past Participles

A participle is a verb used as an adjective to modify a noun or a pronoun, occasionally an entire sentence. The participles are underlined in the following sentence:

> The whispering breeze scattered dust and seeds across the abandoned fields.

Whispering is a present participle, formed by adding *-ing* to the present form of the verb (whisper). **Abandoned** is a past participle, formed by adding *-ed* to the present form of the verb (<u>abandon</u>). Notice that both participles function as adjectives and precede the nouns they modify. Like adjectives, participles may also follow the nouns they modify:

> A small boy, <u>frightened</u> and <u>trembling</u>, was led out of the burning building.

In this sentence, the past participle <u>frightened</u> and the present participle <u>trembling</u> both modify the subject of the sentence, <u>boy</u>.

Present participles always end in *-ing.* Here are some examples:

the <u>laughing</u> lady   the <u>wailing</u> mourners
the <u>falling</u> temperature   the <u>mocking</u> grin
the <u>barking</u> dog   the <u>stinging</u> remark

Practice 1

Convert each simple sentence below to a phrase by adding *-ing* to the verb and moving it in front of the noun.

EXAMPLE

The child <u>cries.</u>
the <u>crying</u> child

a. The toads <u>croak.</u>
b. The salesman <u>whines.</u>
c. The passengers <u>shove.</u>
d. The bears <u>dance.</u>
e. The breeze <u>stings.</u>

The past participles of all regular verbs end in *-ed.* Irregular verbs, however, have various past participle endings (for example, know*n,* beat*en,* done*).* Check your dictionary if you are unsure of a past participle ending. Here are some examples of past participles:

the <u>tired</u> dancer   the <u>stolen</u> car
the <u>prejudiced</u> remark   the <u>swollen</u> ankle
the <u>spilled</u> milk   the <u>torn</u> shirt

Practice 2

Convert each simple sentence below to a phrase by moving the past participle form of the verb in front of the noun.

EXAMPLE

The vase is <u>cracked</u>.
the <u>cracked</u> vase

    a. The player is <u>injured</u>.
    b. The children are <u>excited</u>.
    c. The merchandise has been <u>damaged</u>.
    d. The athlete is <u>determined</u>.
    e. The promise has been <u>broken</u>.

Participle Phrases

Consider how we might combine the three sentences below:

> I guided the pinball through the upper chutes, down a runover lane, off the slingshot bumpers to the flippers.
> I cradled it there.
> I bounced it back and forth until I had a perfect shot through the lighted spinner.

To emphasize the quick, successive actions described in these sentences, we can combine them by turning two of the sentences into *participle phrases*:

> <u>Guiding the ball through the upper chutes, down a runover lane, off the slingshot bumpers to the flippers</u>, I cradled it there, <u>bouncing it back and forth until I had a perfect shot through the lighted spinner</u>.
> (J. Anthony Lukas, "The Inner Game of Pinball")

A participle phrase consists of a participle and its modifiers. In the sentence above, the first participle phrase contains a present participle (<u>guiding</u>) and its object (<u>the pinball</u>), followed by a series of prepositional phrases (<u>through the upper chutes, down a runover lane, off the slingshot bumpers to the flippers</u>). The second participle phrase contains, again, a present participle (<u>bouncing</u>) and its object (<u>it</u>), followed by a pair of adverbs (<u>back and forth</u>) and an adverb clause (<u>until I had a perfect shot through the lighted spinner</u>). Both participle phrases modify <u>I</u>, the subject of the sentence. Notice that the participle phrases cannot stand alone as complete sentences; they must modify a noun or pronoun in the sentence.

Practice 3

Combine the two sentences below by turning the second sentence into a participle phrase (beginning with the past participles <u>jounced and jolted</u>) and placing it after the first sentence.

We sat in the corner of the boxcar on piles of moldy straw.
We were jounced and jolted by the iron wheels, the hard boards, the shaking swaying car.

Arranging Participle Phrases

A participle phrase is a flexible structure, one that can often be placed at the beginning, middle, or end of a sentence. Participle phrases may be arranged to show a sequence of actions, as in the "pinball" sentence just seen. They may also be arranged to show that two or more actions are occurring at the same time, as in this sentence:

The eagles swooped and hovered, <u>leaning on the air</u>, and swung close together, <u>feinting and screaming with delight.</u>
(N. Scott Momaday, *House Made of Dawn*)

In this sentence, the eagles were "leaning on the air" <u>as</u> they "hovered"; they were "feinting and screaming with delight" <u>as</u> they swung close together.

Practice 4

Rewrite the sentence below, shifting the underlined participle phrase to the beginning of the sentence.

The wood ducks come on swift, silent wings, <u>gliding through the treetops as if guided by radar</u>, twisting, turning, never touching a twig in that thick growth of trees that surrounded the lake.
(Jack Denton Scott, "The Wondrous Wood Duck")

Although you can shift a participle phrase to different positions in a sentence, don't risk awkwardness or confusion by placing the phrase too far from the noun it modifies. In particular, a participle phrase that suggests a cause usually precedes the main clause, sometimes follows the subject of the main clause, but only rarely appears at the end of the sentence. For instance, in each sentence below the participle phrase clearly modifies the subject (<u>my younger sister</u>) and suggests a cause for her action.

1. <u>Discouraged by the long hours and low pay,</u> my younger sister finally quit her job at the pet store.
2. My younger sister, <u>discouraged by the long hours and low pay,</u> finally quit her job at the pet store.

But consider what happens when the participle phrase is moved to the end of the sentence:

3. My younger sister finally quit her job at the pet store, <u>discouraged by the long hours and low pay.</u>

Here the logical order of cause-effect is reversed, and thus the sentence is less effective than either sentence 1 or 2.

Practice 5

To clarify the cause-effect relationship in the sentence below, move the underlined participle phrases to the beginning of the sentence.

The Chinese Nationalists were very close to extinction in 1949, <u>humiliated by Communist victories in the homeland, fearing an invasion of Taiwan itself, and smarting under the concerted attack of world opinion.</u>

A participle phrase needs to refer clearly to a noun or pronoun in the sentence. We have to be careful when combining sentences such as the following:

I curled my toes and squinted my eyes.
The doctor prepared to puncture my arm with a hypodermic needle.

Notice what happens if we drop <u>I</u> and change the first sentence to a participle phrase:

<u>Curling my toes and squinting my eyes,</u> the doctor prepared to puncture my arm with a hypodermic needle.

The problem here is that the participle phrases refer to <u>the doctor</u> when they should refer to <u>I</u>—a pronoun not in the sentence. This sentence can be corrected either by adding <u>I</u> to the sentence (as in sentence 1, below) or by rewriting the sentence with an adverb clause instead of a participle phrase (sentence 2):

1. <u>Curling my toes and squinting my eyes,</u> I waited for the doctor to puncture my arm with the hypodermic needle.
2. <u>As I curled my toes and squinted my eyes,</u> the doctor prepared to puncture my arm with the hypodermic needle.

Practice 6

The sentence below is confusing because the participle phrase modifies <u>the sun</u> when it should modify <u>I</u>—a pronoun not in the sentence. Rewrite this sentence in two ways: first, insert <u>I watched</u> between the participle phrase and <u>the sun</u>; and second, change the participle phrase to an adverb clause beginning with <u>As I stood.</u>

<u>Standing on the roof of my apartment building at dawn,</u> the sun rose through crimson clouds.

Summary

Participle phrases add descriptive and informative details to our sentences. They are more economical than clauses (no connecting words are needed), and they may be shifted to various positions in the sentence for reasons of clarity, emphasis, and rhythm. Although they function as adjectives, participles convey the vigor of the verbs from which they are derived.

The exercises that follow will give you practice in building sentences with participle phrases.

Exercise: Sentence Revising

Rewrite each sentence below according to the instructions in parentheses.

1. <u>I listen to my own daughter and others of her generation,</u> and I sense something off, out of focus, growing wrong. *(Change the underlined main clause to a participle phrase beginning with* listening.)

2. One January day, thirty years ago, the little town of Hanover, <u>which was</u> anchored on a windy Nebraska tableland, was trying not to be blown away. *(Change the adjective clause into a participle phrase by eliminating the underlined words.)*

3. Quietly announcing his retirement, <u>Professor Legree peered over the rim of his spectacles.</u> *Turn the underlined main clause into a participle phrase beginning with* peering, *and make the first part of the sentence the main clause.)*

4. A young woman danced with Uncle Gus, <u>wearing a pink party dress.</u> *(Move the underlined participle phrase so that it clearly refers to* a young woman *and not* Uncle Gus.)

5. When I pushed the button under the name plate, the buzzer sounded, the latch gave way, and I mounted two narrow, musty, <u>dimly lighted, creaking</u> flights of stairs. *(Break up the list of modifiers by shifting the underlined participles to the end of the sentence.)*

6. Howard put the ice cream into the toaster oven <u>when he was distracted by the baby's crying.</u> *(Change the underlined adverb clause to a participle phrase beginning with* distracted; *then move the participle phrase to the beginning of the sentence to suggest a logical cause-effect relationship.)*

7. <u>The loud noise frightened Silas,</u> and so he grabbed a rubber knife and hid behind the shower curtain. *(Change the underlined main clause to a participle phrase beginning with* frightened.)

8. <u>Feeling like Emmet Kelly,</u> alone on the stage, trying in vain to sweep up the spotlight *(Turn this word group into a sentence by changing the underlined participle phrase to a main clause with* he *as the subject and* felt *as the verb.)*

9. <u>Swinging from branch to branch,</u> the children watched the monkey. *(Shift the underlined participle phrase to the end of the sentence so that it clearly modifies* the monkey, *not* the children.)

10. The old woman, <u>who was gazing into her crystal ball,</u> predicted that I would soon marry a blacksmith and bear triplets. *(Change the underlined adjective clause to a present participle phrase, and move the phrase to the beginning of the sentence.)*

Exercise: Sentence Building

Combine the sentences in each set into a single, clear sentence with at least one participle phrase. Create a second combination whenever possible.

1. My grandfather sang loudly.
   My grandfather sang out of key.
   My grandfather tapped his cane to the music.

2. The dishwasher was invented in 1889.
   The dishwasher was invented by an Indiana housewife.
   The first dishwasher was driven by a steam engine.

3. Herman tossed a pack of cigarettes.
   He tossed them into the wastebasket.
   Herman announced that he had just quit smoking.

4. A referee is always working before crowds.
   The crowds are unfriendly.
   The crowds are apt to jeer at the first sight of him.
   A referee has orders to exude poise under the most testing circumstances.

5. I washed the windows.
   I whipped the squeegee swiftly up and down the glass.
   I whipped the squeegee in a fever of fear.
   I feared that some member of the gang might see me.

6. The men huddle.
   They are at the cafe tables.
   Their coat collars are turned up.
   They finger glasses of *grog Americain*.
   The newsboys shout the evening papers.
   > (Ernest Hemingway, "Christmas in Paris")

7. The Angelus Building looms on the corner of its block.
   The Angelus Building has seven stories.
   The Angelus Building is thick with dark windows.
   The Angelus Building is caged in a dingy mesh of fire escapes.
   The fire escapes are like mattress springs on a junk heap.
   > (Edmund Wilson, *Travels in Two Democracies*)

145

8. The comedy world of Groucho Marx and his brothers Harpo and
Chico was wildly chaotic.
The comedy world was grounded in slapstick farce.
The comedy world was grounded in free-spirited anarchy.
The comedy world was grounded in zany assaults on the myths
and virtues of middle-class America.

(Albin Krebs, "Master of the Insult")

9. Goldsmith smiled.
He bunched his cheeks.
He bunched them like twin rolls of toilet paper.
His cheeks were fat.
The toilet paper was smooth.
The toilet paper was pink.

(Nathanael West, *Miss Lonelyhearts*)

10. The roaches scurried in and out of the breadbox.
The roaches sang chanteys.
The roaches sang as they worked.
The roaches paused only to thumb their noses.
They thumbed their noses jeeringly.
They thumbed their noses in my direction.

(S. J. Perelman, *The Rising Gorge*)

11. There was a sunset across the sky.
The sunset was wonderful.
The sky was distant.
The sunset was reflected in the sea.
The sunset was streaked with blood.
The sunset was puffed with avenging purple and gold.
It was as if the end of the world had come without intruding on
everyday life.

(Muriel Spark, *The Prime of Miss Jean Brodie*)

12. Great patches of color appear.
The patches are shimmering.
The patches appear over the water.
The patches are expanding.
The patches are contracting.
The patches are doing this in slats.
The slats are like Venetian blinds.

(Annie Dillard, "Mirage")

13. The sun glares down.
    The sun is unpitying.
    It glares down on the corpses.
    The sun speeds their putrefaction.
    The sun rots the hide.
    The sun softens the sinew.
    The sun softens the meat.
    All this is to the vulture's advantage.

    (John D. Stewart, "Vulture Country")

14. Appalachia was the original American frontier.
    Appalachia extends from southern Pennsylvania to northern Alabama.
    Appalachia covers 182,000 square miles of land.
    The land is rich in coal, timber, sandstone, natural gas.
    The land is rich in some of the most magnificent scenery on the continent.

    (Peter Schrag, "Appalachia: Again the Forgotten Land")

15. There is a way we think in dreams.
    This way is also the way we think when we are awake.
    All of these images occur simultaneously.
    Images open up new images.
    The images are charging and recharging.
    This happens until we have a whole field of image.
    It is an electric field.
    The field pulses.
    The field blazes.
    The field takes on the exact character of a migraine aura.

    (Joan Didion, "Making Up Stories")

Exercise: Building Paragraphs and Essays

I. This exercise has been adapted from a paragraph written by Lori Alexander, a student. Combine the sentences into a paragraph containing at least two participle phrases.

Loneliness

1. Loneliness can be described.
   It is a queasy feeling.
   This feeling is in the pit of your stomach.
   Another being is inside of you.
   This is the way you feel.
   This being is a demon.
   The demon is waiting for your insides to come to a boil.
2. He is stirring during the wait.
   He is churning during the wait.
   He is scraping during the wait.
   He is doing these things for a purpose.
   He does not want you to relax.
   He does not want you to escape into sleep.
3. There is a noise.
   The noise is constant.
   The noise is indescribable.
   It is the sound of nothing.
4. This sound could be background music.
   The music would be for a horror movie.
   The movie would be the most terrifying one ever made.
5. Nothing is around you.
   Blank space is around you.
   The space extends for miles and miles.
   The space fills every point in existence.
6. You do not move.
   Your mind races.
   It races through the darkness.
   It searches for the light.
   You want the light to guide you.
   You want to be guided out of your loneliness.

Writing Suggestion

Observe how the writer of "Loneliness" uses physical details to convey the feeling of loneliness. Following her example, write a paragraph in which you describe one of the emotions listed below. Show how the body feels and how the world appears to a person experiencing this emotion.

fear	joy	excitement
nervousness	relief	love
guilt	depression	impatience
sorrow	boredom	

II. This exercise has been adapted from two paragraphs of a chapter in *Report to Greco*, the autobiography of Nikos Kazantzakis. Read the two paragraphs preceding the exercise, and then combine the sentences that follow into two paragraphs containing several participle phrases. There are no sets in this exercise. The conclusion of the episode appears in the paragraphs following the exercise.

Happiness

It was almost nightfall. The whole day: rain, torrents of rain. Drenched to the bone, I arrived in a little Calabrian village. I had to find a hearth where I could dry out, a corner where I could sleep. The streets were deserted, the doors bolted. The dogs were the only ones to scent the stranger's breath; they began to bark from within the courtyards. The peasants in this region are wild and misanthropic, suspicious of strangers. I hesitated at every door, extended my hand, but did not dare to knock.

O for my late grandfather in Crete who took his lantern each evening and made the rounds of the village to see if any stranger had come. He would take him home, feed him, give him a bed for the night, and then in the morning see him off with a cup of wine and a slice of bread. Here in the Calabrian villages there were no such grandfathers.

1. Suddenly I saw a door.
2. The door was open.
3. The door was at the edge of the village.
4. I inclined my head.
5. I looked in.
6. There was a corridor.
7. The corridor was murky.
8. There was a lighted fire at the far end.
9. There was an old lady.
10. She was bent over the fire.
11. She seemed to be cooking.
12. There was not a sound.
13. There was nothing but the burning wood.

14. It was fragrant.
15. It must have been pine.
16. I crossed the threshold.
17. I entered.
18. I bumped against a long table.
19. The table stood in the middle of the room.
20. Finally I reached the fire.
21. I sat down on a stool.
22. I found the stool in front of the hearth.
23. The old lady was squatting.
24. She was on another stool.
25. She stirred the meal.
26. She stirred with a wooden spoon.
27. I felt that she eyed me rapidly.
28. She eyed me without turning.
29. But she said nothing.
30. I took off my jacket.
31. I began to dry it.
32. I sensed happiness.
33. Happiness was rising in me.
34. It rose like warmth.
35. It rose from my feet to my shins.
36. It rose to my thighs.
37. It rose to my breast.
38. I inhaled the fragrance of the steam.
39. The steam rose from the pot.
40. I inhaled hungrily.
41. I inhaled avidly.
42. The meal must have been baked beans.
43. The aroma was overwhelming.
44. Earthly happiness is made to the measure of man.
45. Once more I realized to what an extent this is true.
46. It is not a rare bird.
47. We must pursue a rare bird.
48. We must pursue at one moment in heaven.
49. We must pursue at the next in our minds.
50. Happiness is a domestic bird.
51. This bird is found in our own courtyards.
52. The old lady rose.
53. She took down two soup plates.
54. She took them from a shelf.
55. The shelf was next to her.
56. She filled them.

57. The whole world smelled of beans.
58. She lit a lamp.
59. She placed it on the long table.
60. Next she brought two wooden spoons.
61. She brought a loaf of black bread.
62. We sat down opposite each other.
63. She made the sign of the cross.
64. She glanced rapidly at me.
65. I understood.
66. I crossed myself.
67. We began to eat.
68. We were both hungry.
69. We did not breathe a word.
70. Could she be a mute?
71. I asked myself this.
72. Is she mad perhaps?
73. Is she one of those peaceful, kindly lunatics?
74. Those lunatics are so much like the saints.

As soon as we finished, she prepared a bed for me on a bench to the right of the table. I lay down, and she lay down on the other bench opposite me. Outside the rain was falling by the bucketful. For a considerable time I heard the water cackle on the roof, mixed with the old lady's calm, quiet breathing. She must have been tired, for she fell asleep the moment she inclined her head. Little by little, with the rain and the old lady's rhythmical respiration, I too slipped into sleep. When I awoke, I saw daylight peering through the cracks in the door.

The old lady had already risen and placed a saucepan on the fire to prepare the morning milk. I looked at her now in the sparse daylight. Shriveled and humped, she could fit into the palm of your hand. Her legs were so swollen that she had to stop at every step and catch her breath. But her eyes, only her large, pitch-black eyes, gleamed with youthful, unaging brilliance. How beautiful she must have been in her youth, I thought to myself, cursing man's fate, his inevitable deterioration. Sitting down opposite each other again, we drank the milk. Then I rose and slung my carpetbag over my shoulder. I took out my wallet, but the old lady colored deeply.

"No, no," she murmured, extending her hand.

As I looked at her in astonishment, the whole of her bewrinkled face suddenly gleamed.

"Goodbye, and God bless you," she said. "May the Lord repay you for the good you've done me. Since my husband died I've never slept so well.

Writing Suggestions

1. In a short essay, define what *happiness* means to you. Following the example of Kazantzakis, begin your essay by relating an incident that helped you understand the meaning of happiness.
2. In an essay, describe some encounter you have had with a stranger. Describe the circumstances, your first impressions of the person, and the outcome of the encounter.

III. This exercise has been adapted from the last four paragraphs of an essay by Mary White, a student. Read the first three paragraphs below, and then combine the sentences in each set of the exercise. Several of your sentences should contain participle phrases.

My Home of Yesteryear

Situated on the bend of a horseshoe-shaped dirt road that intersects a back country highway is the place I called home as a child. Here my elderly father raised his two girls without the help or companionship of a wife.

The house is set back about two hundred feet from the road, and as we saunter up the narrow dirt pathway, lined with neat rows of flamboyant orange gladiolas on each side, the tidy appearance of the small, unpainted frame house entices us to enter. Up the steps and onto the porch, we can't help but notice a high-backed rocker on one side and a bench worn smooth by age on the other. Both remind us of the many vesper hours spent here in the absence of modern-day entertainment.

Turning the door knob and entering the parlor is like taking a step back in time. There is no lock on the door and no curtains on the windows, only shades yellowed with age, to be pulled down at night—as if you needed privacy out here in the boondocks. Dad's big over-stuffed armchair is set beside the well-stocked bookcase where he enjoys passing a hot afternoon with a good book. His bed, an old army cot, serves as a couch when company comes. One lone plaque with the words "Home, Sweet Home" adorns the wall over the mantelpiece.

1. A doorway is just to the left.
   The doorway is minus a door.
   The doorway beckons us to investigate the aroma.
   The aroma is drifting our way.

2. We step into the kitchen.
   We are overtaken by the aroma of bread.
   The aroma is rich.
   The bread is freshly baked.
3. Dad is removing the last two loaves.
   He removes them from the belly of Old Bessie.
   Old Bessie is our coal-burning stove.
4. Dad leaves them to cool.
   Dad leaves them in neat rows.
   Dad leaves them on our plank table.
   The table is homemade.
5. We turn toward the back door.
   We see an honest-to-goodness ice box.
   And yes, there's a silver quarter.
   The silver quarter is genuine.
   The quarter is for the ice man.
   He will take the quarter in exchange for fifty pounds of ice.
   The ice is dripping.
6. I can picture him now.
   He snatches the tongs into the frozen block.
   He snatches them tightly.
   This causes tiny slivers of sparkling ice to fly everywhere.
7. He swings it down off the back of his truck.
   It is a chug-a-lug of a truck.
   Instantly he throws his other arm up.
   He does this to gain his balance.
   He staggers with his load.
   He staggers toward the back door.
8. He hoists the block of ice into place.
   He gives a sigh of relief.
   The sigh is long.
   The sigh is loud.
   He drops the shiny quarter into his pocket.
9. We step outside the back door.
   We suddenly realize something.
   There is no running water in the kitchen.
   Here stands the only waterpipe around.
10. Tubs are set upside down by the steps.
    The tubs are galvanized.
    Here is where most of the bathing occurs.
    The tubs indicate this.
11. A footpath leads us to a hand pump.
    The footpath is little.
    The handpump is somewhat rusty.

The handpump still provides a cool refreshing drink.
It provides a drink if we can prime the pump.

12. Dad douses its rusty throat with water.
It gurgles for a minute or two.
Then it belches back a flood of water.
It is sparkling clear spring water.
The water is free from chemicals.
The law requires chemicals in modern water systems.

13. But the pathway doesn't stop here.

14. It winds on out behind a shack.
The shack is dilapidated.

15. No imagination is needed to know where it ends.

16. Dusk approaches.
We must slip around to the front porch.
We relax.
We enjoy a country sunset.

17. The sky is absolutely breathtaking.
The sky has ribbons of orange and violet.
The ribbons are soft.

18. The sun is ablaze with beauty.
The sun casts our long shadows.
It casts them across the porch.
It casts them onto the wall.
The wall is behind us.

19. All around us nature is praising its maker.
Nature is singing its nightsongs.

20. The whippoorwills are off in the distance.
They are just starting their nightly lamentations.

21. The crickets and frogs join in.
Bats dart overhead.
They are in search of a juicy tidbit for breakfast.

22. Bats, you see, begin their day at sunset.

23. The house itself joins in the chorus.
It joins with its creaks and cracks.
These are the sounds of contraction.
The coolness of the evening settles around us.

24. Indeed, a visit to the old home place brings back memories.
The memories are many.
The memories are fond.
A visit almost makes us wish we could turn the clock back a few
years.
Then we might enjoy a few moments of peace.
Then we might enjoy a few moments of innocence.

Writing Suggestions

1. In an essay, describe the house or apartment you grew up in as a child. Provide details that tell us something about the people who lived there and the way they lived.
2. Do one of two things in an essay: either describe a place not ordinarily thought of as attractive and emphasize its positive qualities, or describe an attractive place and emphasize its unpleasant characteristics.

Exercise: Recombining

This exercise has been adapted from three paragraphs of Sharon R. Curtin's "Aging in the Land of the Young." The writer's eighteen original sentences have been combined into seven in the exercise. Untangle these seven sentences by breaking them down into short sentences and then recombining them. Your aim is not to imagine what Curtin's original sentences might be but to create three clear, effective paragraphs. Many combinations are possible.

Aging

1. Painting every action gray, lying heavy on every moment, imprisoning every thought, aging governs each decision with a perversity that is ruthless and single-minded.
2. To age is to learn the feeling of no longer growing, the feeling of struggling to do old tasks, the feeling of struggling to remember familiar actions as the cells of the brain are destroyed with thousands of unfelt tiny strokes, little pockets of clotted blood wiping out memories and abilities without warning.
3. The body seems slowly to give up, randomly stopping, sometimes starting again as if to torture and tease with the memory of lost strength, and the hands become clumsy, frail transparencies, held together with knotted blue veins.
4. Sometimes it seems as if the distance between your feet and the floor were constantly changing, as if you were walking on shifting and not quite solid ground, putting one foot down, slowly, carefully forcing the other foot forward.

5. Not daring to lift your feet from the uncertain earth but forced to slide hesitantly forward in little whispering movements, sometimes you are a shuffler, and sometimes you are able to "step out," but this effort—in fact the pure exhilaration of easy movement—soon exhausts you.

6. With friends and family dying or moving away, the world becomes narrower, and to climb stairs, to ride in a car, to walk to the corner, to talk on the telephone—each action seems to take away from the energy needed to stay alive, and everything is limited by the strength you hoard greedily.

7. Your needs decrease, you require less food, less sleep, and finally less human contact, with this little bit becoming more and more difficult, so that fearing one day you will be reduced to the simple acts of breathing and taking nourishment, dreading this ultimate stage, the period of helplessness and hopelessness, when independence will be over.

Discovery: Self-evaluation

You are probably used to having your writing evaluated by your instructors. The strange symbols, the comments in the margins, the grade at the end of the paper—these all are methods used by instructors to identify what they see as the strengths and weaknesses of your work. Such evaluations can be helpful, but they are no substitute for a thoughtful self-evaluation. As the writer, you can evaluate the whole process of writing a paper, from coming up with a topic to editing the final draft. Your instructor, on the other hand, often can evaluate only the final product.

Make a practice of writing a concise self-evaluation at the end of each of your papers. Try to answer the following four questions, but feel free to add comments not covered by these questions.

1. What part of writing this paper took the most time? (*Perhaps you had trouble finding a topic or expressing a particular idea. Maybe you agonized over a single word or phrase. Be specific when you answer the question.*)

2. What is the most significant difference between your first draft and this final version? *Explain if you changed your approach to the subject, if you reorganized the paper, or if you added or deleted material.)*

3. What is the best part of your paper? (*Explain why a particular word, phrase, sentence, or idea pleases you.*)
4. What part of this paper could still be improved? (*Again, be specific. There may be a troublesome sentence in the paper or an idea that isn't expressed as clearly as you would like it to be.*)

A self-evaluation is neither a defense nor an apology; it is a way of becoming more aware of what you go through when you write and what troubles you run into. You will become more conscious of your strengths as a writer, and you will see more clearly what skills you need to work on. Your comments will guide your instructors as well. By seeing where you are having problems, they may be able to offer helpful advice when *they* come to evaluate your work.

Practice: Sample Combinations

Use the sentences below as a guide after you have completed the Practice exercises in the first part of this chapter. Since in most cases more than one combination is possible, do not think that your sentences are "incorrect" just because they may not be in exact agreement with the ones below.

1. a. the croaking toads
   b. the whining salesman
   c. the shoving passengers
   d. the dancing bears
   e. the stinging breeze
2. a. the injured player
   b. the excited children
   c. the damaged merchandise
   d. the determined athlete
   e. the broken promise
3. We sat in the corner of the boxcar on piles of moldy straw, jounced and jolted by the iron wheels, the hard boards, the shaking swaying car.
4. Gliding through the treetops as if guided by radar, the wood ducks come on swift, silent wings, twisting, turning, never touching a twig in that thick growth of trees that surrounded the lake.
5. Humiliated by Communist victories in the homeland, fearing an invasion of Taiwan itself, and smarting under the concerted attack

of world opinion, the Chinese Nationalists were very close to extinction in 1949.

6. a. Standing on the roof of my apartment building at dawn, I watched the sun rise through crimson clouds.

   b. As I stood on the roof of my apartment building at dawn, the sun rose through crimson clouds.

CHAPTER 8

Building with Absolutes

In this chapter you will practice building sentences with *absolutes*—word groups that modify entire sentences. An absolute always consists of a noun plus at least one other word. These constructions are useful for adding details to a sentence, details that often describe one aspect of something or someone mentioned elsewhere in the sentence.

Building Absolutes

Consider how the pair of sentences below might be combined:

> Bolenciecwcz was staring at the floor now.
> He was trying to think.

Because both sentences refer to the same person, we can combine them by turning the second sentence into a participle phrase:

> Bolenciecwcz was staring at the floor now, trying to think.

Now, what if we wanted to combine the following three sentences and add them to the one above?

> His great brow was furrowed.
> His huge hands were rubbing together.
> His face was red.

The subject is no longer <u>Bolenciecwcz,</u> but particular features of the man. In this case, we can turn the three sentences into absolutes (by omitting the verbs <u>was, were, was</u>) and attach them to our first combination:

> Bolenciecwcz was staring at the floor now, trying to think, <u>his great brow furrowed, his huge hands rubbing together, his face red.</u>
>
> (James Thurber, "University Days")

The sentence now contains three absolutes. The first consists of a noun <u>(brow)</u> followed by a past participle <u>(furrowed)</u>; the second consists of a noun <u>(hands)</u> followed by a present particle <u>(rubbing)</u>; and the third consists of a noun <u>(face)</u> followed by an adjective <u>(red).</u> An adverb or a prepositional phrase can also follow the noun in an absolute. As Thurber's sentence demonstrates, absolutes are useful constructions when we move from a description of a *whole* person, place, or thing to just one or more *parts.*

Practice 1

Combine the two sentences below: turn the second sentence into an absolute by omitting <u>were.</u>

    a. Out of the rainbow a squadron of jacksnipe suddenly banked and veered in perfect formation.
    b. Their white wing patches were flashing.

Arranging Absolutes

Like participle phrases, absolutes may appear at the beginning, in the middle, or at the end of a sentence, as demonstrated below.

> <u>His hair wet from the shower,</u> he walked in the icy air to Luke's Luncheonette, where he ate three hamburgers in a booth with three juniors.
>
> (John Updike, "A Sense of Shelter")

> The train, <u>its metal wheels squealing as they spin along the silver tracks,</u> rolls slower now.
>
> (Roberto Ramirez, "The Woolen Sarape")

North of the house, inside the ploughed fire-breaks, grew a thick-set strip of box-elder trees, low and bushy, <u>their leaves already turning yellow.</u>

(Willa Cather, *My Antonia*)

Note that an absolute, like a participle phrase, is usually set off from the rest of the sentence by a comma or a pair of commas.

Practice 2

a. Combine the two sentences below: turn the second sentence into an absolute and place it in front of the first sentence.

(1). The storks circled above us.
(2). Their slender bodies were sleek and black against the orange sky.

b. Combine the four sentences below: turn the second sentence into an absolute and place it after the verb <u>came up,</u> and turn the fourth sentence into a participle phrase.

(1) For his own reasons Poppa didn't go to the depot, but as my sister and I were leaving he came up.
(2) A cob pipe was jutting from his mouth.
(3) He stood sideways.
(4) He looked over the misty Kansas countryside.

c. Combine the two sentences below: turn the second sentence into an absolute and place it after the first sentence.

(1) On the tops of the hills, the grass stands at its tallest and greenest.
(2) Its new straw-green seed plumes rise through a dead crop of last year's withered spears.

Although most absolutes are flexible, one type appears more often at the beginning of a sentence than in any other position. Observe that the absolute in the following sentence suggests a cause or explanation for the action described in the rest of the sentence.

<u>His right arm imprisoned in a cast,</u> Jimbo was forced to scrawl with his left hand.

Although the absolute could be shifted elsewhere in this sentence, placing it first best conveys the logical order of a cause-effect relationship. As you build sentences with absolutes, try them in different positions until you find an arrangement that is smooth, clear, and logical.

Practice 3

Combine the three sentences below: turn the second and third sentences into absolutes and position them at the beginning of the sentence to establish a clear cause-effect relationship.

    a. Norton vowed never to marry again.
    b. His first marriage ended in divorce.
    c. His second marriage ended in despair.

As we have seen, one or more participle phrases and absolutes may be used together in a sentence. Here is a sentence with a participle phrase followed by three absolutes:

Six boys came over the hill half an hour early that afternoon, <u>running hard, their heads down, their forearms working, their breath whistling.</u>
(John Steinbeck, *The Red Pony*)

Notice how these constructions allow a writer to compress several actions and descriptive details into a single sentence.

Practice 4

Combine the sentences below into a single sentence with a participle phrase and two absolutes.

    a. All afternoon the caravan passed by.
    b. The caravan shimmered in the winter light.
    c. Its numberless facets were gleaming.
    d. The hundreds of wagon wheels were turning in the dust, in slow and endless motion.

Summary

Absolutes are similar to participles (and may, in fact, contain participles) in that they are compact modifying structures that may be placed in various positions in a sentence. Unlike participles, they modify an entire sentence and always begin with a noun.

The exercises that follow will give you practice in building sentences with absolutes.

Exercise: Sentence Revising

Rewrite each sentence below according to the instructions in parentheses.

1. Odysseus comes to shore, <u>and</u> the skin <u>is</u> torn from his hands, <u>and</u> the sea water <u>is</u> gushing from his mouth and nostrils. *(Create two absolutes by eliminating the underlined words.)*
2. The people moved slowly across the horizon at their traditional tasks, their backs bent as they set out the rice, <u>set</u> out the new young trees, <u>pulled</u> their barrows along the narrow path. *(Repeat the absolute* their backs bent *before each of the underlined words.)*
3. When the double giant Ferris wheel circles, <u>the swaying seats are more frightening than a jet plane flying through a monsoon.</u> *(Omit* when *and turn the underlined main clause into an absolute.)*
4. The vulture sidled and circled the dead goat, stood erect to see better, trailed its <u>wing tips</u>, stretched its <u>neck</u> to the full, and swiveled its <u>head</u> rapidly to bring alternate eyes to bear. *(Use the underlined words as nouns in three absolutes; change* stood, trailed, *and* swiveled *to present participles and use* stretched *as a past participle.)*
5. The calm is broken by the arrival of a gray Mustang: <u>the windows are</u> rolled down, <u>the stereo is</u> tuned to the Top Forty, <u>and it is</u> noisily rounding the bend in the dirt road. *(Create two absolutes and a participle phrase by changing the semicolon to a coma and eliminating the underlined words.)*
6. His open mouth <u>met</u> flesh, his numb fingers <u>found</u> a face, and he clawed deeply into an eye, hearing its owner howl as again the heavy club met Kunta's head. *(Create two absolutes by changing the underlined verbs to present participles and eliminating* and.)*

163

7. Jagged pieces of glass stick out of the frames of the hundreds of broken windows in the buildings that sit empty. *(Begin your new sentence with* The buildings sit empty . . . , *and turn the rest of the sentence into an absolute construction.)*

8. Proud of my freedom and bumhood I stood in the doorway of the boxcar, rocking with the motion of the train. <u>My</u> ears <u>were</u> full of the rushing wind and the clattering wheels. *(Combine these sentences by replacing the period with a comma and eliminating the underlined words.)*

9. <u>When the dinosaur ran,</u> its pelvic bones crushed aside trees and bushes, and its taloned feet clawed damp earth, leaving prints six inches deep wherever it settled its weight. *(Turn the underlined adverb clause into a main clause by omitting* when; *follow this with two absolutes.)*

10. Both young and old herd into steaming showers. The young are still building some flesh on straight frames, whereas the old have flat chests, skinny arms, and round sagging bellies. *(Combine these into one sentence beginning* They herd into steaming showers . . . ; *follow this with two absolutes.)*

Exercise: Sentence Building

Combine the sentences in each set into a single, clear sentence with at least one absolute. Create a second combination whenever possible.

1. Victor made a dash for the bedroom.
   Then he swerved away.
   He dove onto the sofa.
   His face was toward the pillows.

2. Arthur Hagenlocher fidgets on his high-legged chair.
   A pencil is poking out from behind his ear.
   Arthur Hagenlocher is in his box-like office.
   His office is in the old Loft's candy factory.
   His office is at 400 Broome Street in the New York City Hall area.
   (N. R. Kleinfield, "Portraits of a Cop")

3. The lions walked slowly.
   The lions walked lazily.
   Their bodies were low slung.

164

Their bodies were dark gold against the pale golden grass.
All twenty of the lions were moving steadily toward the zebras.
(Colin Fletcher, "Morning on the Savanna")

4. I whipped down the Roxbury Road.
I whipped down one sunny morning.
I whipped down on my bicycle.
The front spokes were melting into a saw blade.
The wind was shrilling tunes.
The tunes came through the vent holes.
The vent holes were in my helmet.
(Floyd C. Stuart, "Cyclical Time")

5. There were several species of turtle.
These species took to the sea.
They took to the sea between 90 million and 100 million years ago.
The turtles had stubby legs.
Their legs were adapting into flippers.
The flippers were streamlined.
(Delta Willis, "Prehistoric Encounter")

6. I sat on the steps.
I sat huddled.
My cheeks rested in my palms.
They rested sullenly.
I was half listening to what the grownups were saying.
I was half lost in a daydream.
(Richard Wright, *Black Boy*)

7. Gulls snatch.
Gannets plunge.
The kittiwakes balance delicately.
The kittiwakes are little.
The tails of the kittiwakes are spread.
Their tails are spread like fans.
The fans are made of carved ivory.
(William G. Wing, "Christmas Comes First on the Banks")

8. He leans over a campfire.
He is roasting a pig.
His toes stick through the end of boots.
His toes are dusty.
The boots are almost completely worn away.

John Brown does not suggest the prosperous bank director he once
    was.
John Brown does not suggest the significant figure he is to become.
                (Richard O. Boyer, *The Legend of John Brown*)

9. I can remember Miss May.
   She stood before the handful in the graduating class of her school.
   Her head was tilted slightly to one side.
   Her cheekbones were high and prominent.
   Her cheekbones were beneath the large brown eyes.
   Her eyes searched each pupil's face.
   Her eyes searched for a spark of ambition.
   Her eyes searched for a flicker of hope.
   She had tried to kindle the hope there.
                (Wilma Dykeman, *Look to this Day*)

10. Walt Barnett was sitting behind a desk.
   The desk was cheap.
   He was exactly as I remembered him.
   His body stretched the seams of his suit.
   His body was massive.
   His suit was shiny.
   His suit was navy-blue.
   The cigarette dangled from his lips.
   Even the brown trilby hat was perched on the back of his head.
             (James Herriot, *The Lord God Made Them All*)

11. The woman was elderly.
   She had an ash-blond wig.
   The wig was slightly askew.
   The wig was showing tufts of hair.
   The hair was thin.
   The hair was gray.
   The woman shuffled to a park bench.
   She did this slowly.
   She sat down heavily.
              (Susan Page, "All About Pigeons")

12. There is seldom any real trouble at Stucky's Saloon.
   There is just a lot of foot stomping.
   There is beer drinking.

There are good ole boys.
They are telling each other Friday night lies.
Their elbows are propped on damp tables.
Their faces are sweating.
Their faces are half-hidden in smoke.
The smoke is so thick you could cut it up and make work shirts
    out of it.

                         (Harry Crews, "Running Fox")

13. The men sit on the edges of the pens.
    The fish is between their knees.
    The fish is big.
    The fish is white and silver.
    The men rip with knives.
    The men tear with hands.
    The men heave the bodies into a central basket.
    The bodies are disemboweled.

        (William G. Wing, "Christmas Comes First on the Banks")

14. The golf ball is stroked with a shaft.
    The shaft is slender.
    The shaft is wandlike.
    The shaft is about the length of a cane.
    The bottom end of the shaft is tipped with a blade.
    The blade is variously tilted.
    Or the bottom end is tipped with a knob.
    The knob is fistlike.
    The knob is wooden.

                    (Wright Morris, "Odd Balls")

15. There was a patch of earth outside the hole.
    The patch was small.
    The patch was flat.
    The earth was hard.
    The earth was flat.
    The scorpion stood on the center of this.
    The scorpion stood on the tips of its four pairs of legs.
    Its nerves and muscles were braced for a quick retreat.
    Its senses were questing for the minute vibrations.
    These vibrations would decide its next move.

              (Ian Fleming, *Diamonds Are Forever*)

Exercise: Sentence Expanding

Expand each of the simple sentences below in two ways. First, add at least one participle phrase. Second, add at least one absolute (which may or may not include a participle phrase).

Example

The man sat on the edge of the bed.

EXPANDED WITH PARTICIPLES

1. The man sat on the edge of the bed, *weeping softly as his wife dreamed on beside him.*
2. *Staring at the gun in his hand and thinking about what the doctor had told him that morning,* the man sat quietly on the edge of the bed.

EXPANDED WITH ABSOLUTES

1. The man sat on the edge of the bed, *his eyes closed and his hands folded in prayer.*
2. *His hands clutching the tattered Bible,* the man sat motionless on the edge of the bed.

1. The child hid behind the couch.
2. My grandmother stood by the window.
3. The candidate picked up the baby.
4. The thief pulled out a revolver.
5. The instructor glanced at the student.
6. The detective followed the shoplifter.
7. The driver got out of the car.
8. The deputy examined my license.
9. The reporter scribbled in her notebook.
10. The salesman shook hands with the customer.

Exercise: Building Paragraphs and Essays

I. This exercise has been adapted from a paragraph written by Mary Zeigler, a student. Combine the sentences into a paragraph containing at least two absolutes.

The Waiting Room

1. I was in a dentist's waiting room.
   My sojourn there lasted two hours.
   My sojourn gave me ample opportunity to observe.
   I observed some of the ways human beings demonstrate impatience.
   The ways were obvious.
2. One woman was pale from lack of air.
   This woman showed her impatience by tapping her feet.
   The tapping was rapid.
   She showed her impatience by wiggling around in her chair.
3. She delivered sighs.
   The sighs were long.
   She delivered whines.
   The whines were occasional.
4. A man paced up and down.
   The man was apparently wealthy.
   His mouth was squeezed into a sarcastic smile.
   His eyes were bulging with fury.
5. He glared at the receptionist.
   He glared now and then.
   He glared as if she were responsible for his long wait.
6. The receptionist ignored him.
   She did this carefully.
   Her eyes were focused only on the *National Geographic*.
   The *National Geographic* was ten years old.
   The *National Geographic* was on her desk.
7. A teenage boy stood by the window.
   He sang.
   His singing was loud.
   His singing was off-key.
   He was trying to attract the dentist's attention.
   He was desperate.
8. A woman threatened him.
   The woman was elderly.
   She waved her cane at the body.
   The boy continued his howling.
   His howling was rapid.
9. All this was going on.
   I sat in a corner.
   I sat quietly.
   My arms were crossed.
   My knees were knocking.

10. I was scheduled to have a wisdom tooth removed.
    I was in no hurry to see the dentist.

Writing Suggestion.

Write an essay on *body language*—that is, the gestures and facial expressions we use (deliberately or not) to communicate without words. Once you begin to observe people's behavior carefully, you should have no difficulty in coming up with many examples of body language. You might follow Mary Zeigler's lead and find a particular vantage point from which you can observe the behavior of the people around you.

II. This exercise has been adapted from two paragraphs of "The Well: Drama of India," an article by Peggy and Pierre Streit that first appeared in the *New York Times Magazine* in September 1959. Read the first two paragraphs of the article below, and then combine the sentences that follow into two paragraphs containing several absolutes.

The Well: Drama of India

The hot dry season in India. . . . A corrosive wind drives rivulets of sand across the land; torpid animals stand at the edge of dried-up water holes; newspapers report that in the east wells are empty and villagers have left their fields. The earth is cracked and in the rivers the sluggish, falling waters have exposed the sludge of the mud flats. Throughout the land the thoughts of men turn to water. And in the village of Rampura these thoughts are focused on the village well.

It is a simple concrete affair, built upon the hard earth worn by the feet of five hundred villagers. It is surrounded by a wooden structure over which ropes, tied to buckets, are lowered to the black, placid depths twenty feet below. Fanning out from the well are the huts of the villagers—their walls white from sun, their thatched roofs thick with dust blown in from the fields.

1. The day began at the well.
   The day ended at the well.
2. The men congregated at the water's edge.
   They congregated in the hushed post dawn.
   Their dhotis were wrapped about their loins.
   Their water jugs were in hand.

The jugs were small.
The jugs were made of brass.
Their voices mingled in conversation.
The conversation was quiet.
They rinsed their bodies.
They brushed their teeth.

3. The buffaloes were watered.
   The buffaloes had soft muzzles.
   The muzzles lingered in the buckets.
   Then they were driven off to the fields.

4. Then came the women.
   Their brass pots were atop their heads.
   The women began the ritual of water drawing.
   This ritual began with the careful lowering of the bucket in the well.
   They were careful lest the bucket come loose from the rope.
   Then it hit the water.
   There was the gratifying splash.
   Then there was the maneuvering to make it sink.
   Then the bucket ascended.
   The rope squealed against the pulley.
   The pulley was made of wood.

5. The sun rose higher.

6. Clothes were beaten clean.
   They were beaten on the rocks.
   The rocks surrounded the wall.
   The women gossiped.

7. There was a traveler.
   He was from a near-by road.
   He quenched his thirst from a villager's urn.

8. Two boys dropped pebbles into the water.
   They waited for their hollow splash.
   The splash was far below.
   The boys were little.
   The boys were hot.
   The boys were bored.

9. The afternoon wore on.
   The sun turned orange through the dust.
   The men came back from the fields.

10. They doused the hides of their water buffaloes.
    The hides were parched.
    The hides were cracked.
    They themselves murmured contentedly.
    The water coursed over their own shoulders and arms.

171

11. Finally twilight closed in.
    The evening procession of women came.
    The women were stately.
    The women were graceful.
    Their full skirts swung about their ankles.
    The heavy brass pots were once again balanced on their heads.
12. The day was ended.
    Life was as it always was.

Writing Suggestions

1. In an essay, relate the sequence of events that occur at a particular place during the course of a single day. You might choose a street corner, the library, a fast-food restaurant, or any other familiar spot in your neighborhood. Select the most interesting or significant moments and describe them in detail.
2. Describe a place in an American town or city that serves as the equivalent of an Indian well: a central place where all sorts of people congregate at various times of day. Such places might include a gas station, a laundromat, a twenty-four–hour grocery. Describe some of the various people that visit this place.

III. This exercise has been adapted from five paragraphs in *Fat City*, by Leonard Gardner. In this selection Gardner describes the work of Billy Tully and his fellow "toppers"—migrant onion-pickers. Read the paragraph that precedes the exercise, and then combine the sentences in each set. Several combinations can be made with absolutes and participle phrases.

Topping Onions

The bus rattled past dark houses, gas stations, neon-lit motels, and the high vague smokestack of the American Can Company, past the drive-in movie, its great screen white and iridescent in the approaching dawn, across an unseen creek beneath ponderous oaks, past the cars and trailers and pickup-truck caravans of the gypsy camp on its bank and out between the wide fields. Near a red-and-white checkered *Purina Chows* billboard, it turned off the highway. Down a dirt road it bumped to a barn, and the crew had left the bus and taken bottomless buckets from a pickup truck when the grower appeared and told them they were in the wrong man's onion field. The buckets clattered back into the truckbed, the crew returned to the bus, and the driver, one sideburn hacked unevenly and a bloodstained scrap of toilet paper pasted to his cheek, drove back to the highway swearing defensively while the crew cursed him among themselves. The sky bleached to an almost colorless lavender, except for an orange glow above the distant mountains. As the blazing curve of the sun appeared, lighting the faces of the men jolting in the bus—Negro paired with Negro, white with white, Mexican with Mexican and Filipino with Filipino—Billy Tully took the last sweet swallow of Thunderbird, and his bottle in its slim bag rolled banging under the seats.

1. They arrived at a field.
   The day's harvesting had already begun.
   Tully embraced an armload of sacks.
   Tully ran with the others.
   Tully ran for the nearest rows.
   Tully stumbled over the ground.
   The ground was plowed.
   Tully knocked his bucket with a knee.
   Tully did all this in the bright morning.
   The morning was onion-scented.
2. Tully claimed a row.
   A Negro knelt at the next row.
   The Negro was tall.
   The face of the Negro was covered with scars.
   The scars were thin.
   The Negro had a knife.
   It flashed among the profusion of onions.
   The onions were plowed up.
3. Tully removed his jacket.
   He jerked a sack around his bucket.
   His bucket was bottomless.
   He did this with fierce gasps.
4. He squatted.
   He picked up an onion.
   He severed the top.
   He tossed the onion.
   At the same time he picked up another.
5. The bucket was full.
   Then he lifted it.
   The onions rolled through into the sack.
   This left the bucket once again empty.
6. The driver stood in the distance.
   His hands were inside the waist of his jeans.

173

The waist was mammoth.

He yelled.

"Trim those bottoms!"

7. There was a thumping in the buckets.

The thumping was continuous.

8. The stooped forms inched in a line.

The line was uneven.

The line was like a wave.

The line was across the field.

Their progress was measured by the sacks.

These were the sacks they left behind.

The sacks were squat.

The sacks were upright.

9. There was a drone of tractors.

The drone was faint.

The drone was in the air.

The drone was hardly audible above the hum.

The hum had been in Tully's ears since his first army bouts.

His first army bouts were decades past.

10. He scrabbled on under the arc of the sun.

He cut.

He tossed.

Onion tops were flying.

The knife was fastened to his hand.

It was fastened by draining blisters.

11. His knees were sore.

He squatted.

He stood.

He crouched.

He sat.

He knelt again.

He belched a stinging taste of bile.

He dragged himself through the morning.

12. By noon he had sweated himself sober.

13. The toppers crawled on through the afternoon.

The rows of filled sacks extended farther and farther behind.

14. There was a man half lying near Tully.

He was old.

He was grizzled.

His face was an incredible red.

He was still filling buckets.

He appeared near death.

15. But Tully was standing.

16. He was revived by his lunch.
    He was revived by several cupfuls of warm water.
    The water came from the milk can.
    He was scooping up onions from the straddled row.
    He wrenched off tops.
    He ignored the bottom fibrils.
    Sometimes clods hung there.
    The clods were sometimes as big as the onions themselves.
    He did all this until a sack was full.
17. Then he trimmed several onions.
    He did this thoroughly.
    He placed them on top.
18. There was a gust of wind occasionally.
    He was engulfed by sudden rustlings.
    He was engulfed by flickering shadows.
    A high spiral of onion skins fluttered about him.
    They fluttered like a swarm of butterflies.
19. There were skins left behind.
    The skins were among the discarded tops.
    The skins swirled up with delicate clatters.
    The high, wheeling column moved away.
    It moved across the field.
    It eventually slowed.
    It widened.
    It dissipated.
    The skins hovered weightlessly.
    They then settled back to the plowed earth.
20. There were great flocks of blackbirds overhead.
    The flocks were rising.
    The flocks were falling.
    They streamed past in a melodious din.

Writing Suggestions

1. In a paragraph describe some act of hard physical labor. Use details that not only describe the nature of the work but also show how the worker feels.
2. In an essay describe some experience that left you feeling not just tired but exhausted. In your assay explain the difference between being *tired* and being *exhausted*.

Discovery: Similes and Metaphors

Look again at these two sentences from the last exercise, "Topping Onions":

> The stooped forms inched in an uneven line, <u>like a wave,</u> across the field. . . .

> Occasionally there was a gust of wind and he was engulfed by sudden rustling and flickering shadows as a high spiral of onion skins fluttered about him <u>like a swarm of butterflies.</u>

Each of these sentences contains a *simile:* that is, a comparison (usually introduced by *like* or *as)* between two things that are basically not alike—such as a line of men and a wave; onion skins and a swarm of butterflies. Writers use similes to explain things, to express emotion, and to make their writing more vivid and entertaining. Discovering similes is also a way of discovering new ways to look at a subject.

Metaphors also offer figurative comparisons, but these are implied rather than introduced by *like* or *as.* See if you can identify the implied comparisons in these two sentences:

> The farm was crouched on a bleak hillside, whence its fields, fanged in flints, dropped steeply to the village of Howling a mile away.
> (Stella Gibbons, *Cold Comfort Farm)*

> Time rushes toward us with its hospital tray of infinitely varied narcotics, even while it is preparing us for its inevitably fatal operation.
> (Tennessee Williams, *The Rose Tattoo)*

The first sentence above uses the metaphor of a beast "crouched" and "fanged in flints" to describe the farm and the fields. In the second sentence, time is compared to a doctor attending a doomed patient.

Similes and metaphors are often used in descriptive writing to create vivid sight and sound images, as in these two sentences:

> Over my head the clouds thicken, then crack and split with a roar like that of cannonballs tumbling down a marble staircase; their bellies open—too late to run now!—and suddenly the rain comes down.
> (Edward Abbey, *Desert Solitaire)*

176

The seabirds glide down to the water—stub-winged cargo planes—land awkwardly, taxi with fluttering wings and stamping paddle feet, then dive.

(Franklin Russell, "A Madness of Nature")

The first sentence above contains both a simile ("a roar like that of cannonballs") and a metaphor ("their bellies open") in its dramatization of a thunderstorm. The second sentence uses the metaphor of a "stub-winged cargo plane" to describe the movements of the seabirds. In both cases, the figurative comparisons offer the reader a fresh and interesting way of looking at the thing being described.

Similes and metaphors can be used to convey ideas as well as offer striking images. Consider the simile in the first sentence below and the extended metaphor in the second.

We walk through volumes of the unexpressed and like snails leave behind a faint thread excreted out of ourselves.

(John Updike, "The Blessed Man of Boston")

I am a camera with its shutter open, quite passive, recording, not thinking. Recording the man shaving at the window opposite and the woman in the kimona washing her hair. Some day, all this will have to be developed, carefully printed, fixed.

(Christopher Isherwood, *The Berlin Stories*)

Metaphors and similes can not only make your writing more interesting but also help you to think more carefully about your subject. Similes and metaphors are not just oranaments; they are ways of thinking.

How do you begin to create metaphors and similes? Be prepared to play with language and ideas. For instance, a comparison like the following might appear in an early draft of an essay:

Laura sang like an old cat.

As you revise your work, try adding more details to the comparison to make it more precise and interesting:

When Laura sang she sounded like a cat sliding down a blackboard.

Be alert to the ways other writers use similes and metaphors in their work. Then as you revise your own paragraphs and essays, see if you can make your descriptions more vivid and your ideas clearer by creating original similes and metaphors.

177

Here is an exercise that will give you some practice in creating figurative comparisons. For each of the eight statements below, make up a simile or metaphor that helps to explain each statement and make it more vivid. If several ideas come to you, jot them all down.

Example

George had been working at the same automobile factory six days a week, ten hours a day, for the past twelve years.
(Use a simile or metaphor to show how worn out George was feeling.)

1. George felt as worn out as the elbows on his work shirt.
2. George felt as worn out as an old phonograph record.
3. George felt worn out, like an old punching bag.
4. George felt as worn out as the old Ford that carried him to work every day.
5. George felt as worn out as an old joke.
6. George felt worn out and useless—just a broken fan belt, a burst radiator hose, a stripped wing nut, a discharged battery.

1. Fred had been working all day in the summer sun. *(Use a simile or metaphor to show how hot Fred was.)*
2. This is Nancy's first day at college, and she is in the middle of a chaotic morning registration session. *(Use a simile or metaphor to show either how confused Nancy is or how chaotic the entire session is.)*
3. Victor spent his entire vacation watching quiz shows and soap operas on television. *(Use a simile or metaphor to describe the state of Victor's mind by the end of his vacation.)*
4. Everyone said that Howie was a handsome man, but Howie was convinced that he was ugly. *(Use a simile or metaphor to show just how ugly Howie felt he was.)*
5. After all the troubles of the past few weeks, Sandy felt peaceful at last. *(Use a simile or metaphor to describe how peaceful or relieved Sandy felt).*
6. Silas reached down and touched the forehead of the newborn baby. *(Use a simile or metaphor to describe how gently Silas touched or how delicate the baby was.)*
7. Lou felt out of place and uncomfortable. *(Use a simile or metaphor to show how uncomfortable Lou felt.)*
8. Paula's instructor was boring. *(Use a simile or metaphor to describe how boring Paula's instructor was.)*

Practice: Sample Combinations

Use the sentences below as a guide after you have completed the Practice exercises in the first part of this chapter. Since in most cases more than one combination is possible, do not think that your sentences are "incorrect" just because they may not be in exact agreement with the ones below.

1. Out of the rainbow a squadron of jacksnipe suddenly banked and veered in perfect formation, their white wing patches flashing.

    (Joseph Judge, "New Orleans and Her River")

2. a. Their slender bodies sleek and black against the orange sky, the storks circled above us.

    b. For his own reasons Poppa didn't go to the depot, but as my sister and I were leaving he came up, a cob pipe jutting from his mouth, and stood sideways, looking over the misty Kansas countryside.

    (Gordon Parks, "My Mother's Dream for Me")

    c. On the tops of the hills, the grass stands at its tallest and greenest, its new straw-green seed plumes rising through a dead crop of last year's withered spears.

    (Henry Beston, *The Outermost House*)

3. His first marriage having ended in divorce and his second in despair, Norton vowed never to marry again.

4. All afternoon the caravan passed by, shimmering in the winter light, its numberless facets gleaming, the hundreds of wagon wheels turning in the dust, in slow and endless motion.

    (N. Scott Momaday, *The Names: A Memoir*)

CHAPTER 9

Building with Noun Clauses and Phrases

This chapter will give you practice in building sentences with clauses and phrases that serve as nouns in a sentence. You will work with four constructions that can make your writing more forceful and compact. These four constructions are *wh-* clauses, *that* clauses, gerunds, and infinitives.

Wh- *Clauses*

The words that commonly introduce questions also introduce *wh-* clauses:

who, whose, whoever
what, whatever
which, whichever
where, wherever
when, whenever
why
how (long, far, much, often)

Notice that all of these words (except *how*) begin with *wh-*. One way to think of a *wh-* clause is that it allows us both to ask and to answer a question in the same sentence. Consider, for instance, how we might combine the following question and response:

What will be the most exciting discoveries in physics or biology in the
next quarter of a century?
It seems impossible to predict.

We can combine the sentences by placing the question after the
statement and shifting the position of the verb <u>will be</u>:

It seems impossible to predict <u>what the most exciting discoveries in
physics or biology will be in the next quarter of a century</u>.

Notice that a *wh-* clause, like all clauses, contains its own subject
and verb but must be attached to another sentence to make sense
as a statement, rather than a question.

Practice 1

Combine the following sentences by placing the question after the
statement. Eliminate <u>this</u>, and move the verb <u>will</u> before the verb
<u>be</u>.

a. What will life be like in the American scientific community in the
next quarter of a century?
b. We can be surprisingly confident about this.

We can combine other questions and answers by following this
same procedure. For example, the following set of sentences contains
two questions that can be converted into a single *wh-* clause:

The facts of scientific advance are recognized.
But <u>how</u> do such advances occur?
<u>Why</u> do such advances occur?
There has been relatively little systematic attempt to understand this.

We can combine these sentences by turning the first into an adverb
clause, the second and third into a *wh-* clause, and the last into a
main clause:

Though the facts of scientific advance are recognized, there has been
little systematic attempt to understand <u>how and why such advances
occur</u>.

(Hilary Rose and Steven Rose, *Science and Society*)

181

There is, of course, nothing wrong in first posing a question and then answering it in a separate sentence. This, in fact, can be an effective way of gaining the reader's attention. However, too many questions and answers can make our writing tedious and distracting. Combining a question and answer in one sentence can eliminate unnecessary words and thus make our writing more compact.

Wh- clauses may appear at the beginning, in the middle, or at the end of a sentence—in fact, anywhere an ordinary noun might be found. Here are two examples:

Whatever value there is in studying literature, cultural or practical, comes from the total body of our reading, the castles of words we've built, and keep adding new wings to all the time.

(Northrop Frye, *The Educated Imagination*)

You can tell how healthy a man is by what he takes two at a time—stairs or pills.

(Kin Hubbard)

In the first example, the *wh-* clauses serves as the subject of the sentence. The second sentence contains two *wh-* clauses: one serves as a direct object *(how healthy a man is)* and the other as the object of the preposition by.

Practice 2

a. Combine the following sentences by turning the question into a statement. Eliminate this, and move the verb has in front of the verb thrown.

(1) What has the West thrown on the waters of the world?
(2) This drifts back on a tide of cultural pollution appalling to behold.

b. Combine the following sentences by placing the question before the statement. Eliminate do and this. (Notice that the second sentence below contains a *wh-* clause.)

(1) How do parents actually behave toward members of other groups in the presence of their children?
(2) This influences children more than what parents say about such people.

That *Clauses*

Just as we can think of *wh-* clauses as being based on questions, we can think of *that* clauses as being based on statements that answer questions. Consider how the question and answer below might be combined.

What has been a conspicuous feature of American life? The upper classes have done precious little in this country for the education of anyone but themselves.

We can make one sentence by turning the first into a statement and linking it to the second with the phrase the fact that:

A conspicuous feature of American life has been the fact that the upper classes have done precious little in this country for the education of anyone but themselves.

(James A. Michener, *America Against America*)

That clauses, like *wh-* clauses, may be placed anywhere a noun would normally appear in a sentence, though they appear most often at the end.

Practice 3

Combine the following sentences by omitting what does from the question and linking the two sentences with the fact that:

a. What does the principal determinant of human action spring from?
b. Most people lack the courage to take chances.

The phrase the fact that can often be reduced to a simple that, as shown below.

1. The fact that many Americans will continue to grab for the brass ring while others are letting go in no way invalidates the American Premise that happiness lies just ahead.

2. <u>That</u> many Americans will continue to grab for the brass ring while others are letting go in no way invalidates the American Premise that happiness lies just ahead.

(Leonard Gross, "Is Less More?")

The more concise version is usually the more effective one.

Practice 4

Combine the following sentences by omitting <u>what</u> and <u>of</u> and linking the two sentences with <u>that</u>:

    a. What is humor a reminder of?
    b. No matter how high the throne one sits on, one sits on one's bottom.

Sometimes even <u>that</u> itself can be dropped from the sentence, as long as there is no chance of confusing the reader. For example, we can combine the question and answer below simply by omitting the words <u>What do</u> from the beginning of the question:

What do totalitarian countries say?
They are cooperative societies, even though their regimes coerce their people to work.

The combined form is succinct and clear:

Totalitarian countries say they are cooperative societies, even though their regimes must coerce their people to work.

Practice 5

Combine each set of sentences below. One combination will require the phrase <u>the fact that</u> for the sentence to be clear, but the other combination can omit <u>that</u> altogether.

    a. (1) What do the old people know?
        (2) They will be taken care of if they are sick.
    b. (1) What does much of the abrasiveness, unpleasantness, and costliness of American life come from?
        (2) We are always dealing with strangers.

Gerunds

Phrases as well as clauses may serve as nouns in a sentence. One such phrase is the *gerund*—the present participle *(-ing)* form of a verb used as a noun. We can think of gerunds, like *that* clauses, as constructions that offer answers to questions implied in the rest of the sentence. In fact, the two sentences below can be combined with either a *that* clause or a gerund:

What is the first thing people remember about failing at math?
It felt like sudden death.

The first combination below uses a *that* clause, and the second uses a gerund.

1. The first thing people remember about failing at math is that it felt like sudden death.
2. The first thing people remember about failing at math is the feeling of sudden death.

(Sheila Tobias, "Who's Afraid of Math and Why?")

Gerunds, like present participles, can be used alone or with any number of modifiers.

Practice 6

Combine the following sentences: eliminate How do and insert by at the end of the first sentence; create a gerund by adding -ing to bend.

a. How do giraffes manage to drink?
b. They bend their front knees forward until they can reach the water.

Gerunds, like *wh-* and *that* clauses, may be placed anywhere a noun would normally appear in a sentence. In the following sentence, for example, one gerund appears at the beginning of the sentence as a subject, and another follows the verb:

Coming to New York from the muted mistiness of London is like traveling from a monochrome antique shop to a technicolor bazaar.

(D. H. Lawrence)

Practice 7

Combine the following sentences by changing both <u>prevent</u> and <u>pro-</u><u>tect</u> to gerunds:

    a. What do most parents work hard at?
    b. They either prevent failure or protect their children from the knowl-
       edge that they *have* failed.

Infinitives

An *infinitive* consists of <u>to</u> plus a verb. Often we have a choice between using a gerund or an infinitive as a noun, as shown below.

    1. There is nothing so futile as <u>having the right ideas</u> and <u>getting no</u>
       <u>attention.</u>
    2. There is nothing so futile as <u>to have the right ideas</u> and <u>to get no</u>
       <u>attention.</u>

Like a gerund, an infinitive is often followed by modifiers.

Once again, we can think of an infinitive as either posing or answering a question. By combining the sentences below we can see
that an infinitive can do both in the same sentence.

    What is it like to live without self-respect?
    It is to lie awake some night.
    It is to lie beyond the reach of warm milk.
    It is to lie beyond the reach of phenobarbital.
    It is to lie beyond the reach of the sleeping hand on the coverlet.

We can combine the sentences with an infinitive before and after
the verb:

    To live without self-respect is to lie awake some night, beyond the reach
      of warm milk, phenobarbital, and the sleeping hand on the coverlet.
                                  (Joan Didion, "On Self-Respect")

Practice 8

Use the example above as a model for combining the sentences below with infinitives.

What is it like to live without self-respect?
It is to count up the sins of commission.
It is to count up the sins of omission.
It is to count up the trusts betrayed.
It is to count up the promises subtly broken.

Achieving Balance with Noun Phrases and Clauses

Wh- clauses, *that* clauses, and particularly gerunds and infinitives are often used in pairs—one before and one after the verb—to balance related ideas in a sentence. Some of our common sayings are made of such balanced constructions:

Seeing is believing.
What you see is what you get.
To understand all is to forgive all.

As we first saw in Chapter 3, balanced constructions such as these have a pleasing shape and sound that help call attention to the ideas being connected.

Practice 9

Balance the sentence below by changing the underlined infinitive to a gerund.

To be a writer in a library is rather like being a eunuch in a harem.

Reducing Noun Phrases and Clauses

Although repeating structures to balance related ideas can be an effective technique, we should be careful not to overwork any one structure. Because the words <u>that</u> and <u>to,</u> in particular, are so common, we must take special care with *that* clauses and infinitives. For example, the combination of *that* clauses and adjective clauses in the sentence below is wordy.

> The fact <u>that</u> most people seek after things <u>that</u> they do not possess means <u>that</u> they are thus enslaved by the very things <u>that</u> they want to acquire.

One way to improve this sentence would be simply to omit the last three <u>thats.</u> We can also eliminate <u>the fact that</u> and use a *wh-* clause:

> Most people seek after what they do not possess and are thus enslaved by the very things they want to acquire.
>
> (Anwar Sadat, *In Search of Identity*)

Similarly, we should avoid piling infinitives one on top of the other:

> Environmentalists use the metaphor of the earth as a "spaceship" <u>to</u> <u>try to persuade</u> people <u>to stop</u> wasting and polluting our natural resources.

We can improve the sentence by changing the first infinitive to a gerund:

> Environmentalists use the metaphor of the earth as a "spaceship" <u>in</u> <u>trying</u> to persuade people to stop wasting and polluting our natural resources.

Practice 10

Eliminate one of the distracting <u>tos</u> by replacing the underlined infinitive with a gerund.

<u>To attempt</u> to fly to Chicago in this weather is foolish.

Summary

Noun clauses and phrases are useful constructions in combining sentences to make them compact, clear, and forceful. We have seen how the structures may be paired to give our sentences balance and how they may be mixed to give our sentences variety and to avoid repetition.

The exercises that follow will give you practice in building sentences with *wh-* clauses, *that* clauses, gerunds, and infinitives.

Exercise: Sentence Revising

Rewrite each sentence below according to the instructions in parentheses.

1. <u>When you</u> see your first flock of wood ducks come in to spend the night on an isolated lake, <u>it</u> is like secretly watching a great artist dab his brush in the paints and then slash color on the blank of canvas. *(Change the adverb clause to a gerund: eliminate the underlined words and change* see *to* seeing.)

2. In all areas of our life we make choices about how <u>we should behave,</u> when <u>we should speak,</u> whether <u>we should reveal</u> anger. *(Make this sentence more concise by changing each underlined word group to an infinitive.)*

3. If you have never done any whittling or wood carving before, the first skill to learn is <u>sharpening your knife.</u> *(Replace the underlined gerund with a clause beginning* how to.)

4. <u>Assigning</u> unanswered letters their proper weight, <u>freeing</u> us from the expectations of others, <u>giving</u> us back to ourselves—there lies the great, the singular power of self-respect. *(Change each underlined gerund to an infinitive.)*

5. <u>If you want to know the heart and mind of America,</u> learn baseball, the rules and realities of the game—and do it by watching first some high school or small town teams. *(Change the underlined adverb clause to a* wh- *clause beginning with* whoever; *make any other changes necessary.)*

6. <u>To question</u> the value of old rules is different from simply breaking them. *(Balance this sentence by changing the underlined infinitive to a gerund.)*

7. We <u>define</u> and <u>describe</u> ourselves when we choose clothes, either in a store or at home. *(Begin the sentence with "To choose clothes" and balance it by changing the underlined verbs to infinitives; make any other changes necessary.)*

8. <u>Living</u> with fear and not <u>being</u> afraid is the final test of maturity. *(Change the underlined gerunds to infinitives.)*

9. <u>Those pinpoint-sized twinkles of light all over the night sky</u> that we once believed to be stars turned out to be distant suns, many of them mightier than our own. *(Begin the sentence with "What we once believed to be stars" and follow with the underlined word group as an appositive.)*

10. What do you have left over after you have forgotten everything you have learned? Education. *(Combine the question and response in one sentence beginning "Education is. . . . ")*

Exercise: Sentence Building

Combine the sentences in each set into one clear sentence with at least one noun phrase or noun clause. Turn all questions into statements, and create a second combination whenever possible.

1. One either has or does not have a mathematical mind.
   This is a common myth about the nature of mathematical ability.

2. How does cross-country skiing differ most fundamentally from downhill skiing?
   It differs in the way that you get yourself uphill.

3. What will radar scanning be valuable for?
   It will detect modern waterways lying near the surface in arid areas.
   Geologists believe this.

4. What does the American value?
   The American does not value the possession of money as such.
   The American values his power to make money as a proof of his manhood.

   (W. H. Auden, "The Almighty Dollar")

5. What is the secret of a good life?
   One must have the right loyalties.
   One must hold them in the right scale of values.

   (Norman Thomas, "Great Dissenters")

6. Your authority, if not already gone, is slipping fast.
   What is the best way to learn this?
   Help your eldest son pick a college.

   (Sally and James Reston)

7. What is diplomacy?
   One does the nastiest thing in the nicest way.
   One says the nastiest thing in the nicest way.

8. What should politicians be encouraged to do?
   They should stand for what they believe in.
   They should not formulate their principles on the basis of opinion polls.

9. What is the only thing a man can do for eight hours a day, day after day?
   He can work.
   That is the saddest thing.

   (William Faulkner)

10. How does propaganda work?
    It tricks us.
    It distracts the eye momentarily.
    It distracts while the rabbit pops out from under the cloth.
    (Donna Woolfolk Cross, *Word Abuse*)

11. Troubles come.
    That is not the real problem.
    We don't know how to meet troubles.
    That is the real problem.

12. Do you have what you want?
    That is not happiness.
    Do you want what you have?
    That is happiness.

13. Old people in India know something.
    They have a position of honor in the family.
    They will be needed in diverse matters.
    They will initiate a young bride into the ways and running habits of her new home.
    They will offer experienced business advice.
    They will gauge the proper size of a daughter's dowry.

14. What is the purpose of life?
    Being happy is not the purpose of life.
    The purpose is to matter.
    The purpose is to be productive.
    The purpose is to be useful.
    The purpose is to have it make some difference that you lived at
       all.

    (Leo Rosten)

15. What kind of inner resources do we have?
    What imperishable treasures of mind and heart have we deposited
       in the bank of the spirit against this rainy day?
    The truth is this.
    When we are in trouble we discover these things.
    We discover swiftly.
    We discover painfully.

16. How does the porcupine fight?
    He gets his head under a rock or logs.
    He raises his quills.
    He whips his tail about at lightning speed.
    His tail is quill-filled.
    He waits for someone to come and get it.
          (Robert Thomas Allen, *Children, Wives and Other Wildlife*)

17. Is work useful?
    Or is work useless?
    Is work productive?
    Or is work parasitic?
    In practice nobody cares.
    Work shall be profitable.
    That is the sole thing demanded.
             (George Orwell, *Down and Out in Paris and London*)

18. Do something before you make a major investment in bottled water.
    Check with the manufacturer as to its source.
    Check with the manufacturer as to the type of processing.
    Check with the manufacturer as to results of tests of its content
       and purity.
    Dr. Robert Harris suggests this.
    Dr. Robert Harris is a water specialist at the Environment Defense
       Fund.
    (Jane E. Brody, "How to Make Sure Your Water Is Fit to Drink")

19. What kind of person are you?
    How do you feel about others?
    How will you fit into a group?
    Are you assured?
    Or are you anxious?
    To what degree do you feel comfortable with the standards of your
        own culture?
    Nonverbal communications signal these things to members of your
        own group.

    (Edward T. Hall, "The Sounds of Silence")

20. What is the teacher's task?
    It is not to implant facts.
    It is to place the subject to be learned in front of the learner.
    It is to awaken in the learner the restless drive for answers and
        insights.
    These answers and insights enlarge the personal life.
    These answers and insights give meaning to the personal life.
    The teacher must awaken through sympathy.
    The teacher must awaken through emotion.
    The teacher must awaken through imagination.
    The teacher must awaken through patience.

    (Nathan Pusey)

Exercise: Building Paragraphs and Essays

I. This exercise has been adapted from a paragraph of Anne Roiphe's "Confessions of a Female Chauvinist Sow." Read the paragraph that precedes the exercise, and then combine the sentences in each set, using noun phrases or clauses when appropriate.

Good Girls, Bad Boys

Most people I know have at one time or another been fouled up by their childhood experiences. Patterns tend to sink into the unconscious only to reappear, disguised, unseen, like marionette strings, pulling us this way or that. Whatever ails people—keeps them up at night, tossing and turning—also ails movements no matter how historically huge or

193

politically important. The women's movement cannot remake consciousness, or reshape the future, without acknowledging and shedding all the unnecessary and ugly baggage of the past. It's easy enough now to see where men have kept us out of clubs, baseball games, graduate schools; it's easy enough to recognize the hidden directions that limit Sis to cake-baking and Junior to bridge-building; it's now possible for even Miss America herself to identify what *they* have done to us, and, of course, *they* have and *they* did and *they* are. . . . But along the way we also developed our own hidden prejudices, class assumptions and an anti-male humor and collection of expectations that gave us, like all oppressed groups, a secret sense of superiority (co-existing with a poor self-image—it's not news that people can believe two contradictory things at once).

1. My mother slipped me a few extra dollars.
   It was called mad money.
   My mother did this during my teen years.
   I never left the house on my Saturday night dates without my mother doing this.
2. What was mad money?
   I'll explain for the benefit of a new generation.
   In this new generation people just sleep with each other.
3. The fellow was supposed to bring me home.
   The fellow was supposed to lead me safely through the asphalt jungle.
   He was supposed to protect me from slithering snakes.
   He was supposed to protect me from rapists and the like.
4. But young men were apt to drink too much.
   My mother and I knew that.
   Young men were apt to slosh down so many rye-and-gingers that something might happen.
   Some hero might well lead me in front of an oncoming bus.
   Some hero might smash his daddy's car into Tiffany's window.
   Less gallantly, some hero might throw up on my new dress.
5. What form of insanity did your date happen to evidence?
   It did not matter.
   There was mad money for getting home on your own.
6. Mad money was also a wallflower's rope ladder.
   Perhaps the guy you came with suddenly fancied someone else.
   Well, you didn't have to stay there and suffer.
   You could go home.
7. Boys were fickle.
   Boys were likely to be unkind.
   My mother and I knew that.

We knew that as surely as we knew something else.
Boys tried to make you do things in the dark.
Afterwards, they wouldn't respect you for doing these things.
In fact, they would spread the word.
They would spoil your rep.

8. Boys liked to be flattered.
They would eat out of your hand.
They would do this if you made them feel important.

9. So talk to them about their interests.
Don't alarm them with displays of intelligence.
We all knew that.
We were groups of girls.
We talked into the wee hours of the night.
We talked in a kind of easy companionship.
We thought this companionship was impossible with boys.

10. Boys were prone to have a good time.
Boys were prone to get you pregnant.
Then you came knocking on the door for finances or support.
The boys didn't know your name.
They would pretend this.

11. In short, boys were less moral than we were.
We believed this.

12. They appeared to be hypocritical.
They appeared to be self-seeking.
They appeared to be exploitative.
They appeared to be untrustworthy.
They appeared very likely to be showing off their masculinity.
Their masculinity was precious.

13. A girlfriend would not be unkind.
A girlfriend would not embarrass me in public.
I never had a girlfriend I thought would do this.

14. A girl would not lie to me about her marks.
A girl would not lie to me about her sports skill.
A girl would not lie to me about how good she was in bed.
I never expected a girl to do this.

15. Altogether I gathered that men were sexy.
Men were powerful.
Men were very interesting.
Men were not very nice.
Men were not very moral.
Men were not very humane.
Men were not very tender.
Men were not like us.
No one directly came out and said this.

16. Girls played fairly.
Men, unfortunately, reserved their honor for the battlefield.

Writing Suggestion

In an essay, discuss and compare some of the assumptions about men and women that you were brought up to believe. Explain where those ideas came from and how valid you now think those ideas are.

II. This exercise has been adapted from the five paragraphs of an article by Pamela M. Bischoff that first appeared in the June-July 1978 issue of *Change* magazine. Combine the sentences in each set, using noun phrases and clauses when appropriate.

Increasing Employability

1. There are recent undergraduate enrollment statistics.
The statistics show the steady increase in the popularity of business administration courses.
We need to examine the statistics only superficially to know something.
Choosing the "right" major will lead to obtaining a "good" job upon graduation.
Many students believe this.
2. Similarly, we need to listen to the deliberations of many faculty groups.
We need to listen only briefly.
We know something.
The students' concerns are not always shared by those who teach them.
Indeed, the students' concerns are sometimes deprecated.
3. There is a consumerism movement.
The movement has given impetus to the following notion.
Educational institutions should provide present students with descriptive data.
The descriptive data should include placement statistics.
Prospective students should also be provided with such data.
4. Many students cannot afford to make a poor career decision.
They cannot afford the luxury of this.
This is true particularly of women.

This is true particularly of those who are physically disabled.
This is true of a high percentage of minority group students.

5. The "wrong" major will lead to underemployment.
   The "wrong" major will lead to an inadequate salary.
   The "wrong" major will lead to a certain kind of job.
   This job does not involve self-growth.
   Many students fear these things.

6. Disclosure of information is thus thought to be helpful in decision
   making.

7. Which fields have good prospects?
   Our knowledge of this is woefully inadequate.
   How many persons are preparing for various career areas?
   Our understanding of this is even less certain.
   These are things faculty members rightly protest.
   And, in any event, the purposes of a liberal arts education go far
   beyond simply preparing students for specific careers.

8. Critical modes of thought are taught.
   Problem-solving modes of thought are taught.
   Close familiarity with at least one field is taught.
   The faculty members argue these things.

9. All are useful in preparation for a variety of careers.
   This is what they claim.

10. Our own college communities are so divided.
    What then can we tell students?

11. Here is what we can teach them.
    Self-assessment techniques alone (skills, interests, and values in-
    ventories) should not be the deciding factor in making rational
    career decisions.
    Job availability predictions by themselves should not be the deciding
    factor in making rational career decisions.

12. We of the faculty and professional staff can work cooperatively.
    We can provide helpful direction to students.
    We can do this more than in the past.

13. Employers of all kinds look for resourceful applicants.
    Employers of all kinds look for imaginative applicants.
    We can tell students this.

14. They can increase their employability without changing majors.
    We can focus their concerns on this.

15. There are various means to accomplish this.
    These include helping students to acquire certain things.
    They need well-developed communications skills.
    They need research capabilities.
    They need analytical abilities.

They need fluency in a foreign language.
They need familiarity with computer applications.
They need quantitative competence.
They need the ability to complete independent research projects.

16. We should strongly encourage college-sponsored work internship programs.
    We should strongly encourage field study experiences for credit.
    We should seek out career-related part-time or summer jobs.
    We should support these jobs.
    We should do these things above all else.

17. These things provide a good means of entry to specific jobs.
    They have a salutary side effect.
    They help students make more reasoned personal career decisions.
    These decisions are based upon actual work experiences.

Writing Suggestions

1. In an essay, discuss all the factors you have considered in choosing your major. If you have not yet selected a major, discuss your reasons for attending college.

2. Considering your own attitudes and those of your friends, do you think students today are overly concerned with choosing a major that "will lead to obtaining a 'good' job upon graduation"? Respond in an essay.

3. Do you think the faculty and administration of your college are doing enough to help students make rational career decisions and prepare them for work after college? Before responding to this question in an essay, visit the placement office at your college to find out just what is being done.

III. This exercise has been adapted from seven paragraphs of an article by Phillip Longman that first appeared in the November 1982 issue of the *Washington Monthly*. Read the five paragraphs that precede the exercise, and then combine the sentences in each set, using noun phrases and clauses where appropriate.

Taking America to the Cleaners

Put bluntly, the old have come to insist that the young not only hold them harmless for their past profligacy, but sacrifice their own prosperity to pay for it. And the beauty of it all, at least for the old, is that so far the young have muttered barely a word of protest.

Suffice it to say that by the older generation I refer to those who survived the Depression and World War II to then enjoy the longest sustained period of prosperity in American history. By the young I generally mean those under 30; as for those between the ages of 30 and 50, which includes the first contingent of the much-heralded Baby Boom, their interests are so intertwined with both generations that they have little role in this conflict.

It is upon the youngest that the burden of this new generational politics squarely falls. For with the decline of Youth has come the arrival of an entirely new era in American life, one in which the circumstances of one's age—as much as one's race, sex, or social class—have become a prime determinant of one's economic destiny and political self-interest. If you doubt this, look no further than to how the federal government spends its money.

This year 28 percent of the federal government's outlays will go to social security, medicare, and other transfer payments for the 11 percent of the population over 65—all of that disbursed regardless of need. More than $10 billion in social security checks will go to elderly households whose income already exceeds $25,000 annually; 130,000 of those households, according to the Current Population Survey of the Bureau of Census, have income exceeding $75,000. The federal treasury will forego $2.4 billion to give everyone over 65 an additional income tax deduction, and another $500 million for special tax breaks when those over 55 sell their homes. Indeed, American life is filled with such entitlements, from free health care for all veterans over 65 to reduced bus fares for seniors. All share one thing: eligibility is determined not by one's need but by the date on one's birth certificate. . . .

Today the elderly are not only as well off as the rest of America, during the last decade they were the only major segment of our society that stayed abreast of inflation. This is because 70 percent of America's elderly own their own homes—thereby insulating them against a major component of inflation, high housing costs. Another reason is that most pensions are indexed to the cost of living, which has gone up faster than the salaries of people of working age. Contrary to a popular liberal assumption, "elderly" and "needy" are no longer synonymous.

1. Every old person deserves security from poverty.
   That is indisputable.
   We owe this to all our citizens.
2. Almost a third of the nation's elderly single women, for example, try to eke out an existence on less than $4000 a year.
   This circumstance is made all the more desperate by the natural infirmities of old age.
   It is made all the more desperate by the loneliness.
   Loneliness so often accompanies old age.

3. Such Americans deserve our understanding.
   They deserve the public's subsidy.
4. With this the young should have no quarrel.
5. Do elderly citizens deserve an automatic reward solely for having reached a certain age?
   That is a different credo.
   That is at odds with egalitarian principles.
   American democracy is based on egalitarian principles.
6. If, after all, one falters before reaching age 65, does he deserve any less help from society?
7. Yet a handicapped young adult receives just $284 a month.
   This young adult is dependent today on the government's SSI program.
8. He could be receiving as much as $729 in social security.
   He could if he had managed to complete a career.
   He would have to complete a career before becoming disabled.
9. Are the elderly's entitlements "insurance" and not "welfare"?
   Some argue this.
   It is crucial to understand something.
   This distinction protects certain sensibilities.
   The distinction is more semantic than real.
10. The nation can no longer afford to make this distinction.
11. Social security, for example, is primarily financed by an additional tax.
    Current workers are taxed.
    Current workers must also pay federal income tax.
12. What did the average social security beneficiary today contribute in a lifetime?
    That is what he or she receives in only 19 months.
13. Horace W. Brock is an economic consultant.
    Horace W. Brock has used the social security trustees' own demographic and economic assumptions.
    Today's young workers must force their own children to bear a tax burden three times as large.
    They must do this to realize the same level of retirement benefits.
    Horace W. Brock has calculated that.
14. The current social security system thus does not resemble an insurance scheme.
    It resembles a pyramid game.
    Those who arrive early get far more than they pay in.
15. Later arrivals face a prospect.
    They may get much less.
    They may get nothing at all.

16. Of course, any change in this system must pay decent regard to aroused expectations.

    Those new retired or nearing retirement have these aroused expectations.

17. The necessary reform may be postponed longer.

    The result becomes more inevitable.

    Today's young will be relegated to a certain kind of old age.

    That old age is truly desperate.

    That old age is impoverished.

18. My generation never really knew a different age.

    My generation seeks to live out the values and expectations of that age.

    My generation fails to live out the values and expectations of that age.

    My generation will perceive its true circumstance.

    It is only a matter of time until it does.

19. Was there ever a generation that had reason to take to the streets?

    If there ever was, it is this one.

20. It has not yet happened.

    The young so far have eschewed the streets.

    They have eschewed the halls of Congress.

21. The young have been partly seduced by the ideology of their immediate elders.

    This so often besets quieter generations.

    They inherit a notion from the era of Youth.

    There is little to be found in politics save cause for alienation.

22. But the younger generation must realize something.

    It is unlike a previous generation.

    It does not have the luxury of discounting politics.

23. The government's generosity becomes further limited.

    The old promise to become more militant.

    They will advance their claims of generational privilege.

24. The young must join in this competition for equity.

    The competition is grubby.

    Otherwise, they will find their birthright mortgaged even more.

25. But there is a danger in the younger generation's political awakening.

26. The young may demand nothing less than the same prosperity of their parents.

    That prosperity is reckless.

    They may demand this in frustration.

    The unjust debts of history will compound even further.

    The debts will be passed from one generation to the next.

We will be heavily mortgaged.
We now fear a national decline.
Then the decline will be inevitable.
Then the decline will be irreversible.

27. There is a way to avoid that.
A more fair division of the necessary sacrifices of American life is required.
A more fair division of the ensuing benefits of American life is required.

28. There are those who deserve compassion.
We should be unselfish to them.
We should give to each according to his need.
We should not give to each according to his generation.

Writing Suggestions

1. In a paragraph, summarize the main points raised by Longman in this excerpt from his article "Taking America to the Cleaners."
2. In an essay, carefully evaluate the points raised by Longman. Do you agree that the young generation is being forced unfairly to "sacrifice their own prosperity" for the "past profligacy" of older generations? Or do you believe that the young should assume full responsibility for the care of the old?
3. The increasing proportion of older people in our society is having an effect on employment opportunities, housing development, and many other aspects of American life. Discuss some of these effects in an essay.

Exercise: Recombining

This exercise has been adapted from two paragraphs in "The Hazards of Science," by Lewis Thomas. The writer's sixteen original sentences have been combined into seven in the exercise. Untangle these seven sentences by breaking them down into short sentences and then recombining them. Your aim is not to imagine what Thomas's original sentences might be but to create two clear, effective paragraphs. Many combinations are possible.

Hard Times for the Human Intellect

1. What I consider to be the major discovery of the past hundred years of biology and the only solid piece of scientific truth about which I feel totally confident is that we are profoundly ignorant about nature, and this is, in its way, an illuminating piece of news.

2. Although it would have amazed the brightest minds of the eighteenth-century Enlightenment to be told by any of us how little we know and how bewildering the way ahead seems, it is this sudden confrontation with the depth and scope of ignorance that represents the most significant contribution of twentieth-century science to the human intellect.

3. We are, at last, facing up to it, but we pretended to understand how things worked or we ignored the problem or we simply made up stories to fill the gaps, in earlier times.

4. These are hard times for the human intellect, and it is no wonder that we are depressed, for now that we have begun exploring in earnest, doing serious science, we are getting glimpses of how huge the questions are and how far those questions are from being answered.

5. It is not so bad being ignorant if you are totally ignorant, but the hard thing is knowing in some detail the reality of ignorance, the worst spots and here and there the not-so-bad spots, but no true light at the end of any tunnel nor even any tunnels that can yet be trusted, and so these are hard times, indeed.

6. But we are making a beginning, and there ought to be some satisfaction in that, ought to be some exhilaration even in that—the method works—and there are probably no questions we can think up, sooner or later, that can't be answered, and this includes the matter even of consciousness.

7. To be sure, there may well be questions we can't think up, ever, and there may therefore be limits to the reach of human intellect which we will never know about, but that is another matter, for within our limits, we should be able to work our way through to all our answers, if we keep at it long enough, and if we pay attention.

Discovery: Revision Checklist

To *revise* means to *look again* at what you have written to see how you can improve it. You may begin revising as soon as you begin a rough draft—restructuring and rearranging sentences as you work out your ideas. Then you return to the draft, perhaps several times, for further revisions. Revising is an opportunity to reconsider—in fact, rediscover—your topic, your readers, your purpose for writing. Such a reconsideration may lead you to make major changes in the content and structure of your paper.

Revising involves much more than just recopying a rough draft and correcting errors in grammar, spelling, and punctuation. To emphasize this, we have prepared two checklists: one for revising (below) and one for editing (at the end of the next chapter). Of course, the checklists may be used together: you may edit as you revise, and vice versa. However, you should not waste time carefully editing a paper that you haven't yet revised at all. Because you may end up discarding entire sentences and paragraphs, you should evaluate what you have written before you try to fix it.

The best time to revise is not immediately after you have completed a draft (although at times this will be necessary). Instead, wait a few hours—even a day or two, if possible—in order to gain some distance from your work. This way you will be less protective of your writing and better prepared to make changes.

One more bit of advice: read your paper out loud when you revise. You may *hear* problems that you cannot see.

Study the checklist below, and then read the rough draft that follows it. Use the checklist as a guide while you evaluate the draft. This will prepare you for using the checklist as a guide when you come to revise your own work.

REVISION CHECKLIST

1. Does the essay have a clear and precise main idea? Is this idea made clear to the reader early in the essay?
2. Does the essay have a specific purpose (such as to explain, entertain, evaluate, or persuade)? Is this purpose clear?
3. Does the opening of the essay create interest in the topic and make the reader want to read on?
4. Is there a clear plan to the essay? Does each paragraph develop logically from the previous one?
5. Is each paragraph clearly related to the main idea of the essay? Is there enough information in the essay to support the main idea?
6. Is the main point of each paragraph clear? Is each point adequately and clearly supported?
7. Are there clear transitions from one sentence to the next? Have key words and ideas been given proper emphasis in the sentences and paragraphs?
8. Are the sentences clear and direct? Can they be understood on the first reading? Are the sentences varied in length and struc-

ture? Can they be improved through combining or recombining?

9. Is the language in the essay clear and precise? Does the essay have a consistent tone?

10. Does the essay have an effective conclusion—one that emphasizes the main idea and provides a sense of completeness?

The following rough draft was written by Mark Hulme, a student. A second draft of this essay appears at the end of Chapter 10, and the final version appears as an exercise ("Growing Up at the Victory Drive-In") in Chapter 3. After reading this draft, suggest ways the student might improve his essay. The numbers in the margins refer to questions in the checklist, which you should use as a guide. Then read the student's revised draft ("The Disappearing Drive-In Blues") to see how closely his revision corresponds to your evaluation.

Decline of the Drive-in[*]

3   I am an avid drive-in movie-goer, I have been since I was a kid. You can imagine my distress—how distressed I am by the current decline of the drive-in. As a youth, a highschooler, the drive-in movie house was a frequent activity, past-time, location for frivolarities that I loved to dabble in. Yes, I was a frequent drive-in movie goer, but things are changed now. I've changed and the drive-ins have changed. This essay is about those changes.   1 & 2

When I was young, Mom and Dad use to carry us kids to the drive-in. We went a lot because back then the drive-in movie was just as good as the walk-ins. This is no longer the case. Drive-in movie houses are run down. They are no longer as popular as they once were. Back when my father carried us to the drive-in, the movies were first-rate first-run movies that were run in the house and at the drive-in at the same time. We saw movies like *The Godfather, The Graduate, Airport* and all sorts of great flicks. Nowadays the flicks are horrable wretchedness like *The Valley of the Sabine Women* and *The Man with the Golden Eyesocket,* and other horrable monstronsities that make one wonder if may be home movies might have more merit.

5 (margin)   8 (margin)

Another thing that is horrable about drive-in movies is the food. Egad, you never tasted popcorn as bad as this. Even Palace Cinema, a new theater in town that for it's first few weeks had

[*] A second draft of this essay ("The Disappearing Drive-In Blues") appears at the end of Chapter 10.

popcorn shipped in from Chicago because they didn't have popcorn **9** machines yet was'nt as bad as they stuff they serve now now in the drive-ins. A friend of mine and I have this theory that they the movie people owners, use the leftover popcorn from the walk-in movie houses. They use popcorn that was left over from the day before.

4 Drive-in movies can be a lot of fun. They are a great way to spend one's time. It is a cheap kind of entertainment for all ages. But drive-ins use to be a lot more fun. Unless you are just going there for a cheap date or to drink beer with a friend or just need a place to park the car. Drive-in movies were at one time a popular **6** weekend night activity. They were a place where one could go to **7** see a movie for not much money. But now people don't go to drive-in movies as often because the managers of most of the theaters have let them run down. One wonders if drive-ins are less popular today because the theaters have run down or if the theaters have run down because they aren't as popular as they use to be.

10 Whatever the case, drive-ins just ain't what they use to be.

Practice: Sample Combinations

Use the sentences below as a guide after you have completed the Practice exercises in the first part of this chapter. Since in most cases more than one combination is possible, do not think that your sentences are "incorrect" just because they may not be in exact agreement with the ones below.

1. We can be surprisingly confident about what life will be like in the American scientific community in the next quarter of a century.
2. a. What the West has thrown on the waters of the world drifts back to us on a tide of cultural pollution appalling to behold.
   b. How parents actually behave toward members of other groups in the presence of their children influences children more than what parents say about such people.
3. The principal determinant of human action springs from the fact that most people lack the courage to take chances.
4. Humor is a reminder that no matter how high the throne one sits on, one sits on one's bottom.
5. a. The old people know they will be taken care of if they are sick.
   b. Much of the unpleasantness, abrasiveness, and costliness of American life comes from the fact that we're always dealing with strangers.

6. Giraffes manage to drink by bending their front knees forward until they can reach the water.
7. Most parents work hard at either preventing failure or protecting their children from the knowledge that they *have* failed.
8. To live without self-respect is to count up the sins of commission and omission, the trusts betrayed, the promises subtly broken.
9. Being a writer in a library is rather like being a eunuch in a harem.

(John Braine)

10. Attempting to fly to Chicago in this weather is foolish.

CHAPTER 10

Coherence

Although the emphasis in each of the previous chapters has been on making clear connections within sentences, you have also practiced connecting sentences in paragraphs and paragraphs in essays. Writing that is clearly connected is said to be *coherent.* This chapter will give you additional practice in improving the coherence of your writing. In particular, you will work with signal words and phrases, the repetition of key words, and pronouns—devices that guide the reader from sentence to sentence and paragraph to paragraph.

Unity

Before you can show your readers *how* sentences and paragraphs are connected, you need to be sure that they *are* connected logically. In other words, your writing must be *unified.* Each sentence in a paragraph should contribute to the central purpose and main idea of that paragraph. In the same way, each paragraph in an essay should contribute to the overall purpose and main idea of the whole essay. If you have difficulty making connections, be sure that you are not trying to force together unrelated ideas. If you find that you are, either omit the irrelevant material or shift it to a more appropriate location in your essay.

The paragraph below lacks unity because one of the sentences does not relate directly to the main idea of the paragraph.

Man has credited himself with several talents to distinguish him from all other animals. Once we thought that we were the only creatures to make and use tools. We now know that this is not so: chimpanzees do so and so do finches in the Galapagos that cut and trim long thorns to use as pins for extracting grubs from holes in wood. Even our complex spoken language seems less special the more we learn about the communications used by chimpanzees and dolphins. Dolphins produce an ultra-sound with larynx and maybe an organ in front of the head, the melon. But we are the only creatures to have painted representational pictures and it is this talent which led to developments which ultimately transformed the life of mankind.

(Adapted from *Life on Earth*, by David Attenborough)

The second-to-the-last sentence ("Dolphins produce an ultra-sound . . . ") upsets the unity of the paragraph by adding information that neither illustrates the point raised in the previous sentence (concerning animal communications, not devices of communication) nor relates to the main idea of the paragraph (that many human talents are not unique to humans). We can improve the paragraph by subordinating this sentence or by omitting it altogether.

Practice 1

Create a unified paragraph by arranging *six* of the sentences below in logical order. Begin the paragraph with sentence d, which expresses the main idea, and omit the three sentences that do not relate directly to the main idea of the paragraph.

> a. "Adopt-a-School" programs have flourished over the last three years, with local companies providing personnel and resources to students of a particular school.
> b. "This is the future work force of many businesses in Boston," says Kenneth Rossano, senior vice president of the First National Bank and president of the chamber of commerce.
> c. Florida has established functional-literacy examinations as a requirement for passing the third, fifth, eighth, and eleventh grades—and a sophomore test that university students must take to become juniors.
> d. Businesses are becoming more directly involved in what goes on in the schools, providing funds, professional expertise, and the incentive of jobs.
> e. A study released last fall found that 60 percent of the nation's school districts use computers for learning and that the number of ele-

> mentary schools using them had increased by 80 percent over the year before.
> f. Buckman Laboratories in Memphis, for example, brings kids from Cypress Junior High to its plant for exposure to real-life applications of modern chemistry.
> g. Education rarely commands broad national attention for very long—only, it seems, when the country is in trouble.
> h. The Boston Compact represents a different approach: More than 100 businesses in that city, such as The Boston Globe and Jewish Memorial Hospital, have agreed to give hiring priority and additional training to city-school graduates if standards are raised.
> i. In return, the school system, rated by some the worst in the country, must guarantee that its graduates will have adequate math and verbal skills.

Once you are satisfied that your writing is unified—that every sentence belongs where it is—you can apply the strategies for coherence discussed in the next few pages.

Signal Words and Phrases

Signal words and phrases show the direction of our thought as we move from one sentence to the next. Although they most often appear at the beginning of a sentence, they may appear in the middle (usually after the subject) or even at the end. The following is a list of the common signal words and phrases, grouped according to the type of relationship shown by each:

ADDITION

and	first, second, third
also	in the first place, in the second place,
besides	in the third place
in addition	to begin with, next, finally
furthermore	
moreover	

EXAMPLE

In the first place, no "burning" in the sense of combustion, as in the burning of wood, occurs in a volcano; moreover, volcanoes are not necessarily mountains; furthermore, the activity takes place not always at the summit but more commonly on the sides or flanks; <u>and finally,</u> the "smoke" is not smoke but condensed steam.

(Fred Bullard, *Volcanoes in History, in Theory, in Eruption*)

RESTATEMENT

in other words	that is
in short	to put it differently
in simpler terms	to repeat

EXAMPLE

Anthropologist Geoffrey Gorer studied the few peaceful human tribes and discovered one common characteristic: sex roles were not polarized. Differences of dress and occupation were at a minimum. Society, <u>in other words,</u> was not using sexual blackmail as a way of getting women to do cheap labor, or men to be aggressive.

(Gloria Steinem, "What It Would Be Like If Women Win")

INSISTENCE

in fact	no
indeed	yes

EXAMPLE

A solitary ant, afield, cannot be considered to have much of anything on his mind; <u>indeed,</u> with only a few neurons strung together, he can't be imagined to have a mind at all, much less a thought.

(Lewis Thomas, "On Societies As Organisms")

EXAMPLE

as an illustration	specifically
for example	thus
for instance	to illustrate

EXAMPLE

With all the ingenuity involved in hiding delicacies on the body, this process automatically excludes certain foods. <u>For example,</u> a turkey sandwich is welcome, but the cumbersome cantaloupe is not.

(Steve Martin, "How to Fold Soup")

COMPARISON

by the same token	in the same way
in like manner	likewise
in similar fashion	similarly

211

EXAMPLE

Man is an animal that laughs; <u>likewise,</u> he is an animal that is laughed at.

(Henri Bergson)

CONTRAST

but	on the contrary
however	on the other hand
in contrast	still
instead	yet
nevertheless	

EXAMPLE

By nightfall of an average courting day, a fiddler crab who has been standing on tiptoe for eight or ten hours waving a heavy claw in the air is in pretty sad shape. As in the case of the males of all species, <u>however,</u> he gets out of bed next morning, dashes some water on his face, and tries again.

(James Thurber, "Courtship Through the Ages")

CAUSE-EFFECT

accordingly	consequently
and so	so
as a result	then
for this reason	therefore
hence	thus

EXAMPLE

Stereotypes are a kind of gossip about the world, a gossip that makes us pre-judge people before we ever lay eyes on them. <u>Hence,</u> it is not surprising that stereotypes have something to do with the dark world of prejudice.

(Robert L. Heilbroner, "Don't Let Stereotypes Warp Your Judgments")

CONCLUSION

and so	in closing
after all	in conclusion
at last	on the whole
finally	to conclude
in brief	to summarize

212

EXAMPLE

In all likelihood, corrective measures are being developed for many of
the problems described above, and helpful correspondents will be writing
in to tell me all about it. Yet I remain confident that new examples will
come along to fill the gap. After all, that's progress.

(Alan L. Otten, "This Is Progress?")

TIME

afterward	immediately
at the same time	later
currently	meanwhile
earlier	previously
formerly	simultaneously
in the future	subsequently
in the meantime	then
in the past	until now

EXAMPLE

At first a toy, then a mode of transportation for the rich, the automobile
was designed as man's mechanical servant. Later it became part of the
pattern of living.

PLACE

above	nearby
alongside	on top of
beneath	to the left
beyond	to the right
farther along	under
in back	upon
in front	

EXAMPLE

In the corner next to the toilet was the sink at which we washed, and
the square tub in which my mother did our clothes. Above it, tacked
to the shelf on which were pleasantly ranged square, blue-bordered white
sugar and spice jars, hung calendars from the Public National Bank on
Pitkin Avenue. . . .

(Alfred Kazin, *A Walker in the City*)

Practice 2

Combine the sentences in each set below into *two* clear sentences. Add a signal word or phrase to the second sentence to show how it relates to the first.

a. To be self-centered does not mean to disregard the worth of other people.
   We are *all* self-centered.
   Most psychologists would probably accept this position.

b. There are differences in math performance between boys and girls.
   These differences cannot be attributed simply to differences in innate ability.
   If one were to ask the victims themselves, they would probably disagree.

c. The nuclear believers are like all true believers.
   They have been doing their best to convert everyone to their belief.
   We are constantly exposed to ads and editorials.
   The ads and editorials predict dire consequences if nuclear energy programs are not accelerated.

Repetition of Key Words and Structures

Repeating key words in a paragraph or essay is an important technique for assuring coherence. Used carelessly or excessively, repetition is merely boring. But used skillfully, as in the paragraph below, this technique helps hold our sentences together and focuses the reader's attention on a central idea.

We Americans are a charitable and humane people: we have institutions devoted to every good cause from rescuing homeless cats to preventing World War III. But what have we done to promote the art of <u>thinking</u>? Certainly we make no room for <u>thought</u> in our daily lives. Suppose a man were to say to his friends, "I'm not going to PTA tonight (or choir practice or the baseball game) because I need some time to myself, some time to <u>think</u>"? Such a man would be shunned by his neighbors; his family would be ashamed of him. What if a teen-ager were to say, "I'm not going to the dance tonight because I need some time to think"? His parents would immediately start looking in the Yellow Pages for a psychiatrist. We are all too much like Julius Caesar: we fear and distrust people who think too much. We believe that almost anything is more important than thinking.

(Carolyn Kane, "Thinking: A Neglected Art")

Notice that the writer uses various forms of the same word—think, thinking, thought—to link the different examples and reinforce the main idea of the paragraph. Her repetition of the pronoun we also helps establish clear connections.

A similar way to assure coherence in our writing is to repeat a sentence structure. Although we usually try to vary the length and structure of our sentences, we may, at times, repeat a construction to emphasize connections between related ideas, as in the following example:

> There are couples who dislike one another furiously for several hours at a time; there are couples who dislike one another permanently; and there are couples who never dislike one another; but these last are people who are incapable of disliking anybody.
>
> (George Bernard Shaw, *Getting Married*)

These balanced clauses are closely connected, not only by the semicolons, but by the repeated words and structures as well.

Practice 3

Rewrite the paragraph below, repeating key words and structures to assure coherence. Begin each pair of sentences with once and today. Use the first pair as a model for the next three.

> At the turn of the century, a newborn child could expect to live about to the age of 50; today, the expectancy is about 70. A mother once had sound reason to fear giving birth; death in childbirth is regarded as intolerable today. A full high school education was the best achievement of a minority once; it is the barest minimum today for decent employment and self-respect. The timber and mining barons once stripped away the forests and topsoil wholesale; these companies are confronted by their communities at every other move today.

Coherence with Pronouns

The repetition of key words and structures is an effective technique as long as it is not overworked. Carried on for too long, repetition gets tedious, as in the paragraph below.

> A characteristic human reaction to <u>flies</u> is to eradicate <u>flies.</u> Eradicating <u>flies</u> is deemed a meritorious action. Eradicating <u>flies</u> may be an innate tendency. I have already alluded to the propensity of children for amputating the appendages of <u>flies.</u> Ants amputate the appendages of <u>flies</u> if a <u>fly</u> is unfortunate enough to fall into the ants' clutches. I venture to predict, however, that the <u>fly</u> is in no danger of extinction. The <u>fly</u> has no sociological impediments to reproduction; the <u>fly's</u> food supply is unlimited; the <u>fly's</u> basic requirements, few.

We can maintain the coherence of this paragraph while eliminating the excessive repetition by substituting pronouns for some of the repeated nouns. Consider this revised version of the paragraph:

> A characteristic human reaction to flies is to eradicate <u>them.</u> <u>This</u> is deemed a meritorious action. <u>It</u> may be an innate tendency. I have already alluded to the propensity of children for amputating the appendages of flies. Ants do the <u>same thing</u> if a fly is unfortunate enough to fall into <u>their</u> clutches. I venture to predict, however, that the fly is in no danger of extinction. <u>It</u> has no sociological impediments to reproduction; <u>its</u> food supply is unlimited; <u>its</u> basic requirements, few.
>
> (Vincent Dethier, *To Know a Fly*)

The one thing we must be careful of when using pronouns to assure coherence is that each pronoun clearly refers to an appropriate noun.

Practice 4

Rewrite the paragraph below, replacing the underlined words and phrases with appropriate pronouns.

A society that has no heroes will soon grow enfeebled. <u>That society's</u> purposes will be less elevated; <u>that society's</u> endeavors less strenuous. <u>That society's</u> individual members will "hang loose" and "lay back" and, so mellowed out, the last thing of which <u>that society's individual members</u> wish to hear is heroism. <u>That society's individual members</u> do not want to be told of men and women whose example might disturb <u>that society's individual members</u>, calling <u>that society's individual members</u> to effort and duty and sacrifice or even the chance of glory.

Coherence in the Essay

The same techniques used to connect sentences in a paragraph can also be used to link the beginning of a new paragraph with the one preceding it. The following excerpt from an essay by Isaac Asimov illustrates all of the techniques that have been discussed so far:

[1] When the time comes for the female platypus to produce young, she builds a special burrow, which she lines with grass and carefully plugs. She then lays two eggs, each about three quarters of an inch in diameter and surrounded by a translucent, horny shell.

[2] <u>These</u> the mother platypus places between her tail and abdomen and curls up about them. It takes two weeks for the very young to hatch out. The new-born duckbills have teeth and very short bills, so that they are much less "birdlike" than the adults. They feed on milk. The mother has no nipples, but milk oozes out of pore openings in the abdomen and the young lick the area and are nourished in this way. As they grow, the bills become larger and the teeth fall out.

[3] <u>Yet</u> despite everything zoologists learned about the duckbills, they never seemed entirely certain as to where to place them in the table of animal classification. On the whole, the decision was made because of hair and milk. In all the world, only mammals have true hair and only mammals produce true milk. The duckbill and spiny anteater have hair and produce milk, so they have been classified as mammals.

[4] <u>Just the same, they</u> are placed in a very special position. All the animals are divided into two subclasses. In one of these subclasses ("Prootheria" or "first beasts") are the duckbill and five species of spiny anteater. In the other ("Theria" or just "beast") are all the other 4,231 known species of mammals.

[5] <u>But</u> all this is the result of judging only living <u>species of mammals</u>. Suppose we could study extinct species as well. Would that help us decide on the place of the platypus? Would it cause us to confirm our decision—or change it?

[6] Fossil remnants exist of mammals and reptiles of the far past, but these remnants are almost entirely of bones and teeth. Bones and teeth give us interesting information but they can't tell us everything.

(Isaac Asimov, "What Do You Call a Platypus?")

217

Observe the various ways Asimov has guided the reader from one paragraph to the next. The pronoun these at the beginning of paragraph 2 refers to the two eggs in the last sentence of paragraph 1. The signal word yet links paragraph 3 to paragraph 2. The signal phrase just the same and the pronoun they (referring to the duckbill and spiny anteater) link paragraph 4 to paragraph 3. Paragraph 5 is connected to paragraph 4 by the signal word but and the repetition of the key phrase species of mammals. Finally, paragraph 6 is linked to paragraph 5 because it answers the questions raised at the end of paragraph 5. The result of all these connections is a clear, coherent essay.

Summary

This chapter has considered the need for unity and coherence in our writing and has discussed three strategies that we can use to guide our readers from sentence to sentence and paragraph to paragraph.

The exercises that follow will give you practice in applying these strategies to make your writing clear and coherent.

Exercise: Building and Connecting Sentences

Combine the sentences in each set into *two* clear sentences, and add a signal word or phrase to the second sentence to show how it relates to the first.

1. Retirement should be the reward for a lifetime of work.
   It is widely viewed as a sort of punishment.
   It is a punishment for growing old.

2. In recent years viruses have been shown to cause cancer in chickens.
   Viruses have also been shown to cause cancer in mice, cats, and even in some primates.
   Viruses might cause cancer in humans.
   This is a reasonable hypothesis.

3. We do not seek solitude.
   If we find ourselves alone for once, we flick a switch.

We invite the whole world in.
The world comes in through the television screen.

4. We were not irresponsible.
   Each of us should do something.
   This thing would be of genuine usefulness to the world.
   We were trained to think that.

5. Little girls, of course, don't take toy guns out of their hip pockets.
   They do not say "Pow, pow" to all their neighbors and friends.
   The average well-adjusted little boy does this.
   If we gave little girls the six-shooters, we would soon have double
      the pretend body count.
        (Anne Roiphe, "Confessions of a Female Chauvinist Sow")

6. We drove the wagon close to a corner post.
   We twisted the end of the wire around it.
   We twisted the wire one foot above the ground.
   We stapled it fast.
   We drove along the line of posts.
   We drove for about 200 yards.
   We unreeled the wire on the ground behind us.
        (John Fischer, "Barbed Wire")

7. We know very little about pain.
   What we don't know makes it hurt all the more.
   There is ignorance about pain.
   No form of illiteracy in the United States is so widespread.
   No form of illiteracy in the United States is so costly.
        (Norman Cousins, "Pain Is Not the Ultimate Enemy")

8. Many of our street girls can be as vicious as any corporation pres-
      ident.
   Many of our street girls can be as money mad as any corporation
      president.
   They can be less emotional than men.
   They can be less emotional in conducting acts of personal violence.
        (Gail Sheehy, "$70,000 a Year, Tax Free")

9. The historical sciences have made us very conscious of our past.
   They have made us conscious of the world as a machine.
   The machine generates successive events out of foregoing ones.
   Some scholars tend to look totally backward.

They look backward in their interpretation of the human future.
(Loren Eiseley, *The Unexpected Universe*)

10. Rewriting is something that most writers find they have to do.
They rewrite to discover what they have to say.
They rewrite to discover how to say it.
There are a few writers who do little formal rewriting.
They have capacity and experience.
They create and review a large number of invisible drafts.
They create and review in their minds.
They do this before they approach the page.
(Donald M. Murray, "The Maker's Eye: Revising Your Own
Manuscripts")

Exercise: Revising Paragraphs

Rewrite each paragraph below according to the instructions in parentheses.

1. a. Dr. Edward C. Tolman, after experimenting with rats over a long period of years, found that rats that learned to run a maze under the pressure of hunger took much longer to learn the maze than rats that learned under non-crisis conditions.
   b. The learning that did take place was of a narrow type.
   c. After learning the "right" route, these rats panicked if one avenue were blocked off.
   d. They were not able to survey the field to notice alternative routes.
   e. When the rats were permitted to learn under non-crisis conditions, they later performed well in a crisis.
      (adapted from *How to Study in College*, by Walter Pauk)
      (*Arrange these sentences into a coherent paragraph by adding appropriate signal words or phrases to sentences* b, c, *and* e.)

2. a. The Chinese are adept in the art of taking the kingdom of heaven by storm.
   b. When rain is wanted they make a huge dragon of paper or wood to represent the rain-god, and carry it about in procession.
   c. If no rain follows, the mock-dragon is execrated and torn to pieces.
   d. They threaten and beat the god if he does not give rain.
   e. They publicly depose him from the rank of deity.
   f. If the wished-for rain falls, the god is promoted to a higher rank by an imperial decree.
      (adapted from *The Golden Bough*, by Sir James George Frazer)

220

(Arrange these sentences into a coherent paragraph by adding appropriate signal words or phrases to sentences b, c, d, e, and f.)

3. a. There is a source of energy that produces no radioactive waste, nothing in the way of petrodollars, and very little pollution.
   b. The source can provide the energy that conventional sources may not be able to furnish.
   c. Unhappily, it does not receive the emphasis and attention it deserves.
   d. The source might be called energy efficiency, for Americans like to think of themselves as an efficient people.
   e. The energy source is generally known by the more prosaic term *conservation*.
   f. To be semantically accurate, the source should be called conservation energy, to remind us of the reality—that conservation is no less an energy alternative than oil, gas, coal, or nuclear.
   g. In the near term, conservation could do more than any of the conventional sources to help the country deal with the energy problem it has.

   (adapted from *Energy Future*, by Daniel Yergin)

   (Arrange these sentences into two coherent paragraphs by adding appropriate signal words or phrases to sentences b, c, e, and g.)

4. a. If human beings paid attention to all the sights, sounds and smells that besiege them, their ability to codify and recall information would be swamped.
   b. They simplify the information by grouping it into broad verbal categories.
   c. Human eyes have the extraordinary power to discriminate some ten million colors, but the English language reduces these to no more than four thousand color words, of which only eleven basic terms are used.
   d. A driver stops at all traffic lights whose color he categorizes as *red*, even though the lights vary slightly from one to another in their hues of redness.
   e. Categorization allows people to respond to their environment in a way that has great survival value.
   f. If they hear a high-pitched sound, they do not enumerate the long list of possible causes of such sounds.
   g. They become alert because they have categorized high-pitched sounds as indicators of possible danger.
   h. Words are more than simply labels for specific objects.
   i. They are parts of sets of related principles.

j. To a very young child, the word *chair* may at first refer only to his highchair.

k. He learns that the four-legged object on which his parents sit at mealtime is also called a *chair*.

l. So is the thing with only three legs, referred to by his parents as a *broken chair*, and so is the upholstered piece of furniture in the living room. These objects form a category, *chair*, which is set apart from all other categories by a unique combination of features.

(adapted from *Word Play: What Happens When People Talk*, by Peter Farb)

Arrange these sentences into two coherent paragraphs by adding appropriate signal words or phrases to sentences b, c, d, g, h, i, *and* k.)

Exercise: Building Paragraphs and Essays

I. This exercise has been adapted from a paragraph in *Under the Volcano*, by Malcolm Lowry. Combine the sentences in each set, positioning the signal words and phrases so that your paragraph is clear and coherent.

View from the Parapet of the Hotel Casino de la Selva

1. He rose.
   He went to the parapet.
2. He rested his hands.
   He rested one on each tennis racquet.
   He gazed down.
   He gazed around him.
   He saw the jai-alai courts.
   The courts were abandoned.
   He saw the fountain.
   The fountain was quite near.
   The fountain was in the center of the hotel avenue.
   A cactus farmer was at the fountain.
   The farmer had reined up his horse to drink.
3. He lit a cigarette.

4. There were two volcanoes.
   The volcanoes were Popocatepetl and Ixtaccihuatl.
   The volcanoes were far to his left.
   The volcanoes were in the northeast.
   The volcanoes were beyond the valley.
   The volcanoes were beyond the terraced foothills of the Sierra
   Madre Oriental.
   The volcanoes rose clear and magnificent into the sunset.
5. He made out the village of Tomalin.
   The village was nearer.
   The village was perhaps ten miles distant.
   The village was on a lower level than the main valley.
   The village nestled behind the jungle.
   A scarf of smoke rose from the jungle.
   The scarf was thin and blue.
   The smoke was illegal.
   Someone was burning wood for carbon.
6. Fields and groves spread before him.
   They spread on the other side of the American highway.
   A river meandered through the fields and groves.
   The Alcapancingo road meandered through the fields and groves.
7. The watchtower of a prison rose over a wood.
   The wood was between the river and the road.
   The road lost itself further on.
   The road lost itself where the purple hills of a Doré Paradise sloped
   away into the distance.
8. Quauhnahuac had one cinema.
   The cinema was over in the town.
   The cinema was built on an incline.
   The cinema stood out sharply.
   The lights of the cinema came on suddenly.
   The lights flickered off.
   The lights came on again.

Writing Suggestion

In a paragraph or short essay, describe a view—from a hilltop, a classroom window, or any other vantage point. Use signal words and phrases to assure clarity and coherence.

II. This exercise has been adapted from a paragraph in *Walking the Dead Diamond River*, by Edward Hoagland. Combine the sentences in each set, positioning the pronouns carefully so that your paragraph is clear and coherent.

The Gramercy Gym

1. The Gramercy Gym is two flights up some stairs.
   The stairs are littered.
   The stairs are lightless.
   The stairs look like a mugger's paradise.
   Undoubtedly they are the safest stairs in New York.
2. Two dozen bodies are inside.
   They are chopping up and down.
   They are self-clocked.
   Each fellow is cottoned in his dreams.
3. Some are skipping rope.
   They are turbaned in towels.
   They are wrapped in robes.
   They are dressed this way in order to sweat.
4. These are white-looking figures.
   The men who are about to spar have on dark headguards.
   The headguards close around the face.
   The close grimly.
   They close like an executioner's hood.
5. There are floor-length mirrors.
   There are mattresses.
   These are for exercising.
   These are for rubdowns.
   There are two speedbags.
   They bang like drums.
   There are three heavy bags.
   They swing even between the rounds.
   They swing the momentum of more than a decade of punches.
6. The bell is loud.
   The fighters jerk like eating and walking birds.
   The fighters hiss through their teeth as they punch.
   Their feet sneaker the floor with shuffly sounds.
7. They wear red shoelaces in white shoes.
   They wear gloves.
   The gloves are peanut-colored.
   If they're Irish they're in green.
8. They are learning to move their feet.
   They move to the left.

They move to the right.
They are learning to move in and out.
They are learning to punch over an opponent's guard.
Then they punch under an opponent's guard.
They are learning other repetitive skills.
Without these skills a man in the ring becomes a man of straw.

9. The speedbags teach head-punching.
The heavy bags teach body work.
There is one big bag pinned to the wall.
Both a head and torso are diagrammed on the bag.
The diagram is complete with numbers.
This is so the trainer can shout out what punches his fighter should throw.

10. "Bounce, bounce!" the trainers yell.

Writing Suggestion

In a paragraph or short essay, describe a person or group of people intensely involved in some activity, such as weight lifting, playing a game of chess, or even studying.

III. This exercise has been adapted from an essay written by Patrick Roughen, a student. Read the introductory paragraph, and then combine the sentences in each set of the exercise. Many of the original signal words and phrases have been omitted in the exercise. Add these as necessary, and arrange pronouns and key words carefully so that your paragraphs are clear and coherent.

Worms!

Of all earth's beasts, perhaps the most misunderstood belong to a varied family of animals known to us simply as worms. Ignorance has hidden the worms for hundreds of years in the darkness of death, evil, and disease. Yet they, like all stereotyped beings, deserve an impartial reevaluation so that both sides of their nature might be seen. In short, we must be willing to appreciate the positive and negative qualities of these little crawlers, as well as their poetic wealth as traditional symbols of destruction. Thus, a more realistic perspective of these diverse and intriguing creatures can be attained through an open analysis of their unique characteristics, bringing valuable new insight to one's sense of place in the universal ecosystem.

1. The earthworm needs reexamination.
   Nowhere else is this need more markedly seen.
2. Each earthworm adds much to the soil.
   It adds as much as ten tons of fertile castings.
   It adds digested plants to the soil.
   It adds this every year.
   This is amazing.
   It simultaneously creates ground aeration.
   This makes the farmer's job more successful.
   This makes our stomachs satisfied.
3. The earthworm fills its endless tunnels.
   It fills them with clicking sounds.
   These are chatter-like sounds.
   These sounds are echoes of a primitive form of communications.
   Some people believe this.
4. This denizen of the dirt is conversational.
   This denizen of the dirt is a quite diligent fellow.
   It searches about at night.
   It searches busily.
   It searches for food.
   It postures vividly.
   It postures at the end of a fisherman's hook.
5. Someone may attempt to downgrade this tireless worker.
   Someone might accuse it of being heartless.
   That person should be told something.
   The earthworm has ten hearts instead of one.
   It is really a most sensitive being.
6. The earthworm has a humble appearance.
   The earthworm has an undistinguished carriage.
   These belie a highly developed sense of sexual equality.
   This peculiar folk has both male and female capacities.
7. The earthworm is extremely useful to man.
   His wriggling relations have evil potential.
   This potential cannot be overlooked.
8. Over half the city children of the United States may have pinworms.
   This is true at any particular time.
   Pinworms are an extremely itchy problem.
9. Nematoda can cause damage to foodstuffs.
   They annually cause millions of dollars of damage.
   Nematoda are obliterated by the sweetness of sugar.
   This is ironic.
10. Trichinella can affect people.
    They infect through uncooked meat.
    This results in a disease.

This disease may eventually end in death.
Trichinella are the worst of all mentioned so far.

11. There are worms harmless to man.
These worms are forever cursed.
They must play the part of animated intestines.
Some sympathy can be felt for these worms.

12. Some of these citizens of the soil are in the wrong environments.
These are such mournful states to be in.
There are vinegar and beer worms.
They must spend their lives in some stuff.
They are names for this stuff.
Their lives are hapless.

13. The living standards of the worms might be judged low.
The worms are compensated by attributes.
The worms are compensated by abilites.
These attributes and abilities are outstanding.

14. The Ascaris worm has a racing-stripe.
This worm has prolific powers.
This worm can produce 700,000 eggs.
It can produce these daily.

15. The leech is seemingly senseless.
In reality, it has ten pairs of eyes.
It watches its cousin with these eyes.
Its cousin is the lugworm.
The lugworm enjoys the benefits of thirteen pairs of gills.
The lugworm swims the seas.

16. Worms are far from being stupid.
The planarian is intelligent.
It may be cut in half.
It may be cut after being taught how to navigate a maze.
The separate pieces will regenerate.
The pieces will remember the passage without error.

17. "Shall worms, the inheritors of this excess, eat up thy charge? Is this the body's end?"
William Shakespeare once wrote this.
He continued an ancient practice.
He presented the worm as one of literature's great symbols.
It is a symbol of the inevitability of dissolution.

18. Man has overlooked the worm's essential worth.
Man has overlooked through the ages.
The worm has worth as a member of the world's ecosystem.

19. Our dewy friend is misjudged.
There is the beauty of its folklore.
There is the promise of its power for good and evil.

Our minds should partake of the beauty and the promise.
It is important that we approach our friend with such minds.
It is important that we approach all its relations with such minds.
Its relations belong to the plant and animal kingdom.

Writing Suggestion

Choose a common animal or insect (such as a mouse or a house-fly), and learn what you can about this creature by checking an encyclopedia or a biology text. Find out what unusual and interesting characteristics this creature possesses, and then include this information in an essay that is both informative and entertaining.

Essay Rebuilding

This exercise has been adapted from an essay written by Janice Waters, a student. The introductory paragraph is given as it appears in the original essay. The other sentences in the essay follow the introduction, but not in the original order or in their original form. Rebuild this essay by rearranging the sentences logically, grouping them in paragraphs, and adding signal words and phrases so that the essay is clear and coherent. Feel free to combine and recombine sentences.

How to Bathe a Cat

Bathing the common housecat can be one of the most highly complex, disappointing, and even dangerous chores if done without proper instruction. Therefore, I have set down some guidelines for first-timers to follow until they develop their own techniques. I urge you to read through the instructions carefully and make sure you understand each step completely before you attempt to bathe your cat.

1. Find the cat and lock yourself in the bathroom with him.
2. Clear the bathroom of all objects you do not want broken or wet.
3. Allow the cat to entertain himself.
4. Fill the tub with warm water.
5. If the cat eyes you suspiciously, try to look nonchalant.

6. Get a firm grip on some part of the cat's body (he will wriggle out of a collar); without loosening the grip, put the cat down into the water.
7. Make sure that your arm guard is tightly in place.
8. An arm guard can be purchased from any store that sells archery supplies.
9. Make sure that you hold the cat as far away from your body as possible when you pick him up.
10. If you hold him by the back of his neck, he will not be able to get his claws or teeth close enough to wound.
11. Submerge the cat until he is completely wet.
12. Then, still grasping his neck firmly, rub the shampoo or soap into the fur until a lather is worked up.
13. You should have the soap (liquid soap is convenient) or shampoo within easy reaching distance of the tub.
14. As the lather thickens, the kicking and clawing will subside.
15. It is generally a good idea to keep the cat in a position with the legs extending away from you.
16. If you do not want to get wet, I advise you to wear a wet suit.
17. A wet suit will also keep you from being seriously scratched.
18. The cat may escape while you are attempting to wash him.
19. If you have remembered to lock the bathroom door, you will not have to go far to recapture the cat.
20. If you have a wet suit, by the way, an arm guard is not necessary.
21. Do, however, make sure that you leave the bathroom key with someone else in case you are injured.
22. Once you have washed the cat thoroughly, you are ready to rinse and dry him.
23. Make sure that you have several towels available.
24. If possible, use a hair dryer.
25. First wash away the excess soap with the water from the tub.
26. Then douse the fur thoroughly with warm water from the tap or from the hose you connected to the shower.
27. When the fur is completely free of soap, empty the tub and use a towel to dry the excess water from the fur.
28. Attach one end of the leash to the cat's collar and the other end to a towel rack.
29. Set the hair dryer on "warm," and rub the cat under the warm air until the fur fluffs up.
30. To avoid static cling, leave the fur slightly damp and comb it down.
31. Do not let the cat outside until he is completely dry.
32. If you do, his fur will turn to mud when he rolls along the ground.
33. If the cat does venture outside prematurely, you will have to begin the bathing process from the start.

Discovery: Editing Checklist

After you have revised an essay, perhaps several times, and are satisfied with its basic content and structure, you will still need to edit it. In other words, you will have to examine each sentence so as to eliminate writing faults that might distract or confuse your reader.

You can use the checklist below as a guide when you edit your own work. A writing handbook will provide detailed explanations of each point raised in the list.

To give you practice in using the list, a second draft of Mark Hulme's essay on drive-ins follows the checklist. After you have edited his paper, you should be prepared to edit your own writing with the checklist as a guide.

EDITING CHECKLIST

1. Is each sentence clear and complete?
2. Can any short, choppy sentences be improved by combining them?
3. Can any long awkward sentences be improved by breaking them down into shorter sentences and recombining them?
4. Can any wordy sentences be made more concise?
5. Can run-on sentences be more effectively coordinated or subordinated?
6. Does each verb agree with its subject?
7. Are all verb forms correct and consistent?
8. Do pronouns refer clearly to the appropriate nouns?
9. Do all modifying words and phrases refer clearly to the words they are intended to modify?
10. Is each word in the essay appropriate and effective?
11. Is each word spelled correctly?
12. Is the punctuation logical and necessary?

At the end of the last chapter, you saw the first draft of Mark Hulme's essay on drive-ins. A revised version of that essay follows, but it still requires editing. The numbers in the margins refer to questions in the Editing Checklist. Use these questions as a guide when you edit this second draft. After you have finished working with the draft, go back to Chapter 3 to review the final version of the essay ("Growing Up at the Victory Drive-In"). There you will find that the student did substantially more than just edit this second draft; he once again revised it thoroughly. This demonstrates a point that has been raised before: writing is a continual process of discovering and rediscovering what to say, who to say it to, and how best to say it.

The Disappearing Drive-In Blues

8 Drive-ins were once a popular weekend night activity. A person could go there to see a good movie. He could go with a friend, date, or just by themselves for not too much money. But drive-ins are not as popular and not as much fun as they once were, in fact, drive-ins today are in a dreadful state. The screens are torn up, the sound system is the pits, the snacks are bad, and the movies shown there are awful.

4 One of the more appealing features of drive-ins have always been the huge screens that they show the movies on. Where else can one see a forty-foot Godzilla but on a forty-foot tall screen? Sure, some movie houses have large screens, but unless the theater is the size of a helicopter hangar, you are just not going to get the same big screen effect. Now, however, those huge drive-in screens have begun to deteriorate. They have been wrinkled by rain, shredded by winds, bleached by sun, stained by birds, and pictured by punks armed with beer cans and wine bottles. Watching a movie on one of those mutalated screens is like watching a football game through a snowstorm. The owners are apparently either too broke or too pathetic to make the neccessary repairs.

10 3 Another problem with drive-ins today is that the sound systems are pretty bad. As at our local drive-in the Victory, it has recently converted to a sound system which broadcasts the sound track over an AM radio frequency. One problem with this is that not everyone has a car radio. Sure there are still still a few window speakers available, but these are located in the very back of the parking lot and right next to the snack bar. So, not only is it hard to see because the screen is far away but people are constantly strolling in front of your car as they make their way to the snack bar. For the people who do have radios, there are other problems. Broadcast on such a low frequency, every little airplane, ham radio and CB in the area interfere with the transmission. One has the choice then, of seeing the movie but not hearing it in the front of the lot or hearing the movie without seeing it in the back. The last time I relied on my car radio for sound I up with a dead battery and had to escort my date home on foot.

Another horrable thing about the drive-ins today is the

2 5 6 11 12 9 1

wretched food. Lord knows why so many people trek back and forth to the snack bar. The popcorn is about as tasty as the cardboard containers. And the "piping hot pizzas" taste like frozen styrafoam. The coke is flat but then for 50¢ all you get is a little brown puddle at the bottom of a pound of crushed ice. The candy bars leak like glue on hot summer nights, and the french fries are molded strips of congealed grease.

But the most disappointing thing about drive-ins today is the movies themselves. Back when my father took us to the drive-ins, we saw a fine first-run flick such as *The Godfather, The Graduate,* and *Airport.* Nowadays the drive-ins specialize in such back-lot blockbusters as *The Valley of the Sabine Women* and *The Man with the Golden Eyesocket.* I suppose the owner just can't afford to run first-rate, first-run films.

Drive-ins were once an important part of popular American culture. Now they are just a seedy reminder of what use to be. ⌐ 7

Practice: Sample Combinations

Use the sentences and paragraphs below as a guide after you have completed the Practice exercises in this chapter. Since in most cases more than one version is possible, do not think that your sentences are "incorrect" just because they may not be in exact agreement with the ones below.

1. Businesses are . . . becoming more directly involved in what goes on in the schools, providing funds, professional expertise and the incentive of jobs. "Adopt-a-School" programs have flowered over the last three years, with local companies providing personnel and resources to students of a particular school. Buckman Laboratories in Memphis, for example, brings kids from Cypress Junior High to its plant for exposure to real-life applications of modern chemistry. The Boston Compact represents a different approach. More than 100 businesses in that city, such as The Boston Globe and Jewish Memorial Hospital, have agreed to give hiring priority and additional training to city-school graduates if standards are raised. "This is the future work force of many businesses in Boston, so our interest in improving their education is selfish," says Kenneth Rossano, senior vice president of the First National Bank of Boston and president of the chamber of commerce. In return, the school system, rated by some the worst

in the country, must guarantee that its graduates will have adequate math and verbal skills.

(Dennis A. Williams, "Can the Schools Be Saved?")

2. a. To be self-centered does not mean to disregard the worth of other people. In fact, most psychologists would probably accept the position that we are *all* self-centered.

(Lawrence Casler, "This Thing Called Love Is Pathological")

b. The differences in math performance between boys and girls cannot be attributed simply to differences in innate ability. Still, if one were to ask the victims themselves, they would probably disagree.

(Sheila Tobias, "Who's Afraid of Math, and Why?")

c. Like all true believers, the nuclear believers have been doing their best to convert everyone else to their belief; thus we are constantly exposed to ads and editorials predicting dire consequences if lagging nuclear energy programs are not accelerated.

(Vince Taylor, "The Nuclear Faithful: Time to Face Reality")

3. At the turn of the century, a newborn child could expect to live about to the age of fifty; today, the expectancy is about 70. Once, a mother had sound reason to fear giving birth; today, death in childbirth is regarded as intolerable. Once, a full high school education was the best achievement of a minority; today, it is the barest minimum for decent employment and self-respect. Once, the timber and mining barons stripped away the forests and topsoil wholesale; today, these companies are confronted by their communities at every other move.

(Eric Sevareid, "The World Still Moves Our Way")

4. A society that has no heroes will soon grow enfeebled. Its purposes will be less elevated; its aspirations less challenging; its endeavors less strenuous. Its individual members will also be enfeebled. They will "hang loose" and "lay back" and, so mellowed out, the last thing of which they wish to hear is heroism. They do not want to be told of men and women whose example might disturb them, calling them to effort and duty or sacrifice or even the chance of glory.

(Henry Fairlie, "Too Rich for Heroes")

PART II

Comparing Combinations

CHAPTER 11

Description

Each of the nine chapters in Part II is divided into two parts. The first part consists of Paragraph and Essay Building exercises similar to those in Part I. The second part contains the original paragraphs and essays that served as models for the exercises. This arrangement allows you to compare your work with that of professional writers and other student writers. Be sure to evaluate the original compositions as well as your own, keeping in mind that the original versions are not meant to be interpreted as the "correct answers" to the exercises. Sometimes your work may well be superior to the original.

The essays are loosely organized according to the type of writing and the pattern of organization found in each: description, narration, process analysis, and so on. These divisions are convenient but often arbitrary, as many of the essays are developed and organized in a variety of ways. By the same token, the Writing Suggestions at the end of each chapter are not presented as writing assignments, but as subjects that might be explored through any variety of Discovery techniques introduced in Part I. Nevertheless, the following exercises will give you practice not only in building sentences but in shaping paragraphs and essays as well.

Descriptive Writing

The purpose of descriptive writing is to make our readers see, feel, and hear what we have seen, felt, and heard. Whether we are describing a person, a place, or a thing, our aim is to reveal a subject through vivid and carefully selected details.

Two common forms of description are the *character sketch* and the *place description.* In describing a character, we select details that not only show what an individual looks like but also provide clues to his or her personality. "Nervous Norman" (a description of a school principal in Chapter 2) and "Gregory" (a student's description of her cat in this chapter) are examples of the character sketch. With carefully selected and arranged details, we can also suggest the personality—or mood—of a place. "Antonino's" (in chapter 2), "My Home of Yesteryear" (in Chapter 7), and "The Kitchen" (in this chapter) all provide insights into the lives of the people who occupy the places being described.

Descriptions may also be used to illustrate a point. In "They Also Wait Who Stand and Serve Themselves," Andrew Ward describes a typical service station, past and present, as a way of commenting on the peculiar nature of "progress" in modern America. Ward's lively descriptions make his essay entertaining as well as thought provoking.

Working out the exercises in this chapter should give you ideas on how to select and arrange details in your own descriptive writing. For suggestions on how to probe a subject that you wish to describe, review the Discovery section at the end of Chapter 5.

Exercises

Gregory

BARBARA CARTER

1. Gregory is beautiful.
   Gregory is gray.
   Gregory is a Persian cat.
   Gregory is mine.
2. He walks with pride.
   He walks with grace.
   He performs a dance of disdain.
   He lifts and lowers each paw.

He does this slowly.
He does this with the delicacy of a ballet dancer.
3. His pride does not extend to his appearance.
He spends most of his time indoors.
He spends most of his time watching television.
He spends most of his time growing fat.
4. He enjoys TV commercials.
Some commercials feature Charlie Tuna.
Some commercials feature Morris the cat.
He particularly enjoys those commercials.
5. He is familiar with cat food commercials.
This familiarity has led him to reject generic brands of cat food.
He favors only the most expensive brands.
6. Gregory is finicky about what he eats.
He is just as finicky about visitors.
He befriends some visitors.
He repels other visitors.
7. He may snuggle up against your ankle.
He may beg to be petted.
He may imitate a skunk.
He may stain your trousers.
8. Gregory does not do this to establish his territory.
Many cat experts think that is the reason.
Gregory does this to humiliate me.
He is jealous of my friends.
9. I look at the old fleabag.
I look after my guests have fled.
He is snoozing in front of the television set.
He is smiling in his sleep.
I have to forgive him for his habits.
His habits are obnoxious.
His habits are somehow endearing.

The Kitchen*

ALFRED KAZIN

1. The kitchen held our lives together.
2. My mother worked in it.
She worked all day long.
We ate almost all meals in it.
We did not have the Passover *seder* there.

* This exercise has been adapted from paragraph two of Kazin's essay in the Paragraphs and Essays section of this chapter.

239

I did my homework at the kitchen table.
I did my first writing there.
I often had a bed made up for me in winter.
The bed was on three kitchen chairs.
The chairs were near the stove.

3. A mirror hung on the wall.
The mirror hung just over the table.
The mirror was long.
The mirror was horizontal.
The mirror sloped to a ship's prow at each end.
The mirror was lined in cherry wood.

4. It took the whole wall.
It drew every object in the kitchen to itself.

5. The walls were a whitewash.
The whitewash was fiercely stippled.
My father often rewhitened it.
He did this in slack seasons.
He did this so often that the paint looked as if it had been squeezed
    and cracked into the walls.

6. There was an electric bulb.
It was large.
It hung down at the end of a chain.
The chain had been hooked into the ceiling.
The old gas ring and key still jutted out of the wall like antlers.

7. The sink was in the corner.
The sink was next to the toilet.
We washed at the sink.
The tub was also in the corner.
The tub was square.
My mother did our clothes in the tub.

8. There were many things above the tub.
These things were tacked to a shelf.
Sugar and spice jars were ranged on the shelf.
The jars were white.
The jars were square.
The jars had blue borders.
The jars were ranged pleasantly.
Calendars hung there.
They were from the Public National Bank on Pitkin Avenue.
They were from the Minsker Branch of the Workman's Circle.
Receipts were there.
The receipts were for the payment of insurance premiums.
Household bills were there.
The bills were on a spindle.

Two little boxes were there.
The boxes were engraved with Hebrew letters.
9. One of the boxes was for the poor.
The other was to buy back the Land of Israel.
10. A little man would appear.
The man had a beard.
He appeared every spring.
He appeared in our kitchen.
He would salute with a Hebrew blessing.
The blessing was hurried.
He would empty the boxes.
Sometimes he would do this with a sideways look of disdain.
He would do this if the boxes were not full.
He would bless us again hurriedly.
He would bless us for remembering our Jewish brothers and sisters.
Our brothers and sisters were less fortunate.
He would take his departure until the next spring.
He would try to persuade my mother to take still another box.
He tried in vain.
11. We dropped coins in the boxes.
Occasionally we remembered to do this.
Usually we did this on the morning of "mid-terms" and final examinations.
Those mornings were dreaded.
My mother thought it would bring me luck.
12. She was extremely superstitious.
She was embarrassed about it.
She counseled me to leave the house on my right foot.
She did this on the morning of an examination.
She always laughed at herself whenever she did this.
13. "I know it's silly, but what harm can it do? It may calm God down."
Her smile seemed to say this.

They Also Wait Who Stand and Serve Themselves*

ANDREW WARD

1. Who should take a drive sometime to my neighborhood gas station?
Anyone who is interested in the future of American commerce.
2. It is not much of a place to visit.
It never was.

* This exercise has been adapted from paragraphs one through six of Ward's essay in the Paragraphs and Essays section of this chapter.

3. I first moved here five years ago.
Even then it was shabby.
It was forlorn.
They used to feature garden spots in the commercials.
It was not at all like those spots.
In those spots the men tipped their visors at your window.
The men were trim.
The men were manicured.
The men had cultivated voices.
The men asked what they could do for you.

4. Sal was the owner.
He was a stocky man.
He wore undersized shirts.
The buttons had popped on his shirts.
He wore sagging trousers.
He wore work shoes with broken laces.
The shoes were splattered with oil.

5. "Gas stinks."
That was his motto.
He pumped every gallon into his customers' cars.
Every gallon seemed to take something out of him.

6. "Pumping gas is for morons."
He liked to say this.
He leaned against my rear window.
He leaned indelibly.
He watched the digits fly.
The digits flew on the pump register.

7. "One of these days I'm gonna dump this place on a Puerto Rican, move to Florida, and get into something nice, like hero sandwiches."

8. He had an assistant.
The assistant was nameless.
The assistant was wall-eyed.
The assistant wore a studded denim jacket.
He left a milky film on my windshield.
He did this with his rag and squeegee.
He did this as my tank was filling.

9. There was a German shepherd.
The dog was fume-crazed.
The dog was patchy.
Sal kept the dog chained to the air pump.
There was an office next to the service bays.
The office was overheated.

The office was cluttered.
If you followed Sal into his office you ran a gauntlet of hangers-
 on.
Many of them were Sal's brothers and nephews.
They debated the merits of the driving directions.
Sal gave these directions to travelers.
The travelers were bewildered.
The travelers turned into his station for help.
This is how the hangers-on spent their time.

10. "I don't know."
One of them would say this.
He would pull a bag of potato chips off the snack rack.
"I think I would have put 'em onto 91, gotten 'em off at Willow,
 and then—Bango!—straight through to Hamden."

11. Sal had the rest room key.
He guarded it jealously.
He handed it out with reluctance.
Something in your request had betrayed some dismal aberration.
He acted as if this were the case.

12. The rest room was accessible only through a little closet.
The closet was littered with tires.
It was littered with fan belts.
It was littered with cases of oil cans.

13. The bulb was busted inside.
There were never any towels.
You had to dry your hands on toilet paper.
You did that if Sal wasn't out of toilet paper, too.

14. The soda machine worked for Sal.
It never worked for anyone else.
Complaints were lodged.
He would give the machine a kick.
The kick was full of contempt.
He kicked it as he passed by.
This would dislodge warm cans of grape soda.
When their tops were flipped, they gave off a fine purple spray.

15. There was a machine.
It dispensed peanuts.
This was besides the snack rack.
The machine dispensed them on behalf of the Sons of Garibaldi.

16. There were metal shelves.
The shelves were along the cinderblock wall.
They were sparsely stocked.
They were stocked with cans of windshield de-icer.

They were stocked with cans of antifreeze.
They were stocked with head lamps in boxes.
They were stocked with oil filters in boxes.

17. There was a brass plaque from the oil company.
It hung over the yellow wiper case.
The case was battered.
It hung below the Coca Cola clock.
It was half hidden by a calendar.
The calendar came from a janitorial supply concern.
The plaque had been awarded in recognition of Salvatore A. Castallano's ten-year business association.

Paragraphs and Essays

Gregory

BARBARA CARTER

Gregory is my beautiful gray Persian cat. He walks with pride and grace, performing a dance of disdain as he slowly lifts and lowers each paw with the delicacy of a ballet dancer. His pride, however, does not extend to his appearance, for he spends most of his time indoors watching television and growing fat. He enjoys TV commercials, particularly those featuring Charlie Tuna and Morris the cat. His familiarity with cat food commercials has led him to reject generic brands of cat food in favor of only the most expensive brands. Gregory is as finicky about visitors as he is about what he eats, befriending some and repelling others. He may snuggle up against your ankle, begging to be petted, or he may imitate a skunk and stain your favorite trousers. Gregory does not do this to establish his territory, as many cat experts think, but to humiliate me because he is jealous of my friends. After my guests have fled, I look at the old fleabag snoozing and smiling to himself in front of the television set, and I have to forgive him for his obnoxious, but endearing, habits.

The Kitchen

ALFRED KAZIN

[1] In Brownsville tenements the kitchen is always the largest room and the center of the household. As a child I felt that we lived in a kitchen to which four other rooms were annexed. My mother, a "home"

244

dressmaker, had her workshop in the kitchen. She told me once that she had begun dressmaking in Poland at thirteen; as far back as I can remember, she was always making dresses for the local women. She had an innate sense of design, a quick eye for all the subtleties in the latest fashions, even when she despised them, and great boldness. For three or four dollars she would study the fashion magazines with a customer, go with the customer to the remnants store on Belmont Avenue to pick out the material, argue the owner down—all remnants stores, for some reason, were supposed to be shady, as if the owners dealt in stolen goods—and then for days would patiently fit and baste and sew and fit again. Our apartment was always full of women in their house-dresses sitting around the kitchen table waiting for a fitting. My little bedroom next to the kitchen was the fitting room. The sewing machine, an old nut-brown Singer with golden scrolls painted along the black arm and engraved along the two tiers of little drawers massed with needles and thread on each side of the treadle, stood next to the window and the great coalblack stove which up to my last year in college was our main source of heat. By December the two outer bedrooms were closed off, and used to chill bottles of milk and cream, cold borscht and jellied calves' feet.

[2] The kitchen held our lives together. My mother worked in it all day long, we ate in it almost all meals except the Passover *seder*, I did my homework and first writing at the kitchen table, and in winter I often had a bed made up for me on three kitchen chairs near the stove. On the wall just over the table hung a long horizontal mirror that sloped to a ship's prow at each end and was lined in cherry wood. It took the whole wall, and drew every object in the kitchen to itself. The walls were a fiercely stippled whitewash, so often rewhitened by my father in slack seasons that the paint looked as if it had been squeezed and cracked into the walls. A large electric bulb hung down the center of the kitchen at the end of a chain that had been hooked into the ceiling; the old gas ring and key still jutted out of the wall like antlers. In the corner next to the toilet was the sink at which we washed, and the square tub in which my mother did our clothes. Above it, tacked to the shelf on which were pleasantly ranged square, blue-bordered white sugar and spice jars, hung calendars from the Public National Bank on Pitkin Avenue and the Misker Progressive Branch of the Workman's Circle; receipts for the payment of insurance premiums, and household bills on a spindle; two little boxes engraved with Hebrew letters. One of these was for the poor, the other to buy back the Land of Israel. Each spring a bearded little man would suddenly appear in our kitchen, salute us with a hurried Hebrew blessing, empty the boxes (sometimes with a sidelong look of disdain if they were not full), hurriedly bless us again for remembering our less fortunate Jewish brothers and sisters, and so

245

take his departure until the next spring, after vainly trying to persuade my mother to take still another box. We did occasionally remember to drop coins in the boxes, but this was usually only on the dreaded morning of "mid-terms" and final examinations, because my mother thought it would bring me luck. She was extremely superstitious, but embarrassed about it, and always laughed at herself whenever, on the morning of an examination, she counseled me to leave the house on my right foot. "I know it's silly," her smile seemed to say, "but what harm can it do? It may calm God down."

[3] The kitchen gave a special character to our lives: my mother's character. All my memories of that kitchen are dominated by the nearness of my mother sitting all day long at her sewing machine, by the clacking of the treadle against the linoleum floor, by the patient twist of her right shoulder as she automatically pushed at the wheel with one hand or lifted the foot to free the needle where it had got stuck in a thick piece of material. The kitchen was her life. Year by year, as I began to take in her fantastic capacity for labor and her anxious zeal, I realized it was ourselves she kept stitched together. I can never remember a time when she was not working. She worked because the law of her life was work, work and anxiety; she worked because she would have found life meaningless without work. She read almost no English; she could read the Yiddish paper, but never felt she had time to. We were always talking of a time when I would teach her how to read, but somehow there was never time. When I awoke in the morning she was already to her machine, or conferring over *McCall's* with some neighborhood woman who had come in pointing hopefully to an illustration—"Mrs. Kazin! Mrs. Kazin! Make me a dress like it shows here in the picture!" When my father came home from work she had somehow mysteriously interrupted herself to make supper for us, and the dishes cleared and washed, was back at her machine. When I went to bed at night, often she was still there, pounding away at the treadle, hunched over the wheel, her hands steering a piece of gauze under the needle with a finesse that always contrasted sharply with her swollen hands and broken nails. Her left hand had been pierced through when as a girl she had worked in the infamous Triangle Shirtwaist Factory on the East Side. A needle had gone straight through the palm, severing a large vein. They had sewn it up for her so clumsily that a tuft of flesh always lay folded over the palm.

[4] The kitchen was the great machine that set our lives running; it whirred down a little only on Saturdays and holy days. From my mother's kitchen I gained my first picture of life as a white, overheated, starkly lit workshop redolent with Jewish cooking, crowded with women in housedresses, strewn with fashion magazines, patterns, dress material, spools of thread—and at whose center, so lashed to her machine that

bolts of energy seemed to dance out of her hands and feet as she worked, my mother stamped the treadle against the floor, hard, hard, and silently, grimly at war, beat out the first rhythm of the world for me.

They Also Wait Who Stand and Serve Themselves

ANDREW WARD

[1] Anyone interested in the future of American commerce should take a drive sometime to my neighborhood gas station. Not that it is or ever was much of a place to visit. Even when I first moved here, five years ago, it was shabby and forlorn: not at all like the garden spots they used to feature in the commercials, where trim, manicured men with cultivated voices tipped their visors at your window and asked what they could do for you.

[2] Sal, the owner, was a stocky man who wore undersized popped-button shirts, sagging trousers, and oil-splattered work shoes with broken laces. "Gas stinks" was his motto, and every gallon he pumped into his customers' cars seemed to take something out of him. "Pumping gas is for morons," he liked to say, leaning indelibly against my rear window and watching the digits fly on the pump register. "One of these days I'm gonna dump this place on a Puerto Rican, move to Florida, and get into something nice, like hero sandwiches."

[3] He had a nameless, walleyed assistant who wore a studded denim jacket and, with his rag and squeegee, left a milky film on my windshield as my tank was filling. There was a fume-crazed, patchy German shepherd, which Sal kept chained to the air pump, and if you followed Sal into his cluttered, overheated office next to the service bays, you ran a gauntlet of hangers-on, many of them Sal's brothers and nephews, who spent their time debating the merits of the driving directions he gave the bewildered travelers who turned into his station for help.

[4] "I don't know," one of them would say, pulling a bag of potato chips off the snack rack, "I think I would have put 'em onto 91, gotten 'em off at Willow, and then—Bango!—straight through to Hamden."

[5] Sal guarded the rest room key jealously and handed it out with reluctance, as if something in your request had betrayed some dismal aberration. The rest room was accessible only through a little closet littered with tires, fan belts, and cases of oil cans. Inside, the bulb was busted and there were never any towels, so you had to dry your hands on toilet paper—if Sal wasn't out of toilet paper, too.

[6] The soda machine never worked for anyone except Sal, who, when complaints were lodged, would give it a contemptuous kick as

247

he trudged by, dislodging warm cans of grape soda which, when their pop tops were flipped, gave off a fine purple spray. There was, besides the snack rack, a machine that dispensed peanuts on behalf of the Sons of Garibaldi. The metal shelves along the cinderblock wall were sparsely stocked with cans of cooling system cleaner, windshield de-icer, antifreeze, and boxed head lamps and oil filters. Over the battered yellow wiper case, below the Coca Cola clock, and half hidden by a calendar from a janitorial supply concern, hung a little brass plaque from the oil company, awarded in recognition of Salvatore A. Castallano's ten-year business association.

[7] I wish for the sake of nostalgia that I could say Sal was a craftsman, but I can't. I'm not even sure he was an honest man. I suspect that when business was slow he may have cheated me, but I never knew for sure because I don't know anything about cars. If I brought my Volvo in because it was behaving strangely, I knew that as far as Sal was concerned it could never be a simple matter of tightening a bolt or re-attaching a hose. "Jesus," he'd wearily exclaim after a look under the hood. "Mr. Ward, we got problems." I usually let it go at that and simply asked him when he thought he could have it repaired, because if I pressed him for details he would get all worked up. "Look, if you don't want to take my word for it, you can go someplace else. I mean, it's a free country, you know? You got spalding on your caps, which means your dexadrometer isn't charging, and pretty soon you're gonna have hairlines in your flushing drums. You get hairlines in your flushing drums and you might as well forget it. You're driving junk."

[8] I don't know what Sal's relationship was with the oil company. I suppose it was pretty distant. He was never what they call a "participating dealer." He never gave away steak knives or NFL tumblers or stuffed animals with his fill-ups, and never got around to taping company posters on his windows. The map rack was always empty, and the company emblem, which was supposed to rotate thirty feet above the station, had broken down long before I first laid eyes on it, and had frozen at an angle that made it hard to read from the highway.

[9] If, outside of television, there was ever such a thing as an oil company service station inspector, he must have been appalled by the grudging service, the mad dog, the sepulchral john. When there was supposed to have been an oil shortage a few years ago, Sal's was one of the first stations to run out of gas. And several months ago, during the holiday season, the company squeezed him out for good.

[10] I don't know whether Sal is now happily sprinkling olive oil over salami subs somewhere along the Sun Belt. I only know that one bleak January afternoon I turned into his station to find him gone. At first, as I idled by the no-lead pump, I thought the station had been shut down completely. Plywood had been nailed over the service bays,

248

Sal's name had been painted out above the office door, and all that was left of his dog was a length of chain dangling from the air pump's vacant mast.

[11] But when I got out of the car I spotted someone sitting in the office with his boots up on the counter, and at last caught sight of the "Self-Service Only" signs posted by the pumps. Now, I've always striven for a degree of self-sufficiency. I fix my own leaky faucets and I never let the bellboy carry my bags. But I discovered as I squinted at the instructional sticker by the nozzle that there are limits to my desire for independence. Perhaps it was the bewilderment with which I approach anything having to do with the internal combustion engine; perhaps it was my conviction that fossil fuels are hazardous; perhaps it was the expectation of service, the sense of helplessness, that twenty years of oil company advertising had engendered, but I didn't want to pump my own gas.

[12] A mongrel rain began to fall upon the oil-slicked tarmac as I followed the directions spelled out next to the nozzle. But somehow I got them wrong. When I pulled the trigger on the nozzle, no gas gushed into my fuel tank, no digits flew on the gauge.

[13] "Hey, buddy," a voice sounded out of a bell-shaped speaker overhead. "Flick the switch."

[14] I turned toward the office and saw someone with Wild Bill Hickok hair leaning over a microphone.

[15] "Right. Thanks," I answered, and turned to find the switch. There wasn't one. There was a bolt that looked a little like a switch, but it wouldn't flick.

[16] "The switch," the voice crackled in the rain. "Flick the switch."

[17] I waved back as if I'd finally understood, but I still couldn't figure out what he was talking about. In desperation, I stuck the nozzle back into my fuel tank and pulled the trigger. Nothing.

[18] In the office I could see that the man was now angrily pulling on a slicker. "What the hell's the matter with you?" he asked, storming by me. "All you gotta do is flick the switch."

[19] "I couldn't find the switch," I told him.

[20] "Well, what do you call this?" he wanted to know, pointing to a little lever near the pump register.

[21] "A lever," I told him.

[22] "Christ," he muttered, flicking the little lever. The digits on the register suddenly formed neat rows of zeros. "All right, it's set. Now you can serve yourself," the long-haired man said, ducking back to the office.

[23] As the gas gushed into my fuel tank and the fumes rose to my nostrils, I thought for a moment about my last visit to Sal's. It hadn't been any picnic: Sal claimed to have found something wrong with my

punting brackets, the German shepherd snapped at my heels as I walked by, and nobody had change for my ten. But the transaction had dimension to it: I picked up some tips about antennas, entered into the geographical debate in the office, and bought a can of windshield wiper solvent (to fill the gap in my change). Sal's station had been a dime a dozen, but it occurred to me, as the nozzle began to balk and shudder in my hand, that gas stations of its kind were going the way of the village smithy and the corner grocery.

[24] I got a glob of grease on my glove as I hung the nozzle back on the pump, and it took me more than a minute to satisfy myself that I had replaced the gas cap properly. I tried to whip up a feeling of accomplishment as I headed for the office, but I could not forget Sal's dictum: Pumping gas is for morons.

[25] The door to the office was locked, but a sign directed me to a stainless steel teller's window which had been installed in the plate glass of the front window. I stood waiting for a while with my money in hand, but the long-haired man sat inside with his back to me, so at last I reached up and hesitantly knocked on the glass with my glove.

[26] The man didn't hear me or had decided, in retaliation for our semantic disagreement, to ignore me for a while. I reached up to knock again, but noticed that my glove had left a greasy smear on the window. Ever my mother's son, I reflexively reached into my pocket for my handkerchief and was about to wipe the grease away when it hit me: at last the oil industry had me where it wanted me—standing in the rain and washing its windshield.

Writing Suggestions

Descriptive writing calls for close attention to details. Whether your subject is as small as a roasted peanut or as large as a football stadium, you should begin by observing the subject closely and deciding which details are most significant.

1. A bag of roasted peanuts.
2. A football stadium.
3. A pet.
4. A bowl of fruit.
5. A waiting room.
6. A friend or relative.
7. A sandwich.
8. The contents of your purse or wallet.
9. A plant or tree.
10. A baseball glove.

11. Your secret hiding place as a child.
12. A breakfast table.
13. A character from a book, movie, or television show.
14. A painting.
15. A beer can.
16. A closet.
17. A room in your house.
18. A candle.
19. A photograph.
20. A storefront window.

CHAPTER 12

Narration

The purpose of narrative writing is to show readers what happened at a particular time and place. A narrative is a story—either fiction or nonfiction—that relies on specific details to answer the following questions: What happened? When did it happen? Where did it happen? Who was involved? How did it begin? What was the outcome?

We often think of the story as a form of entertainment, and indeed narratives are frequently used by writers to engage the interest of their readers. But narratives may also be used to create understanding and to explain a subject. The two fictional narratives in this text—"Mrs. Bridge" (Chapter 6) and "Topping Onions" (Chapter 8)—provide insight into the characters described there. In a personal narrative (such as "Happiness" in Chapter 7, and "Salvation" and "The Endless Streetcar Ride into the Night" in this chapter), we may invite our readers to share in an experience of self-discovery. An informative narrative, such as "Of Time and Lizards—and Sex" in this chapter, can make a subject more interesting and easier to comprehend.

The exercises in this chapter will give you practice in organizing narratives and may also remind you of incidents in your own life that you may wish to recount.

Exercises

*Salvation**

LANGSTON HUGHES

1. The preacher preached a sermon.
   The sermon was wonderful.
   The sermon was rhythmical.
   The sermon was all moans.
   The sermon was all shouts.
   The sermon was all cries.
   The sermon was all dire pictures of hell.
   Then he sang a song.
   The song was about the ninety-nine safe in the fold.
   One little lamb was left out in the cold.
2. Then he said something.
   "Won't you come? Won't you come to Jesus? Young lambs, won't you come?"
3. And he held out his arms to all us young sinners.
   We were there on the mourners' bench.
4. And the little girls cried.
5. And some of them jumped up.
   They went to Jesus.
   They went right away.
6. But most of us just sat there.
7. There were a great many old people.
   They came and knelt around us.
   They prayed.
   There were old women.
   They had jet-black faces.
   They had braided hair.
   There were old men.
   They had gnarled hands.
   Their hands were gnarled from work.
8. And the church sang a song.
   The song was about the lower lights.

---

* This exercise has been adapted from paragraphs 3 through 7 of Hughes's essay in the Paragraphs and Essays section of this chapter.

The lower lights are burning.
The song was about some poor sinners.
The sinners are to be saved.

9. And the whole building rocked with prayer.
The building rocked with song.

10. Still I kept waiting to *see* Jesus.

11. Finally all the young people had gone to the altar.
They were saved.
All went but one boy and me.

12. He was a rounder's son.
He was named Westley.

13. Westley and I were surrounded by sisters.
We were surrounded by deacons.
The sisters and deacons were praying.

14. It was very hot in the church.
It was getting late now.

15. Finally Westley said something to me.
He whispered.
"God damn! I'm tired o' sitting here. Let's get up and be saved."

16. So he got up.
He was saved.

17. Then I was left.
I was all alone.
I was on the mourners' bench.

18. My aunt came.
She knelt at my knees.
She cried.
Prayers swirled all around me.
Songs swirled all around me.
They swirled around me in the little church.

19. The whole congregation prayed.
They prayed for me alone.
They prayed in a wail of moans and voices.
The moans and voices were mighty.

20. I kept waiting for Jesus.
I waited serenely.
I was waiting, waiting.
But he didn't come.

21. I wanted to see him.
Nothing happened to me.

22. Nothing!

23. I wanted something to happen to me.
Nothing happened.

Of Time and Lizards—and Sex*

JANE ANN PATCHAK

1. I have logged several hundred hours as a chameleon-watcher.
   I have observed the behavior of chameleons.
   I have observed hunting.
   I have observed stalking.
   I have observed defense.
   I have observed copulation.
2. Once I saw a battle.
   The battle was fierce.
   The battle was between contending males.
3. I broke it up.
   I was ultimately constrained to do this.
   The combatants were unevenly matched.
   They were unevenly matched in size.
   I felt this was the case.
4. One can disturb a chameleon.
   It's easy to do this.
5. Merely touch a finger to the tip of a tail.
   This is all it takes.
6. The big one clamped his jaws about the snout of the smaller one.
   That happened in this battle.
   The big one hung on tenaciously.
   The little chap's hind legs were bouncing on the screen.
7. My intervention gave him a chance to escape.
   Nevertheless, the little bugger leaped back into the fray.
   The little bugger was feisty.
   The little bugger was shortly driven from the field.
8. There was a victor in this struggle.
   He was named Champ.
   He was one tough hombre.
   Champ stayed green all the time, it seemed.
9. He was unmatched for sheer effrontery.
   He claimed the entire back of the house.
   He also claimed the patio.
   He claimed these areas as his territory.
10. He patrolled relentlessly.
    He once chased an interloper.

* This exercise has been adapted from paragraphs 5 through 7 of Patchak's essay in the Paragraphs and Essays section of this chapter.

He chased him all the way to the west end of the house.
He vanished around the corner there.
He was still in hot pursuit.

11. Champ would display at any provocation.
Champ would display even when there was no evident reason.

12. He was a great show-off.
He gave "Hey! Look at me!" macho demonstrations.
These demonstrations wowed most of the females.
These demonstrations scared most of the males.

13. A display involves a series of push-ups.
A display involves a series of head-bobs.
These actions are accompanied by the extension of a throat fan.
Only the males possess a throat fan.
This information is for the benefit of the uninformed.

14. Champs's throat fan was bright orange.
This offered a nice contrast to his hide.
His hide was a brilliant green.

15. Chameleons display during skirmishes.
They display for territory.
They display as part of a courtship ritual.
They are vulnerable to predators when they display.
Supposedly they use up much energy.

16. Champ had energy to spare.
He especially had sexual energy.
In fact, he was downright horny most of the time.

17. Champ was making spectacular leaps.
He was doing this one afternoon.
The afternoon was warm.
The afternoon was sunny.
Champ was in pursuit of *l'amour*.
Champ was leaping between hanging plants.
The plants were as much as two feet apart.
He landed squarely on the back of a hapless female.
He landed with the last leap.

18. She struggled to escape.
She struggled valiantly.
She was a poor dear.
She climbed up the screen.
It was a laborious climb.
He clung to her back.
He bit her on the neck.

19. At one point she even loosened her foothold on the screen.
They fell together.

They landed with a small "thud."
They landed on a ledge.

20. This maneuver failed to dislodge Champ.
    She began another grueling climb.
    She climbed back up the screen.
    That great oaf was still firmly ensconced on her back.
    It was as if he had been glued in place.
    He was biting her neck.

21. Finally, sheer exhaustion overcame her.
    I presume this.

22. Champ then wound his tail around hers.
    Champ braced his feet.
    Champ closed his eyes.
    Champ appeared asleep.

23. She was the one who should have been tired.
    That is how it seemed to me.

24. There was a surprisingly long interlude.
    Then he released her.
    She turned.
    She ate a fly.
    She did this with a good bit of aplomb.

The Endless Streetcar Ride into the Night*

JEAN SHEPHERD

1. Mewling babes.
   Puking babes.

2. That's the way we all start.

3. We cling to someone's shoulder.
   We cling damply.
   We burp weakly.
   We claw our way into life.

4. *All* of us.

5. Then we begin to divide into two streams.
   We divide gradually.
   We divide surely.
   We all march together.
   We march up that road of life.

---

* This exercise has been adapted from the first eight paragraphs of Shepherd's essay in the Paragraphs and Essays section of this chapter.

It is a long yellow brick road.
We march on opposite sides of the street.

6. One crowd goes on to become the Official people.
   They peer out at us from television screens.
   They peer out at us from magazine covers.

7. They are forever appearing in newsreels.
   They carry attaché cases.
   They are surrounded by banks of microphones.
   The world waits for their decisions.
   The world waits for their statements.

8. And the rest of us go on.
   We become . . . just us.

9. They are the Prime Ministers.
   They are the Presidents.
   They are the Cabinet members.
   They are the Stars.
   They are the dynamic molders of the Universe.
   We remain the onlookers.
   We remain this way forever.
   We remain the applauders of their real lives.

10. We ask something down in the dungeons of our souls.
    We ask ourselves.
    We are forever in the dungeons.
    The dungeons are dark.

11. "How did they get away from me? When did I make that first
    misstep that took me forever to the wrong side of the street,
    to become eternally part of the accursed, anonymous Audi-
    ence?"

12. We're all playing around.
    We're around back of the garage.
    It seems like one minute we're doing this.
    We are kicking tin cans.
    We are yelling at girls.
    Then there is the next instant.
    You find yourself doomed to exist as an office boy.
    You are in the Mail Room of Life.
    Meanwhile someone sends down Dicta.
    He is another ex-mewling, puking babe.
    He says "No comment" to the press.
    He lives a real, genuine *Life*.
    His *Life* is on the screen of the world.

13. There are countless sufferers.
    They are spending billions of dollars at this hour.
    They are spending endless man hours.

They are lying on analysts' couches.

They are trying to pinpoint an exact moment.

This is the moment they stepped off the track.

This is the moment they stepped into the bushes forever.

14. It all hinges on one reality.

That reality is sinister.

That reality is rarely mentioned.

It has an implacable inevitability.

It has an irreversible inevitability.

No doubt this is why it is rarely mentioned.

15. These decisions cannot be changed, no matter how many books
we read.

These are brightly cheerful books.

These are buoyantly optimistic books.

These are books on HOW TO ACHIEVE A RICHER, FULLER,
MORE BOUNTIFUL LIFE.

These are books on SEVEN MAGIC GOLDEN KEYS TO IN-
STANT DYNAMIC SUCCESS.

These are books on THE SECRET OF HOW TO BECOME A
MILLIONAIRE.

These decisions cannot be changed, no matter how many classes
are attended.

These classes are for instruction in handshaking.

These classes are for instruction in back-slapping.

These classes are for instruction in making After-Dinner speeches.

16. Joseph Stalin was not a Dale Carnegie graduate.

17. He went all the way.

18. It is an unpleasant truth.

It is swallowed, if at all, like a pill.

The pill is rancid.

The pill is bitter.

19. A star is a star.

A numberless cipher is a numberless cipher.

20. The Great Divide is rarely a matter of talent.

The Great Divide is rarely a matter of personality.

This is an even more eerie fact.

21. Or even luck.

22. Adolf Hitler had a notoriously weak handshake.

23. His smile was, if anything, a vapid mockery.

24. But inevitably his star zoomed higher and higher.

25. There are cinema luminaries of the first order.

They are rarely blessed with even the modicum of Talent.

They have physical beauty.

Often their beauty leaves much to be desired.

26. What is the difference between Us and Them?
    What is the difference between We and They?
    What is the difference between the Big Ones and the rabble?
    The rabble is great.
    The rabble is teeming.

Paragraphs and Essays

Salvation

LANGSTON HUGHES

[1] I was saved from sin when I was going on thirteen. But not really saved. It happened like this. There was a big revival at my Aunt Reed's church. Every night for weeks there had been much preaching, singing, praying, and shouting, and some very hardened sinners had been brought to Christ, and the membership of the church had grown by leaps and bounds. Then just before the revival ended, they held a special meeting for children, "to bring the young lambs to the fold." My aunt spoke of it for days ahead. That night I was escorted to the front row and placed on the mourners' bench with all the other young sinners, who had not yet been brought to Jesus.

[2] My aunt told me that when you were saved you saw a light, and something happened to you inside! And Jesus came into your life! And God was with you from then on! She said you could see and hear and feel Jesus in your soul. I believed her. I had heard a great many old people say the same thing and it seemed to me they ought to know. So I sat there calmly in the hot, crowded church, waiting for Jesus to come to me.

[3] The preacher preached a wonderful sermon, all moans and shouts and lonely cries and dire pictures of hell, and then he sang a song about the ninety and nine safe in the fold, but one little lamb was left out in the cold. Then he said: "Won't you come? Won't you come to Jesus? Young lambs, won't you come?" And he held out his arms to all us young sinners there on the mourners' bench. And the little girls cried. And some of them jumped up and went to Jesus right away. But most of us just sat there.

[4] A great many old people came and knelt around us and prayed, old women with jet-black faces and braided hair, old men with work-gnarled hands. And the church sang a song about the lower lights are burning, some poor sinners to be saved. And the whole building rocked with prayer and song.

[5] Still I kept waiting to *see* Jesus.

[6] Finally all the young people had gone to the altar and were saved, but one boy and me. He was a rounder's son named Westley. Westley and I were surrounded by sisters and deacons praying. It was very hot in the church, and getting late now. Finally Westley said to me in a whisper: "God damn! I'm tired o' sitting here. Let's get up and be saved." So he got up and was saved.

[7] Then I was left all alone on the mourners' bench. My aunt came and knelt at my knees and cried, while prayers and songs swirled all around me in the little church. The whole congregation prayed for me alone, in a mighty wail of moans and voices. And I kept waiting serenely for Jesus, waiting, waiting—but he didn't come. I wanted to see him, but nothing happened to me. Nothing! I wanted something to happen to me, but nothing happened.

[8] I heard the songs and the minister saying: "Why don't you come? My dear child, why don't you come to Jesus? Jesus is waiting for you. He wants you. Why don't you come? Sister Reed, what is this child's name?"

[9] "Langston," my aunt sobbed.

[10] "Langston, why don't you come? Why don't you come and be saved? Oh, Lamb of God! Why don't you come?"

[11] Now it was really getting late. I began to be ashamed of myself, holding everything up so long. I began to wonder what God thought about Westley, who certainly hadn't seen Jesus either, but who was now sitting proudly on the platform, swinging his knickerbockered legs and grinning down at me, surrounded by deacons and old women on their knees praying. God had not struck Westley dead for taking his name in vain or for lying in the temple. So I decided that maybe to save further trouble, I'd better lie, too, and say that Jesus had come, and get up and be saved.

[12] So I got up.

[13] Suddenly the whole room broke into a sea of shouting, as they saw me rise. Waves of rejoicing swept the place. Women leaped in the air. My aunt threw her arms around me. The minister took me by the hand and led me to the platform.

[14] When things quieted down, in a hushed silence, punctuated by a few ecstatic "Amens," all the new young lambs were blessed in the name of God. Then joyous singing filled the room.

[15] That night, for the last time in my life but one—for I was a big boy twelve years old—I cried. I cried, in bed alone, and couldn't stop. I buried my head under the quilts, but my aunt heard me. She woke up and told my uncle I was crying because the Holy Ghost had come into my life, and because I had seen Jesus. But I was really crying because I couldn't bear to tell her that I had lied, that I had deceived

everybody in the church, that I hadn't seen Jesus, and that now I didn't believe there was a Jesus any more, since he didn't come to help me.

Of Time and Lizards—And Sex

JANE ANN PATCHAK

[1] From the vantage of my patio I watch the many-ringed circus of suburban wild life, the aerialists and high wire performers, the balancing acts, and the clowns. There was even a magic act one day when a Luna moth metamorphosed and hung itself to dry on the rubber plant, its luminous four-inch swallow-tailed wings atremble in the slight breeze. My ringside seat affords me much pleasure and a bit of insight as birds and squirrels, butterflies and cats, and lizards, stalk and quarrel, court, and rear their offspring.

[2] It is the chameleons, though, that command much of my attention. Actually, they aren't chameleons at all, but anoles. Chameleons are Old World creatures, and much larger than the small green lizards that dwell in the yard and patio. Nevertheless, I would much prefer to be called a chameleon than an anole, and so, I must presume, would they.

[3] Presently there are six which reside on the patio. They are graduated in size and one has lost part of her tail. I call her Sugar. The very large one is El Groso, and the tiny one I call La Petite. Today I discovered that this is a misnomer, for La Petite is a very young male, and in a gesture of insouciant bravado, he did a couple of quick push-ups and waved a miniscule pink flag at El Groso before scurrying into a crevice in the bricks too small for old fatty to follow. In time these two will likely have a confrontation that will force one to retire from the patio, leaving the other as top dog, to use an inappropriate cliche, with a harem of nubile females.

[4] The other chameleons lack sufficient distinguishing characteristics as yet for naming. They mostly hang out on the periphery, in areas where I have constructed chameleon environments. There's a small rock collection that serves as a miniature mountain range where they can bask in filtered sunlight. At one end of the patio I hung a few twisted branches to provide an escape when life on the screen palls. This morning one was apparently in deep meditation on a branch where he had assumed a Yoga asana, the Pose of the Snake. Then there are the hanging plants where they can lurk and await an unwary bug or a pubescent female.

[5] I have logged several hundred hours chameleon-watching, and have observed hunting, stalking, defense, courtship and copulatory be-

haviors. Once I saw a fierce battle between contending males. I was ultimately constrained to break it up for I felt the combatants were unevenly matched in size. It's easy to disturb a chameleon. The merest touch of a finger to the tip of a tail is all it takes. In this battle the big one clamped his jaws about the snout of the smaller one and hung on so tenaciously that the little chap's hind legs were bouncing on the screen. But despite my intervention, which gave him a chance to escape, that feisty little bugger leaped back into the fray and was shortly driven from the field.

[6] The victor in this struggle, named Champ, was one tough hombre who stayed green all the time, it seemed. He was unmatched for sheer effrontery, and claimed the entire back of the house, as well as the patio, as his territory. He patrolled relentlessly, once chasing an interloper all the way to the west end of the house where he vanished around the corner, still in hot pursuit. Champ would display at any provocation and even when there was no evident reason. He was a great show-off, with his "Hey! Look at me!" macho demonstrations that wowed most of the females and scared most of the males. For the uninformed, a display involves a series of push-ups and head-bobs, accompanied by the extension of a throat fan which only the males possess. Champ's was bright orange, a nice contrast to his brilliant green hide. When chameleons display during skirmishes for territory or as part of a court-ship ritual, they are vulnerable to predators and, supposedly, use up much energy. Champ had energy to spare, especially sexual energy. In fact, he was downright horny most of the time.

[7] One warm sunny afternoon when in the pursuit of *l'amour*, Champ was making spectacular leaps between hanging plants that were as much as two feet apart, and with the last leap he landed squarely on the back of a hapless female. She struggled valiantly to escape, poor dear, climbing laboriously up the screen while he clung to her back and bit her on the neck. At one point she even loosened her foothold on the screen and they fell together, landing with a small "thud" on a ledge. When this maneuver failed to dislodge Champ, she began another grueling climb back up the screen with that great oaf still as firmly ensconced on her back as if he had been glued in place, still biting her neck. Finally, sheer exhaustion, I presume, overcame her and she sub-mited to her fate. Champ then wound his tail around hers, braced his feet, closed his eyes and appeared to sleep. It seemed to me she was the one who should have been tired. After a surprisingly long interlude he released her, and with a good bit of aplomb, she turned and ate a fly.

[8] When I recounted this episode to the psychologists in my de-partment, they suggested that the females probably get their jollies by pretending to resist, which certainly tells you something about psy-chologists, doesn't it? And the biologists prated on about the necessity

of the female being "sexually receptive" and all that for mating to occur. Pooh! I maintain that the female was a reluctant maiden and that her ravaging was nothing short of despoilation.

[9] Later I learned that I was defending my voyeurism to myself, passing it off as the "scientific investigation of the copulatory habits of the *Anolis carolinesis*" rather than prurient interest. This is in addition to justifying the time wasted when I should have been engaged in some sort of productive labor, not lolling on the patio watching lizards. I grew up in an era when girls hastily averted their eyes at the mating behavior of dogs in the schoolyard, while loutish boys shouted and pointed at the offending scene and passed off lewd remarks. They probably grew up to be psychologists. I was also taught that one must earn leisure time, and that time squanderers would be punished in the Hereafter.

[10] Apropos of the cultural concepts of time, I once asked a class if time spent watching chameleons would be considered as frittering. The concensus was that, indeed, it would be frittering, which they thought was worse than puttering. One student did say the expenditure of time could be justified as "learning something about animal behavior." Not one suggested that chameleon-watching in particular, and backyard-watching in general, was okay for the sheer delight it gives me. An interesting commentary on the way Americans regard time and the correct way to use it. I used to keep a balance sheet in my head of time spent, and time frittered was entered in the debit column and had to be balanced by some useful endeavor such as cleaning the bathroom or weeding the garden. But lately I've come around to the conclusion that chameleon watching restores my spirit and lifts my soul; hence, it is therapeutic, and I no longer need to enter it as a debit.

[11] Next time I'll tell you about the head grackle who monopolizes two bird baths, his own and the one I got for the sparrows. Or maybe I'll tell you about the grackle picnic attended by mothers and babies. Or the hummingbird who loses altitude on his backward flight from the nectar feeder. Or . . .

The Endless Streetcar Ride into the Night

JEAN SHEPHERD

[1] Mewling, puking babes. That's the way we all start. Damply clinging to someone's shoulder, burping weakly, clawing our way into life. *All* of us. Then gradually, surely, we begin to divide into two streams, all marching together up that long yellow brick road of life, but on opposite sides of the street. One crowd goes on to become the Official

people, peering out at us from television screens, magazine covers. They are forever appearing in newsreels, carrying attaché cases, surrounded by banks of microphones while the world waits for their decisions and statements. And the rest of us go on to become . . . just us.

[2] They are the Prime Ministers, the Presidents, Cabinet Members, Stars, dynamic molders of the Universe, while we remain forever the onlookers, the applauders of their real lives.

[3] Forever down in the dark dungeons of our souls we ask ourselves:

[4] "How did they get away from me? When did I make that first misstep that took me forever to the wrong side of the street, to become eternally part of the accursed, anonymous Audience?"

[5] It seems like one minute we're all playing around back of the garage, kicking tin cans and yelling at girls, and the next instant you find yourself doomed to exist as an office boy in the Mail Room of Life, while another ex-mewling, puking babe sends down Dicta, says "No comment" to the Press, and lives a real, genuine *Life* on the screen of the world.

[6] Countless sufferers at this hour are spending billions of dollars and endless man hours lying on analysts' couches, trying to pinpoint the exact moment that they stepped off the track and into the bushes forever.

[7] It all hinges on one sinister reality that is rarely mentioned, no doubt due to its implacable, irreversible inevitability. These decisions cannot be changed, no matter how many brightly cheerful, buoyantly optimistic books on HOW TO ACHIEVE A RICHER, FULLER, MORE BOUNTIFUL LIFE or SEVEN MAGIC GOLDEN KEYS TO INSTANT DYNAMIC SUCCESS or THE SECRET OF HOW TO BECOME A BILLIONAIRE we read, or how many classes are attended for instruction in handshaking, back-slapping, grinning, and making After-Dinner speeches. Joseph Stalin was not a Dale Carnegie graduate. He went all the way. It is an unpleasant truth that is swallowed, if at all, like a rancid, bitter pill. A star is a star; a numberless cipher is a numberless cipher.

[8] Even more eerie a fact is that the Great Divide is rarely a matter of talent or personality. Or even luck. Adolf Hitler had a notoriously weak handshake. His smile was, if anything, a vapid mockery. But inevitably his star zoomed higher and higher. Cinema luminaries of the first order are rarely blessed with even the modicum of Talent, and often their physical beauty leaves much to be desired. What is the difference between Us and Them, We and They, the Big Ones and the great, teeming rabble?

[9] There are about four times in a man's life, or a woman's, too,

for that matter, when unexpectedly, from out of the darkness, the blazing carbon lamp, the cosmic searchlight of Truth shines full upon them. It is how we react to those moments that forever seals our fate. One crowd simply puts on its sunglasses, lights another cigar, and heads for the nearest plush French restaurant in the jazziest section of town, sits down and orders a drink, and ignores the whole thing. While we, the Doomed, caught in the brilliant glare of illumination, see ourselves inescapably for what we are, and from that day on skulk in the weeds, hoping no one else will spot us.

[10] Those moments happen when we are least able to fend them off. I caught the first one full in the face when I was fourteen. The fourteenth summer is a magic one for all kids. You have just slid out of the pupa stage, leaving your old baby skin behind, and have not yet become a grizzled, hardened, tax-paying beetle. At fourteen you are made of cellophane. You curl easily and everyone can see through you.

[11] When I was fourteen, Life was flowing through me in a deep, rich torrent of Castoria. How did I know that the first rocks were just ahead, and I was about to have my keels ripped out on the reef? Sometimes you feel as though you are alone in a rented rowboat, bailing like mad in the darkness with a leaking bailing can. It is important to know that there are at least two billion other ciphers in the same boat, bailing with the same leaky can. They all think they are alone and crossed with an evil star. They are right.

[12] I'm fourteen years old, in my sophomore year at high school. One day Schwartz, my purported best friend, sidled up to me edgily outside of school while we were waiting on the steps to come in after lunch. He proceeded to outline his plan:

[13] "Helen's old man won't let me take her out on a date on Saturday night unless I get a date for her girlfriend. A double date. The old coot figures, I guess, that if there are four of us there won't be no monkey business. Well, how about it? Do you want to go on a blind date with this chick? I never seen her."

[14] Well. For years I had this principle—absolutely no blind dates. I was a man of perception and taste, and life was short. But there is a time in your life when you have to stop taking and begin to give just a little. For the first time the warmth of sweet Human Charity brought the roses to my cheeks. After all, Schwartz was my friend. It was little enough to do, have a blind date with some no doubt skinny, pimply girl for your best friend. I would do it for Schwartz. He would do as much for me.

[15] "Okay. Okay, Schwartz."

[16] Then followed the usual ribald remarks, feckless boasting, and dirty jokes about dates in general and girls in particular. It was decided that next Saturday we would go all the way. I had a morning paper

route at the time, and my life savings stood at about $1.80. I was all set to blow it on one big night.

[17] I will never forget that particular Saturday as long as I live. The air was as soft as the finest of spun silk. The scent of lilacs hung heavy. The catalpa trees rustled in the early evening breeze from off the Lake. The inner Me itched in that nameless way, that indescribable way that only the fourteen-year-old Male fully knows.

[18] All that afternoon I had carefully gone over my wardrobe to select the proper symphony of sartorial brilliance. That night I set out wearing my magnificent electric blue sport coat, whose shoulders were so wide that they hung out over my frame like vast, drooping eaves, so wide I had difficulty going through an ordinary door head-on. The electric blue sport coat that draped voluminously almost to my knees, its wide lapels flapping soundlessly in the slightest breeze. My pleated gray flannel slacks began just below my breastbone and indeed chafed my armpits. High-belted, cascading down finally to grasp my ankles in a vise-like grip. My tie, indeed one of my most prized possessions, had been a gift from my Aunt Glenn upon the state occasion of graduation from eighth grade. It was of a beautiful silky fabric, silvery pearl colored, four inches wide at the fulcrum, and of such a length to endanger occasionally my zipper in moments of haste. Hand-painted upon it was a magnificent blood-red snail.

[19] I had spent fully two hours carefully arranging and rearranging my great mop of wavy hair, into which I had rubbed fully a pound and a half of Greasy Kid Stuff.

[20] Helen and Schwartz waited on the corner under the streetlight at the streetcar stop near Junie Jo's home. Her name was Junie Jo Prewitt. I won't forget it quickly, although she has, no doubt, forgotten mine. I walked down the dark street alone, past houses set back off the street, through the darkness, past privet hedges, under elm trees, through air rich and ripe with promise. Her house stood back from the street farther than the others. It sort of crouched in the darkness, looking out at me, kneeling. Pregnant with Girldom. A real Girlfriend house.

[21] The first faint touch of nervousness filtered through the marrow of my skullbone as I knocked on the door of the screen-enclosed porch. No answer. I knocked again, louder. Through the murky screens I could see faint lights in the house itself. Still no answer. Then I found a small doorbell button buried in the sash. I pressed. From far off in the bowels of the house I heard two chimes "Bong" politely. It sure didn't sound like our doorbell. We had a real ripper that went off like a broken buzz saw, more of a BRRRAAAAKKK than a muffled Bong. This was a rich people's doorbell.

[22] The door opened and there stood a real, genuine, gold-plated Father: potbelly, underwear shirt, suspenders, and all.

267

[23] "Well?" he asked.

[24] For one blinding moment of embarrassment I couldn't remember her name. After all, she was a blind date. I couldn't just say:

[25] "I'm here to pick up some girl."

[26] "He turned back into the house and hollered:

[27] "JUNIE JO! SOME KID'S HERE!"

[28] "Heh, heh. . . ." I countered.

[29] He led me into the living room. It was an itchy house, sticky stucco walls of a dull orange color, and all over the floor this Oriental rug with the design crawling around, making loops and sworls. I sat on an overstuffed chair covered in stiff green mohair that scratched even through my slacks. Little twisty bridge lamps stood everywhere. I instantly began to sweat down the back of my clean white shirt. Like I said, it was a very itchy house. It had little lamps sticking out of the walls that looked like phony candles; with phony glass orange flames. The rug started moaning to itself.

[30] I sat on the edge of the chair and tried to talk to this Father. He was a Cub fan. We struggled under water for what seemed like an hour and a half, when suddenly I heard someone coming down the stairs. First the feet; then those legs, and there she was. She was magnificent! The greatest-looking girl I ever saw in my life! I have hit the double jackpot! And on a blind date! Great Scot!

[31] My senses actually reeled as I clutched the arm of that bilge-green chair for support. Junie Jo Prewitt made Cleopatra look like a Girl Scout!

[32] Five minutes later we are sitting in the streetcar, heading toward the bowling alley. I am sitting next to the most fantastic creation in the Feminine department known to Western man. There are the four of us in that long, yellow-lit streetcar. No one else was aboard; just us four. I, naturally, being a trained gentleman, sat on the aisle to protect her from candy wrappers and cigar butts and such. Directly ahead of me, also on the aisle, sat Schwartz, his arm already flung affectionately in a death grip around Helen's neck as we boomed and rattled through the night.

[33] I casually flung my right foot up onto my left knee so that she could see my crepe-soled, perforated, wing-toed, Scotch bluchers with the two-toned laces. I started to work my famous charm on her. Casually, with my practiced offhand, cynical, cutting, sardonic humor I told her about how my Old Man had cracked the block in the Oldsmobile, how the White Sox were going to have a good year this year, how my kid brother wet his pants when he saw a snake, how I figured it was going to rain, what a great guy Schwartz was, what a good second baseman I was, how I figured I might go out for football. On and on I rolled,

like Old Man River, pausing significantly for her to pick up the conversation. Nothing.

[34] Ahead of us Schwartz and Helen were almost indistinguishable one from the other. They giggled, bit each other's ears, whispered, clasped hands, and in general made me itch even more.

[35] From time to time Junie Jo would bend forward stiffly from the waist and say something I could never quite catch into Helen's right ear.

[36] I told her my great story of the time that Uncle Carl lost his false teeth down the airshaft. Still nothing. Out of the corner of my eye I could see that she had her coat collar turned up, hiding most of her face as she sat silently, looking forward past Helen Weathers into nothingness.

[37] I told her about this old lady on my paper route who chews tobacco, and roller skates in the back yard every morning. I still couldn't get through to her. Casually, I inched my right arm up over the back of the seat behind her shoulders. The acid test. She leaned forward, avoiding my arm, and stayed that way.

[38] "Heh, heh, heh. . . ."

[39] As nonchalantly as I could, I retrieved it, battling a giant cramp in my right shoulder blade. I sat in silence for a few seconds, sweating heavily as ahead Schwartz and Helen are going at it hot and heavy.

[40] It was then that I became aware of someone saying something to me. It was an empty car. There was no one else but us. I glanced around, and there it was. Above us a line of car cards looked down on the empty streetcar. One was speaking directly to me, to me alone.

DO YOU OFFEND?

[41] Do I *offend?*!

[42] With no warning, from up near the front of the car where the motorman is steering I see this thing coming down the aisle directly toward *me*. It's coming closer and closer. I can't escape it. It's this blinding, fantastic, brilliant, screaming blue light. I am spread-eagled in it. There's a pin sticking through my thorax. I see it all now.

[43] *I* AM THE BLIND DATE!

[44] ME!!

[45] I'M the one they're being nice to!

[46] I'm suddenly getting fatter, more itchy. My new shoes are like bowling balls with laces; thick, rubber-crepe bowling balls. My great tie that Aunt Glenn gave me is two feet wide, hanging down to the floor like some crinkly tinfoil noose. My beautiful hand-painted snail is seven feet high, sitting up on my shoulder, burping. Great Scot! It is all clear to me in the searing white light of Truth. My friend Schwartz, I can see him saying to Junie Jo:

[47] "I got this crummy fat friend who never has a date. Let's give him a break and. . . ."

[48] *I* AM THE BLIND DATE!

[49] They are being nice to *me*! She is the one who is out on a Blind Date. A Blind Date that didn't make it.

[50] In the seat ahead, the merriment rose to a crescendo. Helen tittered; Schwartz cackled. The marble statue next to me stared gloomily out into the darkness as our streetcar rattled on. The ride went on and on.

[51] I AM THE BLIND DATE!

[52] I didn't say much the rest of the night. There wasn't much to be said.

Writing Suggestions

Although narratives serve a variety of purposes, the most successful ones usually share three basic characteristics: they are clearly organized in time, they make a central point, and they contain specific details relevant to that point. The topics below may remind you of an incident that you can relate in a clearly organized narrative essay.

1. An experience that left you disillusioned.
2. An experience that led to renewed faith.
3. A disastrous date.
4. A day when nothing seemed to go right.
5. A moment of failure.
6. A moment of success.
7. An act of heroism.
8. An act of cowardice.
9. A frightening experience.
10. An embarrassing experience.
11. A memorable journey.
12. An incident that changed your life.
13. An experience that changed your view of someone.
14. Your first day at school or college.
15. Your first night away from home.
16. A traffic accident.
17. A wedding.
18. A funeral.
19. Your first day on a new job.
20. A journey you would like to make.

CHAPTER 13

Process Analysis

Process analysis is writing that explains how to do something or how something works. If you are explaining how to do something, you need to provide clear, step-by-step instructions so that your reader can duplicate the process without further assistance. And if you are explaining how something works, you also must give clear, step-by-step explanations so that your reader understands the process thoroughly.

Like a narrative, a process analysis is organized chronologically. In fact, the student writer of "Fresh Chicken Sam" combines narrative with process analysis: she recalls her own experiences on the farm (narrative) while explaining how to catch, kill, and prepare a chicken (process analysis). "How to Bathe a Cat" (in Chapter 10) and "Crabbing" (in this chapter) are also examples of how-to-do-it essays. "Many Happy Returns" relies on both types of process analysis: the writer explains not only how to throw a boomerang correctly but also how it works.

The writer of an effective process analysis always keeps his or her reader in mind. Too much information can be boring and distracting; but not enough information can be confusing and frustrating to the reader. As you work out the execises in this chapter, evaluate each writer's work by considering the clarity and completeness of the instructions and explanations.

Exercises

Crabbing

MARY ZEIGLER

1. I am a lifelong crabber.
   That is, I catch crabs.
   I am not a chronic complainer.
   I can tell you something.
   Anyone who has patience can join the ranks of crabbers.
   Anyone who has a great love for the river can join.
2. You want your first crabbing expedition to be a successful one.
   You must come prepared.
3. First, you need a boat.
   You do not need just any boat.
4. I recommend a fiberglass boat.
   It should be fifteen-feet long.
   It should have a twenty-five horsepower motor.
   You need extra gas in a steel can.
   You need two thirteen-foot oars.
   You need two steel anchors.
   You need enough cushions for your entire party.
5. Also, you will need scoop nets.
   You will need crab lines.
   You will need bait.
6. Each crab line is made from heavy-duty string.
   Each crab line is attached to a weight.
   The bait is tied around each weight.
   The bait is a chicken neck.
   The chicken neck is slimy.
   The chicken neck is smelly.
   The chicken neck is utterly grotesque.
7. Now you are ready to begin crabbing.
   You are ready once the tide is low.
8. Tie the crab lines to the boat rail.
   Tie them securely.
   Drop your crab lines overboard.
9. Crabs are sensitive to sudden movements.
   Therefore, the lines must be lifted slowly.
   Lift the lines until the chicken necks are visible.
   They should be visible just below the surface of the water.

10. You may spy a crab nibbling at the bait.
    Snatch up the crab with your scoop net.
    Make a quick sweep with your scoop net.
11. The crab will be furious.
    The crab will snap its claws.
    The crab will bubble at the mouth.
12. Drop the crab into a wooden crate.
    Do this before the crab has a chance to get revenge.
13. Leave the crabs in the crate.
    They will brood there.
    Leave the crabs until you get home.
14. Boil the crabs at home.
    Boil them until they turn orange.
    The orange should be a healthy shade.
15. Spread newspapers over the kitchen table.
    Deposit the boiled crabs on the newspapers.
    Enjoy the most delicious meal of your life.

*Many Happy Returns**

DAVID ROBSON

1. There are principles behind the boomerang's comebacks.
   These principles are well understood.
2. The arms of a boomerang are flat on the bottom.
   They are curved on top.
3. The arms cut through the air.
   They generate lift.
   This is like an airplane wing.
4. The boomerang resembles an airplane wing.
   A novice thrower may try to launch it like one.
   He may launch it horizontally.
   He may launch it with the flat bottom parallel to the ground.
5. The lift generated by the wings pushes the boomerang upward.
   This happens on a "flat" launch.
   The result is that it simply climbs steeply.
6. Here is how to launch the boomerang correctly.
   The thrower grasps it near the tip of either arm.

---

* This exercise has been adapted from paragraphs 9 through 12 of Robson's essay in the Paragraphs and Essays section of this chapter.

He releases the boomerang.
It should be nearly vertical.

7. An airplane banks its wings to make a turn.
   In the same way, the boomerang's vertical attitude makes it generate "lift."
   The "lift" pushes it sideways.
   It does not push it up.

8. The sideways-pushing force alone would merely propel the boomerang to another corner of the field.
   What makes the boomerang return?
   It is not the sideways-pushing force.

9. An additional, turning force is needed.
   Gyroscopic precession supplies this force.
   Gyroscopic precession is an enigmatic effect.

10. Precession is a phenomenon.
    It affects all spinning objects.
    It affects gyroscopes.
    It affects bicycle wheels.
    It affects tops.
    It affects planets.

11. Force is applied to the edge of a spinning disk.
    Then the disk will not tilt in the direction of that force.
    It might be expected that it would tilt in that direction.

12. Instead, it will tilt as if a force were applied at a point 90 degrees around the disk.
    This is 90 degrees from where it was pushed.

13. Push a spinning disk.
    Push it at the 12 o'clock position.
    It will behave as though it were pushed at three o'clock.

14. How does a rider turn a bicycle to the left when riding "no-hands"?
    The rider leans to the left.
    This is the same as applying a force to the top of the front wheel.

15. But the front wheel not only leans left.
    It also *turns* left.
    This is because of the effect of precession.

16. What supplies the turning force on a boomerang?
    The uneven lift supplies this force.
    The uneven lift is generated by its spinning wings.

17. The tips of a boomerang's arms spin in the air.
    They spin with a velocity of about 35 miles per hour.
    They form a "wheel."
    The "wheel" lies in a near-vertical plane.

18. What happens when an arm passes the top of this desk?
    The arm is spinning forward.
    The arm spins in the direction of the boomerang's motion.
19. What does this mean?
    The tip of the arm will move through the air with a certain velocity.
    The velocity is a combination of the 35-mile-per-hour spin and the boomerang's 55-mile-per-hour forward velocity.
    In other words, it will move through the air at about 90 miles per hour.
20. What happens when the same arm passes the bottom of the disk?
    The arm is spinning backward.
    It spins opposite the boomerang's forward motion.
21. The arm then moves through the air with a certain velocity.
    The velocity is 55 miles per hour minus 35 miles per hour.
    In other words, the velocity is 20 miles per hour.
22. The boomerang arms have much greater speed through the air at the top of the disk than at the bottom.
    Therefore, the lift they produce is uneven.
    More of the lift is generated at the top.
23. This is the same effect as pushing the wheel at 12 o'clock.
24. The boomerang does not tilt at the top.
    It tilts at the front edge.
    This causes it to turn left.
    This is because of precession.

Fresh Chicken Sam

SYLVIA DRIVER

There are no sets in this exercise. You will need to group the sentences logically before you combine them.

1. I was raised on a farm.
2. The farm is in a little place.
3. The place is called Armuchee.
4. It is in the mountains of northwest Georgia.
5. We had all types of farm animals.
6. Chickens were the most common.
7. We often had fresh chicken for Sunday dinner.
8. We would have fresh chicken on almost every special occasion.
9. My father and I would go out to the chicken coop.
10. We went out on these days.

11. We went out early in the morning.
12. We would get a chicken.
13. Getting a chicken is not as easy as it sounds.
14. You are determined to catch the chicken.
15. He is just as determined that you don't catch him.
16. Catch him sleeping.
17. That is the best method of ambushing your prey.
18. My father picks out a chicken.
19. It is the chicken he wants for that day's meal.
20. We slowly advance towards it.
21. We stealthily advance towards it.
22. We get within grabbing range.
23. We attack.
24. My father usually catches the varmint on the first attack.
25. He misses on rare occasions.
26. Then the chase is on.
27. We chase the stupid chicken.
28. We have spent over an hour doing this.
29. Finally we bag our villain.
30. We are successful.
31. For the poor chicken, it is doomsday.
32. We now move into the more grisly part of preparing a fresh chicken.
33. How do you end a chicken's life?
34. There are two methods.
35. These methods are commonly used.
36. Here is the first method.
37. I call it the "guillotine technique."
38. This method is to chop off the chicken's neck.
39. Do not use an actual guillotine.
40. Use an axe.
41. Place the chicken onto a chopping block.
42. (From now on I will refer to the chicken as "Sam.")
43. The chopping block should be at ground level.
44. Place your left foot on Sam's head.
45. Wear something that you don't mind getting splattered with blood.
46. Be sure to do this.
47. Of course, Sam does not like your foot on his face.
48. He will try very hard to get away.
49. Now here comes the gruesome part.
50. Take the axe in your right hand.
51. The axe is deadly sharp.

52. Raise the axe high above your head.
53. Chop off Sam's head.
54. Do this in guillotine fashion.
55. Then immediately step back.
56. The feathered body of Sam will get up.
57. It will run around the yard.
58. It will run for almost a minute.
59. You will see this to your horror.
60. Do not panic.
61. It is not Sam coming back to haunt you.
62. It is just a nerve-muscle reflex.
63. This reflex causes Sam to keep running.
64. Soon Sam will collapse.
65. You can retrieve his beheaded form.
66. There is a second method of murdering Sam.
67. My father prefers this method.
68. This method is called "wringing the chicken's neck."
69. In this case, Sam's neck is concerned.
70. Simply twist Sam's neck.
71. Twist it until it breaks.
72. Grasp Sam's head in your dominant hand.
73. Swing Sam up and over your head.
74. Swing with one swift motion.
75. Swing in a complete circle.
76. Add a little jerk to the end of the circular motion.
77. Be sure to do this.
78. This will snap Sam's neck.
79. You now have one dead Sam.
80. You have beheaded Sam.
81. Now you are ready to "dress" him.
82. You may have axed Sam's head.
83. Then take him to a nearby tree.
84. Hang him upside down.
85. Hang him by his legs.
86. Let the blood drain out.
87. Then take him back to your chopping block.
88. Cut off his legs.
89. Try to chop them off at the base of the feathers.
90. Now you must remove his entrails.
91. You could wait until after you have plucked him.
92. You might as well gut him right now.
93. Place Sam on the cutting board.
94. Place Sam on his back.

95. Hold him down firmly.
96. Take a sharp knife.
97. Cut off the rest of his neck.
98. Cut it off at the shoulder blades.
99. Place the knife in the center of his chest.
100. Place the knife at the top.
101. Cut him open.
102. Cut him all the way down to his rectum.
103. Reach inside the opening.
104. Remove all of Sam's internal organs.
105. I realize that this is disgusting.
106. Nevertheless, this act must be performed.
107. All of Sam's entrails must be removed.
108. There should be a hollow cavity.
109. Be sure of this.
110. Now comes "Pluck Time."
111. Grip Sam firmly.
112. Pluck off all of his little white feathers.
113. You can make a game out of this.
114. Play, "He loves me, he loves me not."
115. Get to the final "He loves me."
116. Sam is ready to be cleaned up.
117. Now take Sam into the kitchen.
118. Place him in the sink.
119. Run lukewarm water over him.
120. Rinse him off thoroughly.
121. Take a handful of baking soda.
122. Scrub Sam inside and out.
123. Be sure to remove any leftover feathers.
124. Be sure to remove any leftover entrails.
125. Rinse Sam again.
126. This will remove the baking soda.
127. Then take your sharp knife.
128. Cut off Sam's tail.
129. Cut off the fatty parts of his skin.
130. These parts are not wanted.
131. You may remove this skin.
132. You may leave it on.
133. This depends on how you want to cook Sam.
134. Sam is now ready to be cooked.
135. You can prepare him in any fashion you desire.
136. My father and I always try to get mother to make Sam into one of those Southern-fried beauties.

Paragraphs and Essays

Crabbing

MARY ZIEGLER

[1] As a lifelong crabber (that is, one who catches crabs, not a chronic complainer), I can tell you that anyone who has patience and a great love for the river is qualified to join the ranks of crabbers. However, if you want your first crabbing expedition to be a successful one, you must come prepared.

[2] First, you need a boat, but not just any boat. I recommend a fifteen-foot long fiberglass boat complete with a twenty-five horsepower motor, extra gas in a steel can, two wooden thirteen-foot long oars, two steel anchors, and enough cushions for the entire party. You will also need scoops, crab lines, and bait. Each crab line, made from heavy-duty string, is attached to a weight, and around each weight is tied the bait—a slimy, smelly, and utterly grotesque chicken neck.

[3] Now, once the tide is low, you are ready to begin crabbing. Drop your crab lines overboard, but not before you have tied them securely to the boat rail. Because crabs are sensitive to sudden movements, the lines must be slowly lifted until the chicken necks are visible just below the surface of the water. If you spy a crab nibbling the bait, snatch him up with a quick sweep of your swoop net. The crab will be furious, snapping its claws and bubbling at the month. Drop the crab into a wooden crate before it has a chance to get revenge.

[4] You should leave the crabs brooding in the crate until you get back home. There, you will boil them until they turn a healthy shade of orange. Finally, spread newspapers over the kitchen table, deposit the boiled crabs on the newspaper, and enjoy the most delicious meal of your life.

Many Happy Returns

DAVID ROBSON

[1] In New York's Central Park a group of spectators and TV cameramen jockey for position while Barnaby Ruhe, holding a boomerang in his right hand, calmly fastens an apple to the top of his head.

[2] He stands quietly for a few seconds, gauging the wind. The

279

launch is abrupt—the boomerang leaves his hand at 55 miles per hour with an audible *swish!* Spinning nine revolutions a second, it is visible only as a blur. The boomerang flies outward for a second, enters a broad left turn, and heads back towards Ruhe. As it draws near, the cameramen lean back and Ruhe steps forward. *Whack!* Apple pulp sprays all over the spectators, two pieces of apple drop from Ruhe's head, and the boomerang tumbles to the ground.

[3] Ruhe performed this William Tell act last June at the opening of the New York Boomrang Throwing Invitational. "It's a great attention-getter," he says, "and it's not as dangerous as it looks—for an expert thrower."

[4] The apparent danger in knocking an apple off one's head is due partly to the boomerang's reputation as a weapon. "There is a popular myth that the boomerang can be used for hunting and that if it misses the game it will return to the thrower," says Ruhe. "The Australian aborigines used returning boomerangs as playthings—just as we do." Its curved path (which makes it difficult to aim) and light weight (half the weight of a baseball) make it futile for a hunter to throw a boomerang at anything other than a flock of birds.

[5] The game-hunting myth no doubt stems from inaccurate reports from early explorers who confused aboriginal "throw sticks" with returning boomerangs. The throw stick is a curved piece of wood that is larger and heavier than a boomerang. When thrown, it travels waist-high, in a straight line, for up to 200 yards. It is a superb weapon, but it does not return.

[6] For many people, just getting the boomerang to return is pleasure enough. But there are always those who will take a pastime and turn it into a sport. For them, there are boomerang tournaments in Europe, Australia, and the United States with competitions such as the maximum-time-aloft event, in which the thrower not only has to keep the boomerang in the air for as long as possible, he must also catch it (the record is 26 seconds). In the juggling event, a second boomerang is launched while the first is returning. The object is to quickly catch and relaunch it, always keeping one in the air. The world record for juggling is 106 straight catches.

[7] The most demanding event is accuracy throwing. The field is marked with four concentric circles several yards apart. The boomerang is thrown from the bull's-eye, and points are awarded for how close the contestant is standing to the center when the boomerang is caught, combined with how far away from the thrower the boomerang flies.

[8] In 1981 a team of 12 Americans journeyed to Australia for the first international tournament, and to nearly everyone's surprise, won all three matches. The Australian reaction was summarized by the-newspaper, the *Sydney Telegraph:* "Yesterday should be forgotten. It

should be expunged from memory, deleted from the records. It's enough to make any self-respecting Aussie go bush."

[9] The principles behind the boomerang's comebacks are well understood. The arms of a boomerang are flat on the bottom and curved on top. As the arms cut through the air, they generate lift, like an airplane wing. Because the boomerang resembles an airplane wing, a novice thrower may try to launch it like one—horizontally, with the flat bottom parallel to the ground. On a "flat" launch, however, the lift generated by the wings pushes the boomerang upward, with the result that it simply climbs steeply.

[10] To launch correctly, the thrower grasps the boomerang near the tip of either arm and releases the boomerang so that it is nearly vertical. Just as an airplane banks its wings to make a turn, the boomerang's vertical attitude makes it generate "lift" that pushes it sideways instead of up.

[11] But the sideways-pushing force alone would merely propel the boomerang to another corner of the field; it is not what makes the boomerang return. An additional, turning force is needed, and this is supplied by an enigmatic effect called gyroscopic precession. Precession is a phenomenon that affects all spinning objects, be they gyroscopes, bicycle wheels, tops, or planets. If force is applied to the edge of a spinning disk, for example, the disk will not tilt in the direction of that force, as might be expected. Instead, it will tilt as if a force were applied at a point 90 degrees around the disk from where it was pushed. A spinning disk, when pushed at the 12 o'clock position, will behave as though it were pushed at three o'clock. To turn a bicycle to the left when riding "no-hands," a rider leans to the left, which is the same as applying a force to the top of the front wheel. But the front wheel not only leans left; because of the effect of precession, it also *turns* left.

[12] The turning force on a boomerang is supplied by the uneven lift generated by its spinning wings. The tips of a boomerang's arms spin in the air with a velocity of about 35 miles per hour, forming a "wheel" lying in a near-vertical plane. When an arm passes the top of this disk, it is spinning forward, in the direction of the boomerang's motion. This means that the tip of the arm will move through the air with a velocity that is a combination of the 35-mile-per-hour spin and the boomerang's 55-mile-per-hour velocity, or about 90 miles per hour. When the same arm passes the bottom of the disk, it is spinning backward—opposite the boomerang's forward motion. The arm then moves through the air with a velocity of 55 miles per hour minus 35 miles per hour, or 20 miles per hour. Because the boomerang arms have much greater speed through the air at the top of the disk than at the bottom, the lift they produce is uneven, with more of it being generated at the top. This is the same effect as pushing the wheel at 12 o'clock. Because

of precession, the boomerang tilts not at the top but at the front edge, causing it to turn left.

[13] All this, of course, may be of little importance to most people who love to play catch with themselves. Throwing a boomerang seems to appeal more to the irrational side of the psyche. "There is magic in the experience of throwing a boomerang," says Carl Naylor of Brooklyn, New York. "You've done it many times before, but the rational side of your brain still tells you that something that is thrown away shouldn't come back. When it does, it's just a bit awesome. I don't get that feeling playing Pac-Man."

Fresh Chicken Sam

SYLVIA DRIVER

[1] I was raised on a farm in a little place called Armuchee in the mountains of northwest Georgia. We had all types of farm animals, but the most common of these were chickens. Often on Sundays and on almost every special occasion we would have fresh chicken for dinner. On these days my father and I would go out early in the morning to the chicken coop to get a chicken. To get a chicken is not as easy as it may sound.

[2] As determined as you are to catch the chicken, he is just as determined that you don't. The best method of ambushing your prey is to catch him sleeping. So when I say we go out early in the morning, I do mean early. Once my father picks out the chicken he wants for that day's meal, we slowly and stealthily advance towards it. When we are within grabbing range, we attack. My father usually catches the varmint on the first attack, but there are those rare occasions when he misses, and then the chase is on. My father and I have been known to spend at least an hour chasing the stupid chicken before we successfully bag our villain. For the poor chicken, then, it is doomsday.

[3] We now move into the more grisly part of preparing a fresh chicken. There are two methods commonly used to end a chicken's life. The first method, which I call the "guillotine technique," is to chop off the chicken's head. Instead of an actual guillotine, however, you should use an axe. Place the chicken (whom from now on I will refer to as "Sam") onto a chopping block which is at or near ground level. Place your left foot on Sam's head. Be sure to be wearing something that you don't mind getting splattered with blood. Of course, Sam does not like your foot on his face, and he will try very hard to get away. Now here comes the gruesome part: take the deadly sharp axe in your right hand and raise it high above your head. In guillotine fashion, chop off Sam's head—then immediately step back. To your horror you will see the

feathered body of Sam get up and run around the yard for almost a minute. Do not panic: it is not Sam coming back to haunt you, but just a nerve-muscle reflex that causes Sam to keep running. The second method of murdering a chicken is the one my father prefers. This method is called "wringing the chicken's neck"—in this case, Sam's neck. Simply twist his neck until it breaks. Grasp Sam's head in your dominant hand and with one swift motion swing him up and over your head in a complete circle. Be sure to add a little jerk to the end of the circular motion so as to snap Sam's neck. You now have one dead Sam.

[4] After you have beheaded Sam, you are now ready to "dress" him. If you axed his neck, take him to a nearby tree and hang him upside down by his legs and let the blood drain out. If you wrung his neck, you have to cut off his head and then hang him upside down. Leave Sam there for an hour to make sure most of the blood has drained out. Then take him back to your chopping block and cut off his legs. Try to chop them off at the base of the feathers. Now you must remove his entrails. You could wait until after you've plucked him, but you might as well gut him right now. Place Sam on his back on the cutting board and hold him down firmly. Take a sharp knife and cut off the rest of his neck at his shoulder blades. Place the knife in the center of his chest at the top and cut him open all the way down to his rectum. Reach inside the opening and remove all of Sam's internal organs. I realize this is disgusting, but this act must be performed. Be sure all of Sam's entrails have been removed and that you have an empty cavity. Now comes "Pluck Time." Grip Sam firmly and pluck off all of his little white feathers. You can make a game out of this by playing, "He loves me, he loves me not." After you get to the final "He loves me," Sam is ready to be cleaned up.

[5] Now take Sam into the kitchen and place him in the sink. Run lukewarm water over him and rinse him off thoroughly. Take a handful of baking soda and scrub Sam inside and out. Be sure to remove any leftover feathers or entrails. Rinse Sam again to remove the baking soda. Then take your sharp knife and cut off Sam's tail as well as the unwanted fatty parts of his skin. Whether or not you remove the skin altogether depends on how you want to cook the chicken.

[6] Sam is now ready to be cooked. You can prepare him in any fashion you desire, but my father and I always try to get mother to make Sam into one of those Southern-fried beauties.

Writing Suggestions

When writing a process analysis, there are several things to keep in mind. First, be sure to include all steps and arrange them in sequence. Explain why each step is necessary, and include warnings where appropriate. Define any terms that your readers may not be familiar with, and offer clear descriptions of any tools or materials needed to carry out the process. Finally, provide your readers with a way of determining whether or not the process has been carried out successfully. You should not find it difficult to follow these guidelines if you have chosen a subject that you know quite well.

1. How to select a good used car.
2. How to make a pizza.
3. How to survive the weekend on $3.25.
4. How to toilet train a baby.
5. How to flunk out of college.
6. How to avoid a nervous breakdown.
7. How to pitch a knuckleball.
8. How to rob a grave.
9. How to rent an apartment.
10. How to hold a garage sale.
11. How to keep peace with a spouse or roommate.
12. How to win at poker.
13. How to survive babysitting.
14. How to stay sober.
15. How to select a college.
16. How a pocket calculator works.
17. How the registration system system at your college works.
18. How a magician can saw a woman in half.
19. How a microphone works.
20. How a decent person can become corrupted.

CHAPTER 14

Examples

We use examples in our writing to explain ideas and support our arguments. As well as clarifying concepts and observations, examples can also make our writing more interesting. They let us *show* our readers what we mean.

Depending on the subject, examples may be drawn from research or from personal experience. An example may be as brief as a single word or as long as a narrative that covers several paragraphs. "The Waiting Room" (in Chapter 8) relies on a number of short descriptions to illustrate the various types of body language exhibited in a dentist's waiting room. The writer of "Identity" (in this chapter) uses a single narrative example to demonstrate his point that it is important "for a child to be a person in her own right." Both "Watching Out for Loaded Words" and "Superstitions: Old and New" (a student essay) contain a rich variety of examples.

Effective examples, ones that are concise and clearly related to the subject, can help you clarify your ideas and maintain the interest of your readers. You will find them useful in any type of writing that aims to inform or persuade.

Exercises

Identity

ROLLO MAY

1. It is important for a child to be a person in her own right.
   Two little girl twins gave a vivid illustration of this.

2. The little girls were good friends.
How was this fact made especially possible?
They complemented each other.
One was extrovert.
Sometimes people came to visit in the house.
She was always in the center of the crowd.
The other was perfectly happy by herself.
She drew with her crayons.
She made up little poems.

3. The parents had dressed them alike.
Parents generally do this with twins.
The girls were dressed alike when they went out walking.

4. They were about three and a half.
The little extrovert girl began to want something.
She wanted to wear a different kind of dress from her sister.

5. Sometimes she dressed after her sister.
She would wear an older dress.
She would wear a less pretty dress.
She would do this if necessary.
The dress would not be the same as the twin was wearing.

6. Sometimes the sister dressed after her.
She would beg her not to put on the matching dress.
She would beg before they went out.
Sometimes she was weeping.

7. This puzzled the parents.
They were puzzled for days.
The child was not anxious in other ways.

8. Finally, the parents asked the little girl something.
They asked on a hunch.
"When you two go out walking, do you like to have the people on
the street say, 'Look at these nice twins'?"

9. The little girl exclaimed something.
She exclaimed immediately.
"No, I want them to say, 'Look at these two different people!' "

10. The explanation was spontaneous.
Something was very important to the little girl.
It obviously revealed that.
Did the child want attention?
It cannot be explained by saying that.
She would have gotten more attention if she had dressed as a twin.

11. This is what it shows.
She demanded to be a person in her own right.
She demanded to have a personal identity.
This need was more important to her even than attention or prestige.

12. The little girl rightly stated the goal for every human being.
    That is the goal to become a person.

Watching Out for Loaded Words*

FRANK TRIPPETT

1. Words zip into the mind.
   They are words beyond numbering.
   They zip via eye and ear.
   They flash a dizzy variety of meaning.
   The meaning if flashed into the circuits of knowing.
   The circuits are mysterious.
2. Words bring along their meanings.
   A great many of them also bring along some extra freight.
   That is, they bring a load of judgment.
   This load of judgment is a bias.
   The bias plays upon the emotions.
   It does not light up the understanding.
3. These words deserve careful handling.
   They deserve careful minding.
4. They are loaded.
5. Such words babble up in all corners of society.
   They babble up wherever anybody is ax-grinding.
   They babble up wherever anybody is arm-twisting.
   They babble up wherever anybody is back-scratching.
   They babble up wherever anybody is sweet-talking.
6. There are words *(peace, prosperity)* that have moving powers.
   The moving powers outweight exact meanings.
   Political blather leans sharply to such words.
7. Merchandising depends on adjectives *(new, improved)*.
   The adjectives must be continually recharged with notions.
   The notions entice people to buy.
8. There is emotional stuffing in casual conversation.
   The emotional stuffing is lent to words.
   Inflection does this.
   Gesture does this.
   "Thanks a lot" is an innocent phrase.
   The phrase is frequently a vehicle for heaping servings of irritation.
9. Most people are "more anxious to express their approval and dis-
   approval of things than to describe them."

* This exercise has been adapted from the first three paragraphs of Trippett's essay in the
Paragraphs and Essays section of this chapter.

C. S. Lewis put it this way.
Therefore, traffic in opinion-heavy language is universal.

10. Loaded words tend to short-circuit thought.
That is the trouble with them.

11. The words may describe something.
They simultaneously try to seduce the mind.
They want the mind to accept a prefabricated opinion.
The opinion is about the something described.

12. There was a recent survey of public attitudes.
The survey was by the Federal Advisory Commission on Intergovernmental Relations.
The survey incidentally measured the effect of one laden word.

13. Programs are called "aid to the needy."
The same programs are labeled "public welfare."
Many more Americans favor governmental help for the poor when the programs are called "aid to the needy."
The survey found that out.

14. Some citizens prefer H_2O to water.
This finding does not mean merely that.

15. Antipathy has accumulated around the word *welfare*.
The word is benign.
In fact, the finding spotlights the direct influence of that antipathy.

Superstitions: Old and New

DAWN FRAZER

1. There have been notable scientific advances in recent years.
There has been a growth of literacy in recent years.
Most people are still superstitious.
These people are in our society.

2. Some of our superstitions are traditional ones.
These superstitions involve such things as lucky charms.
They involve such things as ill omens.

3. New superstitions have evolved.
They have evolved in recent years.

4. These I call our space-age superstitions.

5. "Step on a crack and break your mama's back."

6. We all sang that.
We sang when we were youngsters.
We were all careful for awhile.
We were careful where we stepped.

288

7. We grew older.
   We learned about mother's backaches.
   Her backaches had nothing to do with how we walked down the
   pavement.
   We outgrew the superstition.
8. But do we really outgrow superstitions?
   Do we just substitute new ones for old ones?
9. I haven't carried a rabbit's foot since I was eleven.
   I do have a lucky penny.
10. My girlfriend has a particular ballpoint pen.
    She reserves the pen only for final examinations.
    My father refuses to lend me his car on any Friday the thirteenth.
11. Most of us have at least a few superstitions.
    The superstitions are silly.
    We swear the superstitions are unimportant.
    But don't dare take away my lucky penny.
12. Not all superstitions are so obviously silly.
13. New superstitions have emerged.
    These superstitions are pseudo-scientific.
    They have emerged in the past few years.
14. People seem to crave mysteries in their lives.
    Science debunks certain notions.
    Yet people still cling to old beliefs.
15. There have been many books in the past ten years.
    Some of the most popular books have promoted space-age super-
    stitions.
    The Bermuda Triangle is one of these superstitions.
    Others concern extraterrestrial visitors to earth.
    Others concern haunted houses in Long Island.
    Still others concern long weekends spent in spaceships.
    The spaceships were bound for Jupiter.
16. Pseudo-science is more popular than true science.
    It is vastly more popular.
17. Most people don't want the truth.
    Most people want mysteries.
18. Perhaps our space-age superstitions are substitutes.
    They are substitutes for ancient beliefs.
    The ancient beliefs have lost their hold on people.
19. Superstitions are harmless.
    They are harmless if we recognize them as odd habits.
    They are harmless if we recognize them as interesting fables.
    They are a poor substitute for genuine knowledge.
    They are poor substitutes for people who mistake them for truth.

Paragraphs and Essays

Identity

ROLLO MAY

[1] Two little girl twins gave a vivid illustration of how important it is for a child to be a person in her own right. The little girls were good friends, a fact made especially possible because they complemented each other, one being extrovert and always in the center of the crowd if people came to visit in the house, the other being perfectly happy by herself to draw with her crayons and make up little poems. The parents, as parents generally do with twins, had dressed them alike when they went out walking. When they were about three and a half, the little extrovert girl began to want always to wear a different kind of dress from her sister. If she dressed after her sister, she would even, if necessary, wear an older and less pretty dress so that it would not be the same as the twin was wearing. Or if the sister dressed after her before they went out, she would beg her, sometimes weeping, not to put on the matching dress. For days this puzzled the parents, since the child was not anxious in other ways. Finally the parents, on a hunch, asked the little girl, "When you two go out walking, do you like to have the people on the street say, 'Look at these nice twins'?" Immediately the little girl exclaimed, "No, I want them to say, 'Look at these two different people!'"

[2] This spontaneous exclamation, obviously revealing something very important to the little girl, cannot be explained by saying that the child wanted attention; for she would have gotten more attention if she had dressed as a twin. It shows, rather, her demand to be a person in her own right, to have personal identity—a need which was more important to her even than attention or prestige. The little girl rightly stated the goal for every human being—to become a person.

Watching Out for Loaded Words

FRANK TRIPPETT

[1] Via eye and ear, words beyond numbering zip into the mind and flash a dizzy variety of meaning into the mysterious circuits of knowing. A great many of them bring along not only their meanings but some extra freight—a load of judgment or bias that plays upon the

emotions instead of lighting up the understanding. These words deserve careful handling—and minding. They are loaded.

[2] Such words babble up in all corners of society, wherever anybody is ax-grinding, arm-twisting, back-scratching, sweet-talking. Political blather leans sharply to words *(peace, prosperity)* whose moving powers outweigh exact meanings. Merchandising depends on adjectives *(new, improved)* that must be continually recharged with notions that entice people to buy. In casual conversation, emotional stuffing is lent to words by inflection and gesture: the innocent phrase, "Thanks a lot," is frequently a vehicle for heaping servings of irritation. Traffic in opinion-heavy language is universal simply because most people, as C. S. Lewis puts it, are "more anxious to express their approval and disapproval of things than to describe them."

[3] The trouble with loaded words is that they tend to short-circuit thought. While they may describe something, they simultaneously try to seduce the mind into accepting a prefabricated opinion about the something described. The effect of one laden term was incidentally measured in a recent survey of public attitudes by the Federal Advisory Commission on Intergovernmental Relations. The survey found that many more Americans favor governmental help for the poor when the programs are called "aid to the needy" than when they are labeled "public welfare." And that does not mean merely that some citizens prefer H_2O to water. In fact, the finding spotlights the direct influence of the antipathy that has accumulated around the benign word *welfare*.

[4] Every word hauls some basic cargo or else can be shrugged aside as vacant sound. Indeed, almost any word can, in some use, take on that extra baggage or bias or sentiment that makes for the truly manipulative word. Even the pronoun *it* becomes one when employed to report, say, that somebody has what *it* takes. So does the preposition *in* when used to establish, perhaps, that zucchini quiche is *in* this year; used just so, *in* all but sweats with class bias. The emotion-heavy words that are easiest to spot are epithets and endearments: *blockhead, scumbum, heel, sweetheart, darling, great human being*, and the like. All such terms are so full of prejudice and sentiment that S. I. Hayakawa, a semanticist before he became California's U.S. Senator, calls them "snarl-words and purr-words."

[5] Not all artfully biased terms have been honored with formal labels. Word loading, after all, is not a recognized scholarly discipline, merely a folk art. Propagandists and advertising copywriters may turn it into a polished low art, but it is usually practiced—and witnessed—without a great deal of deliberation. The typical person, as Hayakawa says in *Language in Thought and Action*, "takes words as much for granted as the air."

291

[6] Actually, it does not take much special skill to add emotional baggage to a word. Almost any noun can be infused with skepticism and doubt through the use of the word *so-called.* Thus a friend in disfavor can become a *so-called friend,* and similarly the nation's leaders can become *so-called leaders.* Many other words can be handily tilted by shortening, by prefixes and suffixes, by the reduction of formal to familiar forms. The word *politician,* which may carry enough downbeat connotation for most tastes, can be given additional unsavoriness by truncation: *pol.* By prefacing liberal and conservative with *ultra* or *arch,* both labels can be saddled with suggestions of inflexible fanaticism. To speak of a pacifist or peacemaker as a *peacenik* is, through a single syllable, to smear someone with the suspicion that he has alien loyalties. The antifeminist who wishes for his (or her) prejudice to go piggyback on his (or her) language will tend to speak not of feminists but of femlibbers. People with only limited commitments to environmental preservation will tend similarly to allude not to environmentalists but to *eco-freaks.*

[7] Words can be impregnated with feeling by oversimplification. People who oppose all abortions distort the position of those favoring freedom of private choice by calling them *pro-abortion.* And many a progressive or idealist has experienced the perplexity of defending himself against one of the most peculiar of all disparaging terms, *do-gooder.* By usage in special contexts, the most improbable words can be infused with extraneous meaning. To speak of the "truly needy" as the Administration habitually does is gradually to plant the notion that the unmodified *needy* are falsely so. Movie Critic Vincent Canby has noticed that the word *film* has become imbued with a good deal of snootiness that is not to be found in the word *movie. Moderate* is highly susceptible to coloring in many ways, always by the fervent partisans of some cause: Adlai Stevenson, once accused of being too moderate on civil rights, wondered whether anyone wished him to be, instead, immoderate.

[8] The use of emotional vocabularies is not invariably a dubious practice. In the first place, words do not always get loaded by sinister design or even deliberately. In the second, that sort of language is not exploited only for mischievous ends. The American verities feature words—*liberty, equality*—that, on top of their formal definitions, are verily packed with the sentiments that cement U.S. society. The affectionate banalities of friendship and neighborliness similarly facilitate the human ties that bind and support. The moving vocabularies of patriotism and friendship are also subject to misuse, of course, but such derelictions are usually easy to recognize as demagoguery or hypocrisy.

[9] The abuse and careless use of language have been going on for a long time; witness the stern biblical warnings such as the one in *Mat-*

thew 12:36: "Every idle word that men shall speak, they shall give account thereof in the day of judgment." Yet the risks of biased words to the unwary must be greater today, in an epoch of propagandizing amplified by mass communications. "Never," Aldous Huxley said, "have misused words—those hideously efficient tools of all the tyrants, warmongers, persecutors and heresy hunters—been so widely and disastrously influential." In the two decades since that warning, the practice of bamboozlement has, if anything, increased. The appropriate response is not a hopeless effort to cleanse the world of seductive words. Simple awareness of how frequently and variously they are loaded reduces the chances that one will fall out of touch with so-called reality.

Superstitions: Old and New

DAWN FRAZER

[1] Despite notable scientific advances and the growth of literacy in recent years, most people in our society are still superstitious. Some of our superstitions are traditional ones involving such things as lucky charms and ill omens. However, new superstitions have evolved in recent years. These I call our space-age superstitions.

[2] "Step on a crack and break your mama's back." We all sang it when we were youngsters, and for awhile we were careful where we stepped. As we grew older and learned that mother's backaches had nothing to do with how we walked down the pavement, we outgrew the superstition. But do we really outgrow superstitions, or do we just substitute new ones for old ones? I haven't carried a rabbit's foot since I was eleven, but I do have a lucky penny. My girlfriend has a particular ballpoint pen that she reserves only for final examinations, and my father refuses to lend me his car on any Friday the thirteenth. Most of us have a few silly superstitions that we swear are unimportant—but don't dare take away my lucky penny.

[3] Not all superstitions are so obviously silly. In the past few years new pseudo-scientific superstitions have emerged. People seem to crave mysteries in their lives, so that even when science debunks certain notions, people continue to cling to their old beliefs. Some of the most popular books in the past ten years have promoted such space-age superstitions as the Bermuda Triangle, extraterrestrial visitors to earth, haunted houses in Long Island, and long weekends spent in spaceships bound for Jupiter. Pseudo-science is vastly more popular than true science. Most people don't want the truth; they want mysteries.

[4] Perhaps the space-age superstitions are substitutes for ancient beliefs that have lost their hold on people. Superstitions are harmless

so long as we recognize them as odd habits and interesting fables, but for people who mistake them for truth, superstitions are a poor substitute for genuine knowledge.

Writing Suggestions

Use the techniques of brainstorming (Discovery, Chapter 4) or probing (Discovery, Chapter 5) to turn one of the subjects or statements below into a topic that can be developed with examples.

1. The Peter principle: "In a hierarchy, every employee tends to rise to his level of incompetence."
2. Parkinson's law: "Work expands so as to fill the time available for its completion."
3. Worth's law: "When something fails to work and you demonstrate it for a repairman, it works better than ever, as if it never failed to work at all."
4. First impressions can be deceiving.
5. Anticipation is often greater than realization.
6. Superstitions.
7. Changing sex roles in America.
8. Contemporary slang.
9. Television commercials.
10. Energy conservation in the home.
11. Unusual hobbies.
12. Useless inventions.
13. How time-saving devices waste time.
14. The worse movies of all time.
15. Adults are merely obsolete children.

CHAPTER 15

Comparison and Contrast

The process of comparing and contrasting—identifying similarities and differences between two subjects—is both a way of thinking and a way of organizing ideas in writing. We use comparison and contrast to evaluate two subjects (people, places, products, services) or to explain one subject by means of another. We may choose to emphasize the differences between two apparently similar subjects or the similarities between apparently different subjects.

Comparisons and contrasts may be organized in two ways: either point by point to emphasize specific details or subject by subject to emphasize overall impressions. "Football and Soccer" (in this chapter) is an example of a simple point-by-point comparison and contrast; "Goodbye Yellow Brick Road" (in Chapter 5) is organized subject by subject. "Watching Baseball, Playing Softball" and "A Tale of Two Professors" (a student essay) both demonstrate that the two methods of organization can be combined. These two essays also show how narratives and examples can be used to support a comparison and contrast.

Working out the exercises in this chapter should give you ideas on how to explore a subject and organize an essay with comparisons and contrasts.

Exercises

Football and Soccer

1. European football is the parent of American football.
   The two games show several major differences.
2. European football is sometimes called association football.
   It is sometimes called soccer.
   It is played in eighty countries.
   It is the most widely played sport in the world.
3. American football is popular in the United States.
   It is popular in Canada.
   It is popular nowhere else.
4. Soccer is played by eleven players.
   It is played with a round ball.
5. Football is also played by eleven players.
   The players are in somewhat different positions.
   The positions are on the field.
   Football is played with an elongated round ball.
6. Soccer has little body contact between players.
   Soccer requires no special protective equipment.
7. Football players make maximum use of body contact.
   They use body contact to block a ball carrier.
   The ball carrier is running.
   They use body contact to block his teammates.
   Football requires special headgear.
   Football requires padding.
8. In soccer, the ball is advanced toward the goal.
   The ball is advanced by kicking it.
   The ball is advanced by butting it with the head.
9. In football the ball is passed from hand to hand.
   The ball is carried in the hands.
   The ball is carried across the opponent's goal.
10. These are just a few of the features.
    These features distinguish association and American football.

Watching Baseball, Playing Softball

TONY CAPPELLA

1. We watch baseball.
   Life should be like baseball.
   That is what we have always imagined.

2. We play softball.
3. It's sloppy.
4. It's more the way life really is.
5. I figured that out a long time ago.
   I figured that out on a soft summer evening.
   I was thirteen years old.
   I was dying of embarrassment.
   I was in center field.
   Our opponents touched us for seventeen runs.
   The runs came in the top half of the first inning.
6. Now I gape at a blank TV screen.
   I do this with beer in fist.
   I await the first major league game of the season.
   What is it I'm waiting for?
   That is what I am trying to define.
7. Baseball is precise.
   Baseball is ceremonial.
8. It is a world bounded by foul lines.
   It is a world marked by fixed positions.
9. The playing field is neatly geometric.
   The game itself is a linear equation.
   It is an equation of batters retired.
   It is an equation of runs batted in.
10. Baseball begins with a song.
    No one can sing this song.
    It ends with whispers.
    The whispers are hoarse.
    "Maybe next year."
11. The purpose of baseball is exquisitely clear.
    The purpose is to meet the ball head on.
    The purpose is to round the bases.
    The purpose is to run home as often as possible.
    There one is greeted by friends.
    These friends suddenly remember how much they have missed
      you.
12. That's baseball.
13. Now softball is quite different.
14. Here is one thing.
    We play wherever we can.
    Usually we play on golden fields.
    They are fields of dog crud.
    They are fields of shattered glass.
    They are bounded by city streets.
    They are bounded by factory parking lots.

15. How do we start?
    We choose sides.
    Who's to be stuck with Arthur Magaffe?
    We argue over this.
    Arthur Magaffe is gimlet-eyed.
    Arthur Magaffe is gimpy.
    And what are we going to use for home plate?
    We argue over that, too.
16. We play until we get too drunk.
    We play until the wives drag us home.
    We play until we lose the ball.
    The ball is somewhere between a trash compactor and a hedge
        row.
17. "It's only a game, fellas."
    Some complacent fool reminds us of this.
    We come close to lopping his head off.
    Of course, we know it's only a game.
    Why else would we take it so seriously?
18. We watch baseball.
19. What would it be like to have the power of Reggie, Mickey, and
        Joltin' Joe?
    We imagine this.
20. We play softball.
    We are more like Larry, Curly, and Moe.
    We discover this.
21. In baseball men are Giants.
    And they are Pirates.
    And they are Tigers.
    And they are Braves.
22. In softball, at best, we're cotter pins.
    We're cotter pins in Corky's Feed, Seed and Hardware.
23. Or, more often, we're just slobs.
    We have beer bellies.
    We wear Disneyworld tee-shirts.
    We wear International Harvester caps.
24. We might just as well be outfitted with party hats.
    We might just as well be outfitted with rubber noses.
    We might just as well be outfitted with long baggy pants.
25. And all the time we imagine grandstands shuddering with
        fans.
    But all we've got is a wino.
    He is in the outfield.
    He is chasing unicorns.

All we've got is Sammy's wife.
She has been brutalized by boredom.
She squats on the hood of their Subaru.
She reads Harold Robbins.
She picks her teeth.

26. What is it we are all waiting for?
Now I remember.
I sit here glaring at the TV.

27. That's why I get up.
I wheeze slightly.
I go to the closet.
I root out a glove.
The glove is stiff.
The glove is old.
The glove has been signed by Hank Bauer.

28. The laces are missing.
All the padding has been squeezed out.
It came out through a hole in the thumb.

29. I follow my belly.
I go across a schoolyard diamond.
There are jackets for bases.
There is a frisbee for home plate.
I wander out to center field.

30. A team is in front of me.
It is a team of obsolete children.
The children are in middle-age.
They are shagging.
They are groaning.
They are slapping their haunches.
They are hollering.
"Way to go! Way to go!"

31. I crouch down.
My hands are on my knees.
I wait.

32. I wait for a ball.
The ball is lopsided.
The ball may come skidding my way.
The ball may come spinning my way.
The ball may come bounding my way.

33. As ever, I will spend the afternoon fumbling.
I will spend the afternoon bobbling.
I will spend the afternoon falling flat on my can.

34. I play softball.

A Tale of Two Professors

WENSLEY HOBBY

1. A professor has a personality.
   A professor has teaching methods.
   These things influence a student's perception.
   They influence the student's perception of the instructor.
   They influence the student's perception of the subject.
   The instructor teaches that subject.

2. How does a professor act?
   What does a professor know?
   A student's success in a course depends on both.
   A student's failure in a course depends on both.

3. I have discovered this.
   I have observed two English professors.
   One is Dr. Axe.
   The other is Dr. Grind.

4. A professor has mannerisms.
   The mannerisms can help communication.
   They can hinder communication.
   The communication is in the classroom.
   They can show if the professor is interested in his subject.
   They can show if the professor is interested in his students.
   They can show if the professor is not interested.

5. Consider the behavior of Dr. Axe.
   Consider his behavior in the classroom.
   Dr. Axe was my English 100 instructor.

6. He would trudge into the classroom.
   He would be late.
   This was habitual.
   He would be unshaven.
   He wore a blue beach shirt.
   He wore seersucker pants.
   He wore no socks.
   He wore a pair of sandals.

7. He would drag himself to the center of the room.
   He would drop his attaché case on the desk.
   He would call the roll.
   He never smiled.
   He never said good morning.

8. He would collapse in his chair.
   He would sigh.
   The sigh was weary.

He would read an essay.
He read out loud.
He read to the class.

9. Now and then he paused.
He gazed at the floor.
The floor was scuff-marked.
He gazed as if he were drifting off.
He drifted on a cloud.
He drifted off to Venus.

10. Then he would continue reading.
He paused every few minutes.
He entertained a reverie.

11. Dr. Grind was in sharp contrast.
Dr. Grind was my English 101 instructor.
He entered the classroom.
He entered briskly.
He wore a sports coat.
It was plaid.
He wore a dress shirt.
The shirt was white.
He wore slacks.
The slacks were neatly pressed.
He wore Hush Puppy shoes.

12. He reached the podium.
He checked his seating chart.
He checked it quickly.
He checked it for absentees.
He smiled.
He greeted the class.

13. Then he might read to the class.
He might initiate a class discussion.
He might give a pop quiz.
He might discuss a writing assignment.
What would he do next?
We never knew.
The routine was varied.

14. Sometimes he would pace the floor.
He was waiting for an answer to a question.
Sometimes he would shake a student's hand.
The student had given a correct answer.

15. He looked at a book.
The book was on the podium.
Dr. Grind had a habit.
He would shift his spectacles.

He would shift them up and down.
He shifted them as he pondered.
What would he say next?
That is what he pondered.

16. He was restless.
He was always fiddling.
He was always twiddling.
He was always moving around.
He kept the class awake.

17. The same cannot be said of Dr. Axe.

18. Mannerisms may break the barriers.
Mannerisms may create the barriers.
The barriers are between students and teachers.
An instructor's teaching technique is also important.
This technique may mean the difference between ignorance and understanding.

19. Dr. Axe's technique was to dictate.
His technique was not to discuss.

20. Here is an example.
He taught the basic essay format.
This format includes an introduction.
This includes three body paragraphs.
This includes a conclusion.

21. This is the only way to write an essay.
He insisted on this.

22. He also insisted that we use correct grammar.
He did not enjoy teaching grammar.
He taught it in a perfunctory way.
He did not teach it very often.

23. He preferred to read his poetry.
He read his poetry to the class.
Sometimes he read chapters.
The chapters were from *Zen and the Art of Motorcycle Maintenance.*

24. Dr. Grind was altogether different.

25. Dr. Grind encouraged his students.
He encouraged them to experiment with their writing.
He enforced no strict limitations.
There were no limitations on the number of paragraphs.

26. He also insisted on correct grammar.
He enjoyed teaching it.
He drilled the class with grammar exercises.
He drilled the class three times a week.

27. Dr. Grind would ask students to label the parts of speech.
    The parts of speech were in a sentence.
    Then he would ask another student if she agreed or disagreed.
28. Sometimes this technique was embarrassing.
    It embarrassed both students.
    The technique was very effective.
    It taught English grammar effectively.
29. I respected both of these professors.
    I learned much from them.
    I had greater respect for Dr. Grind.
    I learned more from him.
30. Dr. Grind was encouraging.
    Dr. Grind was critical.
    Dr. Axe was aloof.
    Dr. Axe appeared indifferent.
    He was indifferent to his students' progress.
31. They had contrasting personalities.
    They had dissimilar teaching techniques.
    These reflected their different attitudes.
    Their attitudes were toward the students.
    Their attitudes were toward the subject.

Paragraphs and Essays

Football and Soccer

Although European football is the parent of American football, the two games show several major differences. European football, sometimes called association football or soccer, is played in eighty countries, making it the most widely played sport in the world. American football, on the other hand, is popular only in the United States and Canada. Soccer is played by eleven players with a round ball. Football, also played by eleven players in somewhat different positions on the field, is played with an elongated round ball. Soccer has little body contact between players, and therefore requires no special protective equipment. Football, in which players make maximum use of body contact to block a running ball carrier and his teammates, requires special headgear and padding. In soccer, the ball is advanced toward the goal by kicking it or by butting it with the head. In football, on the other hand, the ball is passed from hand to hand across the opponent's goal. These are just a few of the features that distinguish association and American football.

Watching Baseball, Playing Softball

TONY CAPPELLA

[1] We watch baseball: it is what we have always imagined life should be like. We play softball. It's sloppy. It's more the way life really is.

[2] I figured that out a long time ago, on a soft summer evening when I was thirteen years old and dying of embarrassment in center field as our opponents touched us for seventeen runs in the top half of the first inning. Now, beer in fist, gaping at a blank TV screen as I await the first major league game of the season, I am trying to define just what it is I'm waiting for.

[3] Baseball, we know, is precise, ceremonial. It is a world bounded by foul lines, marked by fixed positions. The playing field is neatly geometric, while the game itself is a linear equation of batters retired and runs batted in. It begins with a song no one can sing, and it ends with hoarse whispers of "Maybe next year." The purpose of baseball is exquisitely clear: to meet the ball head on, to round the bases, and to run home as often as possible, there to be greeted by friends who suddenly remember how much they have missed you.

[4] That's baseball. Now softball is quite different. For one thing we play wherever we can, usually on golden fields of dog crud and shattered glass, bounded by city streets and factory parking lots. We start by choosing sides, arguing over who's to be stuck with Arthur Magaffe, gimlet-eyed and gimpy, and what we are going to use for home plate. We play until we get too drunk or until the wives drag us home or until we lose the ball somewhere between a trash compactor and a hedge row. And whenever some complacent fool reminds us, "It's only a game, fellas," we come close to lopping his head off because, of course, we know it's only a game. Why else would we take it so seriously?

[5] We watch baseball. We imagine what it would be like to have the power of Reggie, Mickey, and Joltin' Joe. We play softball and we discover ourselves to be more like Larry, Curly, and Moe. In baseball men are Giants—and Pirates and Tigers and Braves. In softball, at best, we're cotter pins in Corky's Feed, Seed and Hardware. Or, more often, we're just beer-bellied slobs in Disneyworld tee-shirts and International Harvester caps. We might just as well be outfitted with party hats, rubber noses, and long baggy pants. And all the time we imagine grandstands shuddering with fans, all we've got is a runny-nosed wino chasing unicorns in the outfield, and Sammy's wife, brutalized by boredom, squatting on the hood of their Subaru, reading Harold Robbins and picking her teeth.

[6] But now, as I sit here glaring at the TV, I remember what it is we're all waiting for. That's why I get up, wheezing slightly, go to the closet and root out a stiff old glove signed by Hank Bauer. The laces are missing and all the padding has been squeezed out through a hole in the thumb. I follow my belly across a schoolyard diamond—jackets for bases, a frisbee for home plate—and I wander out to center field. In front of me a team of obsolete children in middle-age are shagging, groaning, slapping their haunches, hollering "Way to go! Way to go!" I crouch down with my hands on my knees and I wait. I wait for a lopsided ball to come skidding or spinning or bounding my way. And, as ever, I will spend the afternoon fumbling and bobbling and falling flat on my can.

[7] I play softball.

A Tale of Two Professors

WENSLEY HOBBY

[1] A professor's personality and teaching methods influence a student's perception of both the instructor and the subject he or she teaches. A student's success or failure in a course depends on how a professor acts as well as on what he or she knows. I have discovered this through observing two English professors, Dr. Axe and Dr. Grind.

[2] A professor's mannerisms can either help or hinder communication in the classroom, and they can show whether or not he is interested in the students or the subject. Consider the classroom behavior of Dr. Axe, my English 100 instructor. Unshaven, wearing a blue beach shirt, seersucker pants, and a pair of sandals with no socks, Dr. Axe would habitually trudge into the classroom late. After dragging himself to the center of the room and dropping his attaché case on the desk he would call the roll—never smiling, never saying good morning. He would collapse in his chair with a weary sigh and proceed to read an essay out loud to the class. Now and then, as if he were drifting off on a cloud to Venus, he would pause to gaze at the scuff-marked floor. Then he would continue reading, pausing every few minutes to entertain a reverie.

[3] In sharp contrast was Dr. Grind, my English 101 instructor, who would enter the classroom briskly, wearing a plaid sports coat, white dress shirt, neatly pressed slacks and Hush Puppy shoes. Upon reaching his podium he would quickly check his seating chart for absentees, and then smile as he greeted the class. Then he might read to the class, initiate a class discussion, give a pop quiz, discuss a writing assignment: the routine was so varied that we never knew what he would do next. Sometimes he would pace the floor while waiting for an answer

to a question; other times he would shake the hand of a student who had given him a correct answer. When looking at a book on the podium, Dr. Grind had a habit of shifting his spectacles up and down as he pondered what he would say next. Always fiddling, twiddling, moving around, Dr. Grind kept the class awake with his restless behavior. The same cannot be said of Dr. Axe.

[4] Just as mannerisms may either create or break barriers between students and teachers, so an instructor's teaching technique may mean the difference between ignorance and understanding. Dr. Axe's technique was to dictate, not discuss. For example, he insisted that the only way to write an essay is according to the basic format of an introduction, three body paragraphs, and a conclusion. And although he insisted that we use correct grammar, he did not teach it very often, and when he did it was in a perfunctory way because he did not enjoy teaching it. He preferred to read his poetry to the class; sometimes he read chapters from *Zen and the Art of Motorcycle Maintenance*.

[5] Dr. Grind was altogether different. He encouraged his students to experiment with their writing and enforced no strict limitations on the number of paragraphs. Though he also insisted on correct grammar, he enjoyed teaching it and drilled the class with grammar exercises three times a week. He would ask students to label the parts of speech in a sentence, and then he would ask another student if she agreed or disagreed with the answers. Sometimes this technique was embarrassing to both students, but it was a very effective way of teaching English grammar.

[6] Although I respected and learned much from both of these professors, I had greater respect for Dr. Grind and learned more from him. Dr. Grind was both encouraging and critical, while Dr. Axe was aloof and appeared indifferent to his students' progress. Their contrasting personalities and dissimilar teaching techniques reflected their different attitudes toward their students and their subject.

Writing Suggestions

To write an effective comparison and contrast, your subjects should be logically comparable, and your essay should have a clear purpose. Remember that the topics below are merely suggestions, not restrictions.

1. Two places you have visited.
2. A place you have visited at two different times.
3. Two stages of a person's life.
4. Two ball players.

5. Two teachers or professors.
6. Two family members.
7. Two neighborhoods.
8. Two close friends.
9. Your experiences before and after giving up a bad habit.
10. Two places where you have worked.
11. Two books or movies or plays.
12. Two automobiles.
13. Two bars or restaurants.
14. Two pets.
15. Two views of your parents: before and after you left home.

CHAPTER 16

Classification

Classifying is a way of analyzing a subject, either by arranging many items into a few groups or by dividing one item into parts. The aim of classification is to reach a clearer understanding of a subject by considering its parts individually and in relation to one another.

To be effective, a classification should have a clear purpose and be guided by a single principle. "Growing Up at the Victory Drive-In" (in Chapter 3) identifies three distinct stages in the writer's life. In this chapter, Larry McMurtry classifies "Houston Bars" according to the social class of their patrons; "The Plot Against People" by Russell Baker considers the various ways inanimate objects "resist" and "defeat" us, and "In the Locker Room," a student essay, classifies high school athletes according to their different methods of preparing for a ball game. As all of these essays demonstrate, classification can be a means of entertaining as well as informing the reader.

Classifying should not be confused with stereotyping. It is not a process of generalizing and oversimplifying, but an opportunity to examine a subject from a fresh perspective. Your work with the exercises in this chapter should make that clear.

Exercises

Houston Bars

LARRY MCMURTRY

1. One can choose a single aspect of Houston.
   One can characterize the city from that aspect.
   If one were forced to choose a single aspect, I think I would choose
      its bars.
   To be fully accurate, I would choose its bars and clubs.
2. The upper class inhabits the upper air.
   This is true for the most part.
3. Their clubs are very posh.
   They are posh in a somewhat River Okie way.
   They tend to be altitudinally remote.
4. There are tall buildings in town.
   There is a club on top of almost every one.
   The clubs provide elevation.
   The elevation is physical.
   The elevation is psychological.
5. There is a hunger for heights.
   The hunger can seize one in a city.
   The city is only forty-one feet above sea level.
   The clubs help relieve the hunger.
   The clubs also put their members well above the masses.
   The masses cannot afford such relief.
6. There are hundreds of middle-class clubs.
   These are generally one-story affairs.
   They are squat.
   They are converted restaurants.
   They have imitation Las Vegas furniture.
   They have deafening acoustics.
7. The Texas liquor laws are neolithic.
   The middle-class clubs provide a certain relief from these laws.
   The clubs are rather rigidly divided as to clientele.
   They are divided between "swinging couples" (their phrase) and
      uneasily-marrieds.
   The uneasily-marrieds have just noticed middle-age.
   Middle-age is crooking his finger at them.
8. The poor have beer-bars.

There are hundreds of beer-bars.
The beer-bars are seldom fancy.
They are reliably dim.
They are cool.

9. Most of them are equipped with jukeboxes.
Most of them are equipped with shuffleboards.
Most of them are equipped with jars of pig's feet.
Most of them are equipped with drunks.
The drunks are talkative.

10. There are lots of bar burlesques.
Girls gyrate from 3 P.M. on.
They gyrate at one's elbow.
They gyrate with varying degrees of grace.

11. There are open-air bars.
There are a fair number of them.
They are on the East side.
There are those who like to watch the traffic.
They can sit.
They can drink Pearl.
They can listen to the jukebox.

12. Louisiana is just down the road.
A lot of the men wear Cajun sideburns.
They leave their shirttails out.

13. Cowboys are common on the West side.

14. There are members of the cross-continental hitch-hiking set.
They congregate on Franklin Street.
They congregate at places like The Breaking Point Lounge.

15. Symbolic *latinos* slip over to the Last Concert.
This is on the North side.
They may be especially bold.
Then they go all the way to McCarty Street.
There is Mexican saloon-and-whorehouse architecture.
There is the most extraordinary example of this architecture north of the border.

The Plot Against People

RUSSELL BAKER

1. Inanimate objects are classified scientifically.
They are classified into categories.
There are three major categories.
There are inanimate objects that break down.

There are inanimate objects that get lost.
There are inanimate objects that don't work.

2. Inanimate objects resist man.
Ultimately they defeat man.
This is the goal of all inanimate objects.
Each object uses a method to achieve its purpose.
The three major classifications are based on that method.

3. Any object is capable of breaking down.
It breaks down at the moment when it is most needed.
If it can break down it will do so.
This is a general rule.

4. The automobile is typical of the category.

5. The automobile enters a filling station.
The station has a large staff of mechanics.
The mechanics are idle.
The automobile has the cunning peculiar to its breed.
It never breaks down while entering a filling station.

6. The automobile waits.
It reaches a downtown intersection.
This happens in the middle of the rush hour.
Or the automobile may be fully loaded with family and luggage.
The automobile may be on the Ohio Turnpike.

7. It creates maximum inconvenience.
It creates maximum frustration.
It creates maximum irritability.
It reduces its owner's lifespan.

8. There are washing machines and garbage disposals.
There are lawn mowers, furnaces, and TV sets.
There are tape recorders and slide projectors.
These all are in league with the automobile.
They take their turn at breaking down.
They do this whenever life threatens to move smoothly for their enemies.

9. Many inanimate objects, of course, find it extremely difficult to break down.

10. Pliers are an example.
Gloves and keys are examples.
They are almost totally incapable of breaking down.

11. They resist man.
They have had to evolve a different technique for doing this.

12. They get lost.

13. How do they do it?
Science has still not solved the mystery.
No man has ever caught any one of them in the act.

14. Have they developed a secret method of locomotion?
    Are they able to conceal this method from human eyes?
    This is the most plausible theory.
15. A pair of pliers may climb all the way from the cellar to the attic.
    This is not uncommon.
    The pair of pliers has a single-minded determination to raise its
      owner's blood pressure.
16. Keys may burrow three feet under mattresses.
    They have been known to do this.
17. Women's purses frequently travel through six or seven rooms.
    They do this to find hiding space under a couch.
    They do this despite their great weight.
18. Things that break down virtually never get lost.
    Things that get lost hardly ever break down.
    Scientists have been struck by this fact.
19. A furnace is an example.
    It will invariably break down at the depth of the first winter cold
      wave.
    It will never get lost.
20. Does this constitute evidence that inanimate objects are not entirely
      hostile to man?
    Some persons believe this.
21. They point something out.
    A furnace could infuriate a man even more thoroughly.
    Instead of breaking down it could get lost.
    A glove could upset him far more.
    Instead of getting lost it could break down.
22. Does this indicate a conciliatory attitude?
    Not everyone agrees.
23. Many say it merely proves something.
    Furnaces, gloves, and pliers are incredibly stupid.
24. There are objects that don't work.
    Here is the third class of objects.
    This class is the most curious of all.
25. These include such objects as barometers, car clocks, cigarette
      lighters, flashlights, and toy-train locomotives.
26. It is inaccurate, of course, to say that they *never* work.
27. They work once.
    They usually work for the first few hours after being brought home.
    Then they quit.
28. Thereafter, they never work again.
29. Are they built for the purpose of not working?
    That is widely assumed, in fact.
30. Some people have reached advanced ages.

They have never seen some of these objects in working order.
Barometers are an example of these objects.
31. Science is utterly baffled by the entire category.
32. There are many theories about it.
33. Here is the most interesting theory.
The things that don't work have attained the highest state possible
for an inanimate object.
Things that break down can only aspire to this state.
Things that get lost can only aspire to this state.
34. They have truly defeated man.
They have conditioned him.
He never expects anything of them.
35. His cigarette lighter won't light.
His flashlight fails to illuminate.
This does not raise his blood pressure.
36. Objects that don't work have given man peace.
This is the only peace he receives from inanimate society.

In the Locker Room

WENSLEY HOBBY

1. Man follows some ritual.
The ritual is in preparation for a physical contest.
Man has done this since the first Olympic games.
2. Football may not carry as much glamour as the Olympic games.
Football may not carry as much prestige as the Olympic games.
Football does require just as much preparation.
The preparation is by the players.
The preparation is before a game.
3. I participated in this ritual.
I participated during my own high school football days.
Players prepared themselves for a game in many ways.
I had the opportunity to observe these various ways.
4. There were four basic approaches.
These approaches were represented by four players.
These players were rather remarkable.
5. There are calm, humorous types.
These types are special.
They do not think about the danger.
The danger awaits them.
The danger is on the field.
6. Keith Mack was the son of a farmer.
He was an excellent example of this type.

313

7. He would stroll into the locker room.
   He chewed tobacco.
   He spit the juice into his cup.
   It was a paper cup.
   It was a Garfield cup.
8. He had a chat with the assistant coach.
   The chat was brief.
   The chat was about a prospective coon hunt.
   He would then wander over to his locker.
   He would tell jokes to his teammates.
   He put on his equipment.
9. Keith would then saunter out of the locker room.
   He was still chewing his tobacco.
   He would chew until the game started.
10. Later he would be aggressive.
    He would be aggressive during the game.
    He was as aggressive as a tomcat.
11. We were still laughing at Keith's wisecracks.
    Wendall Holmes would arrive.
    Wendall would mumble to himself.
    Wendall would never speak to us.
12. He would proceed to his small shower cubicle.
    He went there solemnly.
    He would turn on his tape player.
    He listened to Richard Pryor.
    Richard Pryor talked about sexual morality.
13. Wendall only listened.
    He never laughed.
14. The tape player stopped.
    Wendall was ready then.
    We always knew that.
    He was ready to "crush some bones."
15. Timmy Lundell took the preparation session seriously.
    He was just as serious as Wendall.
    He had his own ritual.
16. He was an avid follower of Zen.
    He followed the art of meditation.
17. Timmy would open the door of the locker room.
    Often he was angry.
    He would retire to his shower cubicle.
18. He would sit down in the stall.
    He would reach into his blue backpack.
    He would take out a red can of incense.

He placed the can in front of him.
He lit it.

19. Timmy possessed a varied collection of incense cans.
The cans came in different colors.
He had them for each day of practice.
He usually saved the red cans.
He used the red cans before a game.

20. Then he would close his eyes.
He hummed some Indian words.
We did not understand the words.

21. He did that for about fifteen minutes.
Then he would extinguish the incense.
He would walk out of the locker room.
He was relaxed.
He was at peace with himself.

22. Charles Brown, on the other hand, never relaxed.

23. He was our first-string center.
He would get high-strung before a game.
We would have to leave him alone.

24. Charles was mean before a game.
He once kicked a stray cat.
He kicked it onto the hood of a car.

25. Charles would storm into the locker room.
He acted as if he were furious about everything.
He was furious with his teammates.
He was furious with his coaches.
He was furious with the color of the sky.

26. He put on his equipment.
He would walk outside to the blocking machine.
He would start hitting the machine.
He hit it with his shoulder pads.
He hit it until his nervousness subsided.

27. Charles would then run out to the field.
He was calm.
He was ready to kill.

28. These are examples of football players.
These are their methods of preparing for a game.
I remember these four examples fondly.

29. Our world is crazy.
People are tormented by the stress of their jobs.
They tend to let this happen.
Financial worries torment them also.

30. Perhaps people could adapt these methods of preparation.

They could use these methods in their everyday lives.
The methods could help them cope with the world around them.
That world is much tougher than any football game.

Paragraphs and Essays

Houston Bars

LARRY MCMURTRY

[1] If one were forced to choose a single aspect of Houston and from that aspect . . . characterize the city I think I would choose its bars, or, to be more fully accurate, its bars and clubs. The upper class, for the most part, inhabits the upper air. Their clubs are very posh, if in a somewhat River Okie way, and tend to be altitudinally remote. There is a club on top of almost every tall building in town; the elevation they provide is both physical and psychological. They help relieve the hunger for heights that can seize one in a city only forty-one feet above sea level; and they also put their members well above the masses who cannot afford such relief.

[2] The hundreds of middle-class clubs are generally squat one-story affairs, converted restaurants with imitation Las Vegas furniture and deafening acoustics. They provide a certain relief from the neolithic Texas liquor laws and are rather rigidly divided as to clientele between "swinging singles" (their phrase) and uneasily-marrieds who have just noticed middle-age crooking his finger at them.

[3] The poor have beer-bars, hundreds of them, seldom fancy but reliably dim and cool. Most of them are equipped with jukeboxes, shuffleboards, jars of pig's feet and talkative drunks. There are lots of bar burlesques, where from 3 P.M. on girls gyrate at one's elbow with varying degrees of grace. On the East side there are a fair number of open-air bars—those who like to watch the traffic can sit, drink Pearl, observe the wrecks, and listen to . . . the jukebox. Louisiana is just down the road, and a lot of the men wear Cajun sideburns and leave their shirttails out. On the West side cowboys are common. Members of the cross-continental hitch-hiking set congregate on Franklin Street, at places like The Breaking Point Lounge. Symbolic *latinos* slip over to the Last Concert, on the North side; or, if they are especially bold, go all the way to McCarty Street, where one can view the most extraordinary example of Mexican saloon-and-whorehouse architecture north of the border.

316

The Plot Against People

RUSSELL BAKER

[1] Inanimate objects are classified scientifically into three major categories—those that break down, those that get lost, and those that don't work.

[2] The goal of all inanimate objects is to resist man and ultimately to defeat him, and the three major classifications are based on the method each object uses to achieve its purpose. As a general rule, any object capable of breaking down at the moment when it is most needed will do so. The automobile is typical of the category.

[3] With the cunning peculiar to its breed, the automobile never breaks down while entering a filling station which has a large staff of idle mechanics. It waits until it reaches a downtown intersection in the middle of the rush hour, or until it is fully loaded with family and luggage on the Ohio Turnpike. Thus it creates maximum inconvenience, frustration, and irritability, thereby reducing its owner's lifespan.

[4] Washing machines, garbage disposals, lawn mowers, furnaces, TV sets, tape recorders, slide projectors—all are in league with the automobile to take their turn at breaking down whenever life threatens to flow smoothly for their enemies.

[5] Many inanimate objects, of course, find it extremely difficult to break down. Pliers, for example, and gloves and keys are almost totally incapable of breaking down. Therefore, they have had to evolve a different technique for resisting man.

[6] They get lost. Science has still not solved the mystery of how they do it, and no man has ever caught one of them in the act. The most plausible theory is that they have developed a secret method of locomotion which they are able to conceal from human eyes.

[7] It is not uncommon for a pair of pliers to climb all the way from the cellar to the attic in its single-minded determination to raise its owner's blood pressure. Keys have been known to burrow three feet under mattresses. Women's purses, despite their great weight, frequently travel through six or seven rooms to find hiding space under a couch.

[8] Scientists have been struck by the fact that things that break down virtually never get lost, while things that get lost hardly ever break down. A furnace, for example, will invariably break down at the depth of the first winter cold wave, but it will never get lost. A woman's purse hardly ever breaks down; it almost invariably chooses to get lost.

[9] Some persons believe this constitutes evidence that inanimate objects are not entirely hostile to man. After all, they point out, a furnace could infuriate a man even more thoroughly by getting lost than by

317

breaking down, just as a glove could upset him far more by breaking down than by getting lost.

[10] Not everyone agrees, however, that this indicates a conciliatory attitude. Many say it merely proves that furnaces, gloves, and pliers are incredibly stupid.

[11] The third class of objects—those that don't work—is the most curious of all. These include such objects as barometers, car clocks, cigarette lighters, flashlights and toy-train locomotives. It is inaccurate, of course, to say that they *never* work. They work once, usually for the first few hours after being brought home, and then quit. Thereafter, they never work again.

[12] In fact, it is widely assumed that they are built for the purpose of not working. Some people have reached advanced ages without ever seeing some of these objects—barometers, for example—in working order.

[13] Science is utterly baffled by the entire category. There are many theories about it. The most interesting holds that the things that don't work have attained the highest state possible for an inanimate object, the state to which things that break down and things that get lost can still only aspire.

[14] They have truly defeated man by conditioning him never to expect anything of them. When his cigarette lighter won't light or his flashlight fails to illuminate, it does not raise his blood pressure. Objects that don't work have given man the only peace he receives from inanimate society.

In the Locker Room

WENSLEY HOBBY

[1] Since the first Olympic games man has followed some ritual in preparation for a physical contest. Although football may not carry as much glamour or prestige as the Olympic games, it does require just as much preparation by the players before a game. I participated in this ritual during my own high school football days and had the opportunity to observe the various ways players prepared themselves for a game. The four basic approaches were represented by four rather remarkable players.

[2] The calm, humorous types are special because they seem not to think about the danger that awaits them on the field. Keith Mack, a farmer's son, was an excellent example of this type. He would stroll into the locker room chewing tobacco and spitting the juice into his Garfield paper cup. After a brief chat with the assistant coach about a

prospective coon hunt, he would wander over to his locker and tell jokes to his teammates as he put on his equipment. Keith would then saunter out of the locker room, chewing his tobacco until the very moment the game started. During the game itself, however, he would be as aggressive as a tomcat.

[3] While we were still laughing at Keith's wisecracks, Wendall Holmes would arrive, mumbling to himself and never speaking to us. He would then proceed solemnly to his small shower cubicle, turn on his tape player and listen to Richard Pryor talk about sexual morality. Wendall only listened; he never laughed. When the tape player stopped we knew that Wendall was ready to "crush some bones."

[4] Timmy Lundell took the preparation session just as seriously as Wendall, but he had his own ritual. Tim was an avid follower of Zen and the art of meditation. After angrily opening the door of the locker room and retiring to his shower cubicle, he would sit down, reach into his blue backpack for a red can of incense, place the can in front of him, and light it. Timmy possessed a collection of variously colored incense cans, one for each day of practice; he usually saved the red cans for preparation before a game. After lighting the incense he would close his eyes and hum some Indian words that none of us understood. He did that for about fifteen minutes, and then he would extinguish the incense and walk out of the locker room, relaxed, at peace with himself.

[5] Charles Brown, on the other hand, never relaxed. Our first-string center, Charles would get so high-strung before a game that we had to leave him alone. He was so mean that he once kicked a stray cat onto the hood of a car. Charles would storm into the locker room as if he were furious about everything—his teammates, the coaches, the color of the sky. After putting on his equipment he would walk outside to the blocking machine and start hitting it with his shoulder pads until his nervousness subsided. Then, calm, ready to kill, Charles would run out to the field.

[6] I remember fondly these football players and their methods of preparing for a game. In our crazy world, people have a tendency to let financial worries and the stress of their jobs torment them. Perhaps people could adapt these methods of preparation for use in their everyday lives to help them cope with the world around them—a world much tougher than any football game.

Writing Suggestions

Many subjects can be explored through classification. The suggestions below may help you choose a topic that particularly interests you.

1. Advertisements.
2. On-campus jobs for students.
3. Reasons for attending college.
4. Styles of eating in the cafeteria.
5. Drug users.
6. Baseball pitchers or football quarterbacks.
7. Visitors to an art museum.
8. Smokers.
9. College students or instructors.
10. Drinkers.
11. Cheaters.
12. Television comedies.
13. Smiles.
14. Dogs.
15. Roommates.

CHAPTER 17

Definition

We rely on definitions in our writing to identify the essential characteristics or various meanings of abstract words or concepts. Although a simple definition may be expressed in just a few words, an extended definition can serve as the subject of an entire essay. In either case, the aim of definition is to clarify the meaning of a word or concept that our readers might otherwise misunderstand or not fully comprehend.

Any one or more of the organizing techniques discussed so far may be used to develop and shape a definition: there is no set format to be followed. A writer may simply enumerate some of the unique characteristics of his or her subject, as Alexander Theroux does in "How Curious the Camel" (in Chapter 5), or provide descriptive details, as in the definition of "Loneliness" (in Chapter 7). In this chapter, "Appetite" is defined with examples, and "Wanted: One Good Teacher" (a student essay) uses contrast to distinguish a good teacher from a bad one. Finally, Gustave Simons combines classification and process analysis to define a "heavy drinker" in the essay "The Mad Dog's Hair: Alcoholism." As the titles of these essays suggest, definitions may give us new insights into familiar terms as well as clarify less familiar words and concepts.

The exercises in this chapter will show you the value of definition and review some familiar sentence and paragraph structures.

Exercises

*Appetite**

LAURIE LEE

1. Appetite is one of the major pleasures in life.
   We should preserve appetite.
   That should be one of our major duties.
2. Appetite is the keenness of living.
   It is one of the senses.
   It tells you that you are still curious to exist.
   You still have an edge on your longings.
   You want to bite into the world.
   You want to taste its flavors and juices.
   Its flavors and juices are multitudinous.
3. By appetite, of course, I don't mean just the lust for food.
   I mean any condition of unsatisfied desire.
   I mean any burning in the blood.
   This burning proves you want more than you've got.
   You haven't yet used up your life.
4. Wilde said something.
   He felt sorry for certain people.
   They never got their heart's desire.
   He felt sorrier still for those who did.
5. I got mine once only.
   It nearly killed me.
   Since then I've always preferred wanting to having.
6. To me, appetite is this state of wanting.
   This state keeps one's expectations alive.
7. I learned this lesson long ago.
   I learned this lesson as a child.
   I remember it.
   Treats and orgies were few.
   The greatest pitch of happiness was not in actually eating a toffee.
   The greatest pitch of happiness was in gazing at it beforehand.
   I discovered this.
8. The first bite was delicious.
   This was true.
   Once the toffee was gone one was left with nothing.

---

* This exercise has been adapted from the first four paragraphs of Lee's essay in the Paragraphs and Essays section of this chapter.

There was no toffee.

There was no lust.

9. Besides, the whole toffeeness of toffees was imperceptibly diminished.

The gross act of having eaten it diminished the toffeeness.

10. No, the best was in wanting it.

The best was in sitting and looking at it.

Then one tasted a treasure-house of flavors.

The treasure-house was inexhaustible.

11. There is the wanting.

That remains one of the keenest pleasures of appetite for me.

The pleasure is not the satisfaction.

12. This is true in wanting a peach.

This is true in wanting a whisky.

This is true in wanting a particular texture or sound.

This is true in wanting to be with a particular friend.

13. The object of desire is always at its most flawlessly perfect.

It is most perfect in this condition.

I know that.

14. Which is why I would carry the preservation of appetite to the extent of deliberate fasting.

The appetite is too good to lose.

It is too precious to be bludgeoned into insensibility.

Satiation bludgeons it.

Over-doing it bludgeons it.

Wanted: One Good Teacher

ELLISON MINGLEDORF

There are no sets in this exercise. You need to group the sentences logically before combining them.

1. I judge teachers by their ability to motivate their students.
2. I judge teachers by their ability to interest their students.
3. A teacher may be knowledgeable.
4. But she must be able to transmit her fascination with a subject.
5. She must transmit this fascination to others.
6. Otherwise, the class will be just another required course.
7. This course must be plowed through.
8. I also value a sense of humor.
9. I value a willingness to admit to errors.
10. Such qualities distinguish the good teacher from another sort of teacher.

11. This other sort is all too typical.
12. This other sort is the pick-up-the-paycheck-and-run teacher.
13. All subjects are potentially interesting.
14. I believe this.
15. The teacher must kindle that interest.
16. I sympathize with "teacher burnout."
17. Teachers have to deal with pressures.
18. I sympathize with that too.
19. But a teacher may be too tired to inspire her students.
20. She may be too bored to inspire her students.
21. Then she isn't kindling anything.
22. She is only kindling resentment in her students.
23. Fortunately, I have had a few good teachers.
24. They were excited about their subject.
25. I had considered the subject (for example, history) to be dull.
26. I became interested enough to do some extra research on the subject.
27. A sense of humor is another characteristic of the good teacher.
28. The teacher doesn't have to be a clown.
29. The teacher doesn't have to be a cheap entertainer.
30. In fact, the teacher shouldn't be these things.
31. She should be able to see the lighter elements of a subject.
32. She should be able to point out these elements.
33. Similarly, a teacher should have a good attitude toward her students.
34. This should be a tolerant attitude.
35. The tolerance should be mixed with a keen sense of the ridiculous.
36. People can be very strange at times.
37. A teacher may take the peculiarities of people too seriously.
38. Then she cannot maintain a good attitude while working with people.
39. Some teachers remain remote and aloof from their students.
40. I cannot tolerate such teachers.
41. Every teacher was once an ignorant student.
42. Some teachers seem to have forgotten this.
43. A teacher may adopt an air of superiority.
44. A teacher may be unwilling to admit to error.
45. Insecurity makes a teacher do this.
46. Some teachers encourage their students to communicate with them.
47. Some teachers encourage their students to work with them.
48. I have benefited the most from these teachers.
49. One type of teacher can recognize her students' difficulties.
50. This type of teacher can offer assistance.
51. She assists students who are willing to work.
52. This type of teacher is a good teacher.
53. A teacher's job is very demanding.

54. I recognize this.
55. Teachers should periodically take time off.
56. They should do this in order to appreciate the benefits of a teaching job.
57. What are the chief characteristics of a good teacher?
58. Enthusiasm for her subject is one characteristic.
59. Empathy with her students is another characteristic.
60. However, good teachers can turn bad.
61. They must be given enough time for rest and relaxation.

The Mad Dog's Hair: Alcoholism

GUSTAVE SIMONS

1. Drinkers can be classified under three categories.
   There are moderate drinkers.
   Moderate drinkers take two cocktails before dinner.
   There are heavy drinkers.
   Heavy drinkers take two or three cocktails before lunch.
   Heavy drinkers take two more cocktails before going home.
   Heavy drinkers take another two at home before dinner.
   There are alcoholics.
   Their intake may begin with a shot or two of bourbon.
   The shot goes in their morning coffee.
   This continues through the morning.
   This continues through lunch.
   This continues through the afternoon.
   This continues through the evening.
   They fall into bed.
   They have no recollection whatever the next morning.
   They do not know where they have been.
   They do not know what they have done.
   They do not remember the day before.
2. These are the problems.
   These are the dangerous ones.
   These are alcoholics.
   They are a constant danger.
   They are a danger to themselves.
   They are a danger to their families.
   They are a danger to their business associates.
   They are possibly a danger to the community where they live.
3. Is this quantitative definition of an alcoholic too limited?
   Is it too rigid?
   That has been argued.

4. I agree.
   This is the case.
   The definition should be wider.
   The definition should be less simplistic.
5. Perhaps this might be a better definition.
   An alcoholic is a person.
   By reason of his drinking he functions significantly less adequately
      than would otherwise be the case.
   He functions this way at home.
   He functions this way at the office.
6. There is a quantitative definition.
   There is a qualitative definition.
   Use a combination of the definitions.
   This might be the best solution.
7. We may be limited to one definition.
   We may be limited to the other.
   There are enough cases where alcohol is indisputably present.
   There are enough cases to merit our attention.
8. Can a moderate drinker develop into a heavy drinker?
9. Frequently.
   Not necessarily.
   Pressure in a job can cause the conversion.
   Tension at home can cause the conversion.
   Worry over finances can cause the conversion.
10. One can raise the day's quota.
    One can raise it from two drinks to five or seven or more.
    This is not too difficult.
11. Most heavy drinkers have no temptation to drink before
       lunch.
    These are heavy drinkers I have known.
    They have told me this.
    They get home.
    Only then do they let down the bars.
12. "Of course I drink only Scotch and water."
13. There are men who drink this amount daily.
    They show no loss of ability in their work.
    They appear at their office on time.
    Their desks are clear at the end of the day.
14. Some of them are walking along the edge of a precipice.
    This is not necessarily a majority.
    This is a fair percentage.
15. There will be an unusually heavy evening.
    Then there will be that first early morning.

326

What lies ahead through the day?
That thought is quite impossible to face.

16. A bracer will be tough to take (swallow it with a shudder!).
    It is down.
    Life takes on a more cheerful aspect.

17. Take one more.
    Do this before the lady of the house comes down.
    She will come to drink coffee.
    She will come to eat breakfast.

18. She has noticed nothing.
    The new cure works wonderfully.

19. Everything goes well at the office.
    (What was I worried about this morning?)
    Everything goes well until about eleven.

20. At eleven there is a little let-down.

21. The bistro opens at exactly eleven.
    It is around the corner from the office building.
    Why shouldn't a shot restore the circulation?
    There is no reason.
    The shot is quick.
    The shot is short.

22. Other executives are there.
    They seem to require the same restorative.
    They are sprinkled among taxi drivers.
    There are a couple of policemen.
    It is surprising how many other executives are there.

23. Then lunch.

24. The afternoon seems to drag.
    Once home, be more tired than usual.
    Have two stiff jolts before dinner.
    Have three more before bed.
    The jolts mark the end of an unexpectedly pleasant day.

25. The heavy drinker shifts into alcoholism here.
    He shifts quietly.
    He shifts relentlessly.

26. Before he swallowed his before-breakfast shots with distaste.
    Now he looks forward to them.
    He looks with pleasure.
    He looks with anticipation.

27. But now they have become necessary.

28. He sometimes exhibits odd exhilaration.
    He does this when he says goodbye.
    His wife may wonder at this.

She is used to Harry's moods.
After all, he is a splendid provider.
She may be worried about those five drinks in a single evening.
She knows better than to protest.

29. Harry has become the silent alcoholic.
Harry has become the secret alcoholic.

30. How many drinks does he put away in the course of a day?
No one knows.
He himself does not know.

31. He may go undetected for years.
He conceals his deterioration from his employer.
He conceals his deterioration from his family.
But eventually there will be unmistakable signs.
He is not the man he once was.
His looks will show the signs.
Probably his health will show signs.
His relations with his wife will show signs.
His handling of some important matter in his office will show signs.

Paragraphs and Essays

Appetite

LAURIE LEE

[1] One of the major pleasures in life is appetite, and one of our major duties should be to preserve it. Appetite is the keenness of living; it is one of the senses that tells you that you are still curious to exist, that you still have an edge on your longings and want to bite into the world and taste its multitudinous flavors and juices.

[2] By appetite, of course, I don't mean just the lust for food, but any condition of unsatisfied desire, any burning in the blood that proves you want more than you've got, and that you haven't yet used up your life. Wilde said he felt sorry for those who never got their heart's desire, but sorrier still for those who did. I got mine once only, and it nearly killed me, and I've always preferred wanting to having since.

[3] For appetite, to me, is this state of wanting, which keeps one's expectations alive. I remember learning this lesson long ago as a child, when treats and orgies were few, and when I discovered that the greatest pitch of happiness was not in actually eating a toffee but in gazing at it beforehand. True, the first bite was delicious, but once the toffee was gone one was left with nothing, neither toffee nor lust. Besides, the

whole toffeeness of toffees was imperceptibly diminished by the gross act of having eaten it. No, the best was in wanting it, in sitting and looking at it, when one tasted an inexhaustible treasure-house of flavors.

[4] So, for me, one of the keenest pleasures of appetite remains in the wanting, not the satisfaction. In wanting a peach, or a whisky, or a particular texture or sound, or to be with a particular friend. For in this condition, of course, I know that the object of desire is always at its most flawlessly perfect. Which is why I would carry the preservation of appetite to the extent of deliberate fasting, simply because I think that appetite is too good to lose, too precious to be bludgeoned into insensibility by satiation and over-doing it.

[5] For that matter, I don't really want three square meals a day— I want one huge, delicious, orgiastic, table-groaning blowout, say every four days, and then not be too sure where the next one is coming from. A day of fasting is not for me just a puritanical device for denying oneself a pleasure, but rather a way of anticipating a rarer moment of supreme indulgence.

[6] Fasting is an act of homage to the majesty of appetite. So I think we should arrange to give up our pleasures regularly—our food, our friends, our lovers—in order to preserve their intensity, and the moment of coming back to them. For this is the moment that renews and refreshes both oneself and the thing one loves. Sailors and travellers enjoyed this once, and so did hunters, I suppose. Part of the weariness of modern life may be that we live too much on top of each other, and are entertained and fed too regularly. Once we were separated by hunger both from our food and families, and then we learned to value both. The men went off hunting, and the dogs went with them; the women and children waved goodbye. The cave was empty of men for days on end; nobody ate, or knew what to do. The women crouched by the fire, the wet smoke in their eyes; the children wailed; everybody was hungry. Then one night there were shouts and the barking of dogs from the hills, and the men came back loaded with meat. This was the great reunion, and everybody gorged themselves silly, and appetite came into its own; the long-awaited meal became a feast to remember and an almost sacred celebration of life. Now we go off to the office and come home in the evenings to cheap chicken and frozen peas. Very nice, but too much of it, too easy and regular, served up without effort or wanting. We eat, we are lucky, our faces are shining with fat, but we don't know the pleasure of being hungry any more.

[7] Too much of anything—too much music, entertainment, happy snacks, or time spent with one's friends—creates a kind of impotence of living by which one can no longer hear, or taste, or see, or love, or remember. Life is short and precious, and appetite is one of its guardians, and loss of appetite is a sort of death. So if we are to enjoy this short

329

life we should respect the divinity of appetite, and keep it eager and not too much blunted.

[8] It is a long time now since I knew that acute moment of bliss that comes from putting parched lips to a cup of cold water. The springs are still there to be enjoyed—all one needs is the original thirst.

Wanted: One Good Teacher

ELLISON MINGLEDORF

[1] I judge teachers by their ability to motivate and interest their students. No matter how knowledgeable a teacher is, if she can't transmit her fascination with that subject to others, the class will be just another required course to plow through. I also value a sense of humor and a willingness to admit to errors. Such qualities distinguish the good teacher from the all too typical pick-up-the-paycheck-and-run teacher.

[2] I believe that all subjects are potentially interesting, but it is the teacher who must kindle that interest. I sympathize with "teacher burn-out" and the pressures teachers have to deal with, but if a teacher is either too tired or too bored to inspire her students, then she isn't kindling anything but resentment in her students. Fortunately, I have had a few teachers who were so excited about what I had considered to be a dull subject (for example, history), that I became interested enough to do some extra research on the subject.

[3] A sense of humor is another characteristic of the good teacher. The teacher doesn't have to be (in fact, shouldn't be) a clown or a cheap entertainer, but she should be able to see and point out the lighter elements of a subject. Similarly, a teacher should have a good attitude toward her students, an attitude of tolerance mixed with a keen sense of the ridiculous. People can be very strange at times, and a teacher cannot maintain a good attitude while working with people if she takes their peculiarities too seriously.

[4] I cannot tolerate a teacher who remains remote and aloof from her students. Every teacher was once an ignorant student, but some teachers seem to have forgotten this. It is insecurity that makes a teacher adopt an air of superiority and be unwilling to admit to error. I have benefited the most from teachers who encouraged their students to communicate with them and work with them. A good teacher is one who can recognize her students' difficulties and offer assistance to those students who are willing to work.

[5] I recognize that a teacher's job is very demanding. I feel that teachers should periodically take time off to refresh themselves and even work at other jobs in order to appreciate the benefits of a teaching job.

A teacher's enthusiasm for her subject and empathy with her students are the chief characteristics of a good teacher. However, good teachers can turn bad if not given enough time for rest and relaxation.

The Mad Dog's Hair: Alcoholism

GUSTAVE SIMONS

[1] There are three categories under which drinkers can be classified: moderate drinkers, who take two cocktails before dinner; heavy drinkers, who take two or three cocktails before lunch, two more cocktails before going home, and another two at home before dinner; and alcoholics, whose intake may begin with a shot or two of bourbon in their morning coffee and continue through the morning, lunch, the afternoon, and evening until they fall into bed with no recollection whatever the next morning as to where they have been or to what they have done during the day before. These are the problems, the dangerous ones; these are the alcoholics, a constant danger not only to themselves, but to their families, their business associates, and possibly to the community where they live.

[2] It has been argued that this quantitative definition of an alcoholic is too rigid and limited. I agree that this is the case and that the definition should be wider and less simplistic. Perhaps a better definition might be one in which an alcoholic is defined as a person who, by reason of drinking, functions at home, and even more in his office, significantly less adequately than would otherwise be the case. However, this definition can also be criticized as too broad and too vague in many situations. Perhaps the best solution is to use a combination of the quantitative and qualitative definitions. However, even if we are limited to one or the other, there are enough cases where alcoholism is indisputably present to merit our attention.

[3] Can a moderate drinker develop into a heavy drinker? Frequently, but not necessarily; pressure in a new job, tension at home, worry over finances, all can cause the conversion. It is not too difficult to raise the day's quota from two drinks to five or seven or more. Most heavy drinkers I have known have told me they have no temptation to drink before lunch, and it is only when they get home that they let down the bars. "Of course I drink only Scotch and water." Most men who drink this amount daily show no loss of ability in their work; they appear at their office on time and their desks are clear at the end of the day.

[4] But some of them, not necessarily a majority but a fair percentage, are walking along the edge of a precipice. There will be that first early morning, after an unusually heavy evening, when the thought

of what lies ahead through the day is quite impossible to face. A bracer will be tough to take (swallow it with a shudder!), but once it is down, life takes on a more cheerful aspect. One more, before the lady of the household comes down to drink coffee and have breakfast. She has noticed nothing, and the new cure works wonderfully. At the office, everything goes well (what was I worried about this morning?) until about eleven. At eleven there is a little let-down. There is a bistro around the corner from the office building that opens at exactly eleven, and there is no reason why a quick, short shot should not restore the circulation. It is surprising how many other executives, sprinkled among taxi drivers and a couple of policemen, seem to be requiring the same restorative. Then lunch. The afternoon seems to drag, but once home, more tired than usual, two stiff jolts before dinner and three more before bed mark the end of an unexpectedly pleasant day.

[5] This is where the heavy drinker shifts quietly and relentlessly into alcoholism. Where before he swallowed his before-breakfast shots with distaste, he now looks forward to them with pleasure and anticipation. But now they have become necessary. His wife may wonder at the odd exhilaration he sometimes exhibits when he says goodbye, but she is used to Harry's moods (after all, he is a splendid provider), and if she is worried by those five drinks in a single evening, she knows better than to protest.

[6] Harry has become the silent, secret alcoholic. No one knows, he himself does not know, how many drinks he puts away in the course of a day. He may go undetected for years, concealing his deterioration from his employer and his family, but eventually his looks (and probably his health), his relations with his wife, his handling of some important matter in the office, will begin to show unmistakable signs that he is not the man he was.

Writing Suggestions

Abstract and controversial terms can be clarified through extended definitions. The concepts listed below have interested many writers representing divergent points of view. See if you can add to the list.

1. Maturity.
2. Responsibility.
3. A sense of humor.
4. Freedom.
5. Integrity.
6. Cheating.

7. Sportsmanship.
8. Guilt.
9. Sophistication.
10. Friendship.
11. Success.
12. Courage.
13. Dedication.
14. Pornography.
15. Sexism.
16. Racism.
17. A happy marriage.
18. A good parent.
19. A good leader.
20. Peace of mind.

CHAPTER 18

Cause and Effect

Whenever we ask the question "Why?" about a subject, we begin to explore its causes. When we ask "So what?" we consider the effects. Cause-and-effect writing involves drawing connections between events or conditions or actions so as to achieve a clearer understanding of the subject.

Whether we choose to focus on causes (the reasons for something) or on effects (the consequences of something) depends on our subject and our purpose for writing. In practice, however, the relation of cause to effect is often so close that one cannot be considered independently of the other. In this chapter, John Holt's "How Teachers Make Children Hate Reading" proceeds logically from one paragraph on causes to another on effects. Both "Out of Work" and "Ear Quirk" (a student essay) are developed along a chain of cause-and-effect relationships, in which one effect produces another.

As you work out the exercises in this chapter, keep in mind that clear connections between ideas should be represented by clear connections between sentences and paragraphs.

Exercises

How Teachers Make Children Hate Reading

JOHN HOLT

1. We make books and reading a constant source of failure.
   They are a constant source of public humiliation.
   We do this from the very beginning of school.
2. We make little children read aloud.
   They read before the teacher.
   They read before other children.
   They read so that we can be sure of something.
   They must "know" all the words they are reading.
3. Here is what this means.
   They may not know a word.
   Then they are going to make a mistake.
   They make it right in front of everyone.
4. They have done something wrong.
   They are made to realize this instantly.
5. Perhaps some of the other children will begin to wave their hands.
   The children will say, "Ooooh! O-o-o-oh!"
6. Perhaps they will just giggle.
   Perhaps they will nudge each other.
   Perhaps they will make a face.
7. "Are you sure?"
   Perhaps the teacher will say that.
   Perhaps the teacher will ask someone else what he thinks.
8. Perhaps the teacher is kindly.
   She will smile.
   The smile is sweet.
   The smile is sad.
   This is often one of the most painful punishments.
   A child suffers these punishments in school.
9. In any case, the child has made the mistake.
   He knows he has made it.
   The child feels foolish.
   The child feels stupid.
   The child feels ashamed.
   Any of us would feel the same way in his shoes.
10. Children associate books with mistakes.
    Children associate reading with mistakes.

Children do this before very long.
The mistakes may be real.
The mistakes may be feared.
They associate books and reading with penalties.
They associate books and reading with humiliation.

11. This may not be sensible.
    It is natural.

12. A cat sat on a hot stove.
    It would never sit on a hot one again after this.
    It would never sit on a cold one either.
    Mark Twain once said that.

13. As true of children as of cats.

14. Leave all books alone.
    That is the safest thing to do.
    Children are likely to decide that.
    They will decide that if they, so to speak, sit on a hot book a few times.
    They will decide that if books cause them humiliation.
    They will decide that if books cause them pain.

Out of Work*

JAN HALVORSEN

1. The loss of a job is rejection.
   It results in hurt feelings.
   It is as if a friend had told you to "bug off."

2. Only this "friend" filled up 40 to 60 (or more) hours of your week.

3. There are constant references to the staff as "family."
   These references only accentuate the feeling of desertion.
   These references only accentuate the feeling of deception.

4. Here is how you picture yourself.
   You are going home to your parents or spouse.
   You are informed of something.
   "Your services as our daughter/my wife are no longer required.
   Pick up your baby pictures as you leave."

5. Each new affirmation of unemployment renews the pain.
   There is the first trip to the unemployment office.
   There is the first interview.
   There is the first trip to the unemployment office.
   This is the most dreaded of all.

* This exercise has been adapted from paragraphs 6 through 11 of Halvorsen's essay in the Paragraphs and Essays section of this chapter.

6. You stand in line at the unemployment office.
   You feel very much the same as you did the first time you ever
   flunked a class or a test.
   You feel as if you had a big red "F" printed across your forehead.
   The "F" is for "Failure."
7. I stand at the end of the line.
   This is how I fantasize myself.
   I am in a blue suit.
   The suit is crisp.
   The suit is efficient.
   My chin is up.
   I am neat.
   I am straight.
   I am like a corporate executive.
8. I move down the line.
   I start to come unglued.
   I finally reach the desk.
   This is half an hour later.
   I am slouching.
   I am sallow.
   I am in torn jeans.
   I am wearing tennis shoes.
   I am wearing a jacket from the Salvation Army.
   I carry my worldly belongings in a shopping bag.
   I am unable to speak.
9. You do eventually become accustomed to being unemployed.
   You might accept a bad limp in the same way.
10. You gradually quit beating yourself.
    You were beating yourself for not having been somehow indispen-
    sable.
    Or you were beating yourself for not having become an accountant.
11. You tire of straining your memory for possible infractions.
12. You recover some of your confidence.
    Your confidence always told you how good you were at your job.
    You accept what the supervisor said: "This doesn't reflect on your
    job performance; sales are down 30 per cent this month."
13. You recover that self-esteem.
    That self-esteem is hallowed.
    Each time you do you renew a fight to maintain it.
14. You go to a job interview.
    You give them your best.
    They hire someone else.
    Then you go another round with yourself.
    You go another round with your self-esteem.

15. Your unemployment seems to drag on beyond all justification.
16. You start to glimpse a stranger in your rearview mirror.
17. The stranger suddenly looks like a bum.
18. You look at her with clinical curiosity.
19. Hmmm.
20. Obviously into the chronic stages.
21. Definitely not employable.
22. We unemployed have a social stigma.
    The rape victim has a social stigma.
    We share a similar social stigma.
23. The public is driven by the work ethic.
    Much of the public feels that you've somehow "asked for it."
    They feel that you've secretly wanted to lose your job.
    They feel that you've "flirted" with unemployment through your
       attitude.
    They feel you were probably dressed in a way to invite it.
    You may have left the vest unbuttoned on your three-piece suit.
    The public may feel this consciously.
    The public may feel this subconsciously.

Ear Quirk

BARBARA CARTER

1. I am a fading female.
   My bait has grown old.
   Why should I worry about the beauty of my ears?
2. This is the reason.
   People laughed at my ears.
   These people included my mother.
   My ears were extra large.
   This happened when I was a child.
3. Their laughter was cruel.
   Their laughter rang in my ears.
   Their laughter changed me.
   I had been a happy child.
   I had been a carefree child.
   I became withdrawn.
   I became self-conscious.
4. The peels of laughter started a pattern of behavior.
   The behavior was self-centered.
   The behavior was bizarre.
   The behavior was the result of attempts to do something.

338

The attempts were senseless.
I tried to keep my "aliens" hidden from human eyes.

5. I was not aware of being physically deformed.
Then something happened in my fourth year.
My mother decided that my hair looked awful.
My hair was stringy.

6. She plaited my hair.
She pinned the two braids together.
She pinned them on the crown of my head.
She stepped back to view her handiwork.

7. Suddenly mama's laughter filled my ears.
She said something.
She spoke in a gasping voice.
"My lord, youngun, you look like you are fixin' to fly."

8. Tears streamed down her cheeks.
They were tears of laughter.
She unplaited my hair.
She rearranged my hair.
She did this in an attempt to cover my ears.

9. My sense of deformity became an obsession.
It became an obsession that day.

10. I made furtive comparisons.
I realized something.
The realization was sad.
Mine were the most outstanding ears in the family.

11. I then began a pattern of doing something.
I kept my hair pulled tight.
I kept my hair over my ears.
I used my hands to do this.

12. I could practice this hands-on defense at home.
But I was forced to surrender my hands to a pencil.
I was forced to surrender my first day of school.

13. I kept my head bent down.
My head was stringy.
I went through grammar school in this way.

14. Other little girls had great curls.
These were Shirley Temple curls.
My ears were bigger than the curls.

15. Everyone stared at my alien ears.
I knew this.
They were too timid to say anything.

16. There was some comfort in cold weather.
I could wear ear muffs.

In warm weather my ears were bare.
I felt naked.
I felt ashamed.

17. I requested plastic surgery.
My parents laughed at the request.
Then I became an expert at ear flattening.

18. I bought head bands.
I bought silk scarves.
I bought Ear Glue.
Ear Glue was a phony miracle product.

19. I avoided swimming.
I avoided spirited runs along the beach.
I avoided motorcycle riding.
I avoided any other hair-raising activity.
Such an activity would reveal my aliens.

20. There was the fear of being rejected by boys.
This was the greatest of all my fears.

21. I moved up through my teenage years.
I had my fair share of dates.
No boy ever whispered sweet nothings in my ears.
I would not allow this.

22. What if he ever saw the true dimensions of my ears?
He would turn.
He would run.
I was certain of this.

23. One fellow did accept me.
He accepted me in spite of my bizarre behavior.
He accepted my huge ears.
He accepted all.

24. Soon I was married.
I wore a pair of ear muffs.
The ear muffs were fragrant.
The ear muffs were made out of flowers.

25. My first child was born.
I scrutinized his ears.
I did this anxiously.
I did this before I counted his fingers and toes.

26. My daughter was born a few years later.
I repeated the examination.

27. I was relieved.
My alien trait had not dominated.
Both infants were born with normal ears.

28. My children grew.
I listened to their laughter.

Their laughter was musical.
I could hear them speak their first words.
I came to ask myself something.
How could I be so ashamed of two healthy parts of my body?
These parts received such marvelous sounds of life.

29. It was just vanity.
I decided this.

30. I had to look beyond appearances, especially my own.

31. Now my ears are just as big as they ever were.

32. I do my best to disguise their great size.
I disguise them with careful hair fashioning.
I admit this.

33. But my big ears are really a small thing.
They are too small for me to worry about anymore.

34. They are not aliens.
They are a part of me.
I have learned to accept them.
I have tried to cast aside my vanity.

Paragraphs and Essays

How Teachers Make Children Hate Reading

JOHN HOLT

[1] From the very beginning of school we make books and reading a constant source of possible failure and public humiliation. When children are little we make them read aloud, before the teacher and other children, so that we can be sure that they "know" all the words they are reading. This means that when they don't know a word, they are going to make a mistake, right in front of everyone. Instantly they are made to realize that they have done something wrong. Perhaps some of the other children will begin to wave their hands and say, "Ooooh! O-o-o-oh!" Perhaps they will just giggle, or nudge each other, or make a face. Perhaps the teacher will say, "Are you sure?" or ask someone else what he things. Or perhaps, if the teacher is kindly, she will just smile a sweet, sad smile—often one of the most painful punishments a child can suffer in school. In any case, the child who has made the mistake knows he has made it, and feels foolish, stupid, and ashamed, just as any of us would in his shoes.

[2] Before long many children associate books and reading with mistakes, real or feared, and penalties and humiliation. This may not

seem sensible, but it is natural. Mark Twain once said that a cat that sat on a hot stove would never sit on one again—but it would never sit on a cold one either. As true of children as of cats. If they, so to speak, sit on a hot book a few times, if books cause them humiliation and pain, they are likely to decide that the safest thing to do is to leave all books alone.

Out of Work

JAN HALVORSEN

[1] Layoffs, unemployment and recession have always affected Walter Cronkite's tone of voice and the editorial page. And maybe they affected a neighborhood business or a friend's uncle. But these terms have always been just words, affecting someone else's world, like a passing ambulance. At least they were until a few weeks ago, when the ambulance came for me.

[2] Even as I sat staring blankly at my supervisor, hearing, "I've got bad news: we're going to have to let you go," it all still seemed no more applicable to my daily life than a "60 Minutes" exposé. I kept waiting for the alternative—"but you can come back after a couple of months," or "you could take a salary cut, a different position," or even, "April fool." But none of these came. This was final. There was no mistake and no alternative.

[3] You find yourself going back over it in your idle moments. There wasn't so much as a "Thank you" for the long nights working alone, the "Sure, no problem, I'll have it tomorrow," the "Let me know if I can help," the "I just went ahead and did it this weekend" and, especially, for the "You forgot to tell me it changed? Oh, that's all right, I'll just do it over. No big deal."

[4] No big deal. How it all echoes through your evenings and awakens you in the morning. The mornings are probably the worst—waking up with the habitual jar, for the first two weeks, thinking, "I'm late!" Late for what? The dull ache in your lower stomach reminds you: late for nothing.

[5] Again, you face the terms. "Loss of self-esteem and security, fear of the future, stress, depression." You wonder dully if eating a dozen chocolate-chip cookies, wearing a bathrobe until 4, combing your hair at 5, cleaning behind the stove (twice) and crying in an employment-agency parking lot qualify as symptoms of stress or maybe loss of self-esteem. Fighting with your spouse/boyfriend? Aha—tension in personal relationships.

[6] The loss of a job is rejection, resulting in the same hurt feelings

as if a friend had told you to "bug off." Only this "friend" filled up 40 to 60 (or more) hours of your week. Constant references to the staff as "family" only accentuate the feeling of desertion and deception. You picture yourself going home to your parents or spouse and then being informed, "Your services as our daughter/my wife are no longer required. Pick up your baby pictures as you leave."

[7] Each new affirmation of unemployment renews the pain: the first trip to the employment agency, the first friend you tell, the first interview and, most dreaded of all, the first trip to the unemployment office.

[8] Standing in line at the unemployment office makes you feel very much the same as you did the first time you ever flunked a class or a test—as if you had a big red "F" for "Failure" printed across your forehead. I fantasize myself standing at the end of the line in a crisp and efficient blue suit, chin up, neat and straight as a corporate executive. As I move down the line I start to come unglued and a half hour later, when I finally reach the desk clerk, I am slouching and sallow in torn jeans, tennis shoes and a jacket from the Salvation Army, carrying my worldly belongings in a shopping bag and unable to speak.

[9] You do eventually become accustomed to being unemployed, in the way you might accept a bad limp. And you gradually quit beating yourself for not having been somehow indispensable—or for not having become an accountant. You tire of straining your memory for possible infractions. You recover some of the confidence that always told you how good you were at your job and accept what the supervisor said: "This doesn't reflect on your job performance; sales are down 30 per cent this month."

[10] But each time you recover that hallowed self-esteem, you renew a fight to maintain it. Each time you go to a job interview and give them your best and they hire someone else, you go another round with yourself and your self-esteem. Your unemployment seems to drag on beyond all justification. You start to glimpse a stranger in your rearview mirror. The stranger suddenly looks like a bum. You look at her with clinical curiosity. Hmmm. Obviously into the chronic stages. Definitely not employable.

[11] We unemployed share a social stigma similar to that of the rape victim. Whether consciously or subconsciously, much of the work-ethic–driven public feels that you've somehow "asked for it," secretly wanted to lose your job and "flirted" with unemployment through your attitude—probably dressed in a way to invite it (left the vest unbuttoned on your three-piece suit).

[12] But the worst of it isn't society's work-ethic morality; it's your own, which you never knew you had. You find out how much self-

satisfaction was gained from even the most simple work-related task: a well-worded letter, a well-handled phone call—even a clean file. Being useful to yourself isn't enough.

[13] But then almost everyone has heard about the need to be a useful member of society. What you didn't know about was the loneliness. You've spent your life almost constantly surrounded by people, in classes, in dorms and at work. To suddenly find yourself with only your cat to talk to all day distorts your sense of reality. You begin to worry that flights of fancy might become one way.

[14] But you always were, and still are, stronger than that. You maintain balance and perspective, mainly through resorting frequently to sarcasm and irreverence. Although something going wrong in any aspect of your life now seems to push you into temporary despair much more easily than before, you have some very important things to hang on to—people who care, your sense of humor, your talents, your cat and your hopes.

[15] And beyond that, you've gained something—a little more knowledge and a lot more compassion. You've learned the value of the routine you scorned and the importance of the job you took for granted. But most of all, you've learned what a "7.6 per cent unemployment rate" really means.

Ear Quirk

BARBARA CARTER

[1] Why should I, a fading female whose bait has grown old, worry about the beauty of my ears? Because when I was a child, people—including my mother—laughed at my extra-large ears. Their cruel laughter rang in my ears and changed a happy, carefree child into a withdrawn and self-conscious person. The critical peals of laughter also started a pattern of bizarre and self-centered behavior that was the result of senseless attempts to keep my "aliens" hidden from human eyes.

[2] I was not aware of being physically deformed until my fourth year when my mother decided that my stringy hair looked awful. She plaited my hair, pinned the two braids together upon the crown of my head, and stepped back to view her handiwork. Suddenly mama's laughter filled my ears and she said with a gasping voice, "My lord, youngun, you look like you are fixin' to fly." Tears of laughter streamed down her cheeks as she unplaited and rearranged my hair in an effort to cover up my ears. That day my sense of deformity became an obsession. After making furtive comparisons, I sadly realized that mine were the most outstanding ears in the family. I then began a pattern of

using my hands to keep my hair pulled tight over my ears. I could practice this hands-on defense at home, but my first day of school I was forced to surrender my hands to a pencil.

[3] I went through grammar school with my stringy head bent down. While other little girls had great Shirley Temple curls, my ears were bigger than the curls. I knew that everyone was staring at my alien ears, though they were too timid to say anything. There was some comfort in cold weather—I could wear ear muffs—but in warm weather my ears went bare and I felt naked and ashamed.

[4] When my parents laughed at my request for plastic surgery, I became an expert at ear flattening. I bought head bands, silk scarves, and some phony miracle product called Ear Glue. I avoided swimming, spirited runs along the beach, motorcycle riding, and any other hair-raising activity that would reveal my aliens. Of all my fears, though, the greatest was the fear of being rejected by boys. As I moved up through my teenage years I had my fair share of dates, but I never once allowed a boy to whisper sweet nothings in my ear. I was certain he would turn and run if he ever saw their true dimensions. In spite of my bizarre behavior, one fellow did accept me—huge ears and all. I was married, wearing a pair of fragrant ear muffs made out of flowers.

[5] When my first child was born I anxiously scrutinized his ear size before I counted his fingers and toes. I repeated the examination a few years later when my daughter was born. To my relief, I discovered that my alien trait had not dominated and both infants were born with normal ears. As my children grew and I listened to their musical laughter and could hear them speak their first words, I came to ask myself how I could be so ashamed of two healthy parts of my body that received such marvelous sounds of life. It was just vanity, I decided. I had to look beyond appearances, especially my own.

[6] Now my ears are just as big as they ever were. And I admit I do my best to disguise their size with careful hair fashioning. But my big ears are really too small a thing for me to worry about anymore. They are not aliens, but a part of me that I have learned to accept as I have tried to cast aside my vanity.

Writing Suggestions

Although some of the topics below call attention to causes and others to effects, keep in mind that the two are closely related and not always easily separated.

1. Why teenagers run away from home.
2. The effect of a parent, teacher, or friend on your life.

3. Why students drop out of high school or college.
4. The effects of peer pressure.
5. Why people keep pets.
6. The effects of poverty on an individual.
7. Why people smoke cigarettes.
8. The effects of smoking.
9. Why you selected your major.
10. The effects of computers on our everyday lives.
11. Why gossip magazines are so popular.
12. The effect of a book or movie on your life.
13. Why one college course is more enjoyable than another.
14. The effects of growing up in front of the television set.
15. Why many people don't bother to vote in local elections.
16. The effects of too much drinking.
17. Why people drink alcohol.
18. The effects of cramming before an exam.
19. Why some students cheat.
20. The effects of music on an individual.

CHAPTER 19

Argument

The primary aim of most of the essays considered so far has been to inform the reader, often in an entertaining way. However, an argument aims to do more than inform and entertain: it attempts to convince the reader that a certain point of view is valid. In an argument, information is not an end in itself, but a means to defend or attack an attitude or proposition.

A convincing argument must be supported with sound evidence that is organized clearly and logically. This evidence is often arranged in a pattern of cause and effect, as seen in "Taking America to the Cleaners" (in Chapter 9) and in Gore Vidal's "Drugs" (in this chapter). Both Vidal's essay and "Video Mania" (a student essay) share two other characteristics of arguments: a statement of the writer's credentials and some recognition of opposing points of view. "The First Step to the Cemetery" demonstrates how an essay can be organized by building one argument on top of another. And the final exercise in this chapter, "The Reporter," offers a very practical form of argument—the job application.

Working out the exercises in this chapter should give you ideas on how to select and arrange support for your own arguments. For suggestions on how to probe an argument topic, review the Discovery section at the end of Chapter 5.

Exercises

*The First Step to the Cemetery**

KENNETH BERNARD

There are no sets in this exercise. You will need to group the sentences logically before combining them.

1. In America you are primarily valued not for your good deeds.
2. You are primarily valued not for your good character.
3. You are valued for money.
4. This is the money that you command.
5. The more money you have, the better you are treated.
6. Everyone treats you better.
7. Your local cop treats you better.
8. Your congressman treats you better.
9. You may doubt this.
10. If so, go to any store.
11. Go to any social agency.
12. Go, for example, to any urban clinic.
13. See what it is like to be old.
14. See what it is like to be sick.
15. See what it is like to be poor.
16. There is a living hell.
17. You do not get kindness.
18. You do not get respect.
19. You do not get service.
20. You may take a step toward that condition.
21. You may take a step voluntarily.
22. To do this you have to be blind.
23. To do this you have to be mad.
24. Your ability to command money decreases.
25. At the same time your stature as a human being decreases.
26. You are less important to doctors.
27. You are less important than the forms.
28. They must process these forms.
29. They do this to get money for their services.
30. To landlords, you are a barrier to high rents.
31. Retirees band together in colonies.

* This exercise has been adapted from the third paragraph of Bernard's essay in the Paragraph and Essays section of this chapter.

32. Retirees band together in clubs.
33. Retirees band together in homes.
34. Retirees band together in hospitals.
35. It is small wonder that they band together.
36. They want to belong.
37. They can do so only with their own kind.
38. Everywhere else, their money will be taken.
39. Everywhere else they will be shut out.

Drugs

GORE VIDAL

1. There is drug addiction in the United States.
   It is possible to stop most of it.
   It can be stopped within a very short time.
2. Simply make all drugs available.
   Sell them at cost.
3. Label each drug.
   Put a precise description on it.
   Describe the effect—good and bad.
   It will have this effect on the taker.
4. This will require heroic honesty.
5. Don't say that marijuana is addictive.
   Don't say that marijuana is dangerous.
   It is neither.
   Millions of people know this.
   This is unlike "speed."
   Speed kills most unpleasantly.
   This is also unlike heroin.
   Heroin is addictive.
   Heroin is difficult to kick.
6. This is for the record.
   I have tried—once—almost every drug.
   I have liked none.
   This disproves the popular Fu Manchu theory.
   According to this theory a single whiff of opium will enslave the
       mind.
7. The United States was the creation of men.
   What did these men believe?
   Each man has a right.
   He can do what he wants with his own life.
   He can do this under one condition.
   He must not interfere with his neighbor's pursuit of happiness.

(That his neighbor's pursuit of happiness is persecuting others does confuse matters a bit.)
It might be good for our citizens to recall this.

8. This is a startling notion.
The current generation of Americans finds this startling.

9. There is a system of public education.
The current generation reflects this system.
This system has made the Bill of Rights, literally, unacceptable.
It is unacceptable to a majority of high school graduates.
These graduates now form a "silent majority."
The "silent majority" is a phrase.
Richard Nixon took the phrase from Homer.
Richard Nixon is an underestimated wit.
Homer used the phrase to describe the dead.

10. Now one can hear the warning rumble again.
If everyone is allowed to take drugs everyone will.
The GNP will decrease.
The Commies will stop us from making everyone free.
We shall end up a race of zombies.
We will passively murmur "groovie" to one another.

11. Alarming thought.

12. Yet will a reasonably sane person become a drug addict if he knows in advance what addiction is like?
It seems most unlikely.

13. Is everyone reasonably sane?

14. No.

15. Some people will always become drug addicts.
Similarly, some people will always become alcoholics.
It is just too bad.

16. However, every man has the power to kill himself.
Every man should have the legal right also.
He can do this if he chooses.

17. But most men don't.
They won't become mainliners either.

18. People like things.
People think they might enjoy things.
Forbidding these things only makes them want those things all the more.

19. This is a psychological insight.
It is, for some mysterious reason, perennially denied our governors.

20. Our country has always existed in a kind of time vacuum.
This is a lucky thing for the American moralist.
We have no public memory of anything.
Anything happened before last Tuesday.

21. What happened during the years alcohol was forbidden to people?
    No one in Washington today recalls this.
    Alcohol was forbidden by Congress.
    Congress thought it had a divine mission.
    Its mission was to stamp out Demon Rum.
    In the process it launched the greatest crime wave in the country's history.
    It caused thousands of deaths from bad alcohol.
    It created a general (and persisting) contempt for the laws of the United States.
    The contempt was among the citizenry.
22. The same thing is happening today.
    There have been past attempts at prohibition, not to mention repression.
    The government has learned nothing from these attempts.
23. Last year the supply of Mexican marijuana was slightly curtailed by the Feds.
    The pushers got the kids hooked on heroin.
    Deaths increased dramatically.
    Deaths increased particularly in New York.
24. Whose fault?
25. Evil men like the Mafiosi?
26. Permissive Dr. Spock?
27. Wild-eyed Dr. Leary?
28. No.
29. Who was responsible for those deaths?
    The Government of the United States.
30. There is a bureaucratic machine.
    It has a vested interest in playing cops and robbers.
31. The Bureau of Narcotics wants strong laws.
    The Mafia wants strong laws.
    They want laws against the sale of drugs.
    They want laws against the use of drugs.
    There is a reason for this.
    If drugs are sold at cost there would be no money in it for anyone.
32. What if there was no money in it for the Mafia?
    There would be no friendly playground pushers.
    Addicts would not commit crimes to pay for the next fix.
33. What if there was no money in it?
    Finally, the Bureau of Narcotics would wither away.
    They are not about to do this without a struggle.
34. Will anything sensible be done?
    Of course not.
    The American people are devoted to the idea of sin.

351

They are devoted to the idea of the punishment of sin.
They are just as devoted to making money.
Fighting drugs is nearly as big a business as pushing drugs.
35. The combination of sin and money is irresistible.
It is particularly irresistible to the professional politician.
The situation, therefore, will only grow worse.

Video-Mania

JANICE WATERS

1. Video games have become increasingly popular.
They are popular in arcades.
They are popular in the average American home.
2. People are enjoying hours of entertainment.
These are people of all ages.
These are people from all walks of life.
These people feed their time into the machines.
These people feed their quarters into the machines.
The machines flash.
The machines beep.
3. What gives Pac Man, Centipede, and a multitude of other popular games their appeal?
Their appeal is magnetic.
They appeal to millions of players.
Many skeptics have asked this question.
Many prospective arcade owners have asked this question.
4. I am a video player myself.
There are many answers to that question.
I believe this.
Three reasons are outstanding.
There is the rising cost of entertainment.
There are rapid advancements.
These advancements have been made in computer technology.
There is the psychological effect.
The games have this effect on their players.
5. There are traditional forms of entertainment.
One should consider the rising costs of these forms.
These costs are rising in a society being devoured by inflation.
One should consider the costs before an attack is launched.
This is a full-scale attack.
The attack is launched against young video players.
The players are "throwing away" their quarters.

6. Eighteen holes of miniature golf will cost the player at least two dollars.
   Ten frames of bowling will cost the player at least two dollars.
   One movie costs four bucks.
7. A video player can get at least eight games for two dollars.
   He gets better at the game.
   Then he can play longer.
8. Compare that record with the game of miniature golf.
   One becomes better in miniature golf.
   He then gets to play a shorter amount of time.
9. The games are less expensive than other forms of entertainment.
   The games are also more in tune with the issues of the day.
   These issues are important.
10. Science has had much influence on our lives today.
    People are beginning to appreciate this.
    These people have never been interested in science.
11. Commercial shuttles in space are realities.
    Colonies in space are realities.
    These realities are exciting.
    These realities would have been considered impossible dreams.
    They would have been considered dreams thirty years ago.
12. Computers are no longer scientific fancies.
    Solar power is no longer a scientific fancy.
    Ordinary families can afford to use them.
13. Rapid advancements have been made in electronics.
    Rapid advancements have been made in computer technology.
    Business may be conducted faster than ever.
14. Video games are the products of advanced technology.
    Video games are the products of uncontrolled imagination.
    Video games have brought today's youth closer than ever to the exciting world of science.
    Video games involve youths in dramatic battle.
    Video games involve youths in new concepts of computer science.
    These concepts are sophisticated.
15. There are new home video sets.
    These sets have superior graphics.
    These sets have a wider variety of games than ever before.
16. There are cartridges.
    They teach gamers how to program computers.
17. It is exciting to be involved with the ideas of the day.
    These ideas are up to date.
    Video games help provide people with the opportunity to be involved.

18. Video games help people to understand modern technology.
    Video games help people to become involved with modern technology.
    Video games also provide an outlet.
    They are an outlet for the emotions.
    They are an outlet for the ego.
19. A man might get frustrated with his boss.
    He can go to the arcade.
    He can go after work.
    He can destroy enemy cruisers.
    He can do this rather than drown his anxieties in liquor.
20. Some people feel that they are not capable of excelling at anything.
    The games provide challenges for these people.
    These challenges are easily mastered.
    They are mastered with patience.
    They are mastered with practice.
21. A person has broken his own record.
    A person has broken the record of someone else.
    Knowing this gives a person a good feeling.
22. I have set forth reasons.
    These are reasons for the popularity of video games.
    These reasons are valid.
    I know this.
    I enjoy playing video games.
23. There are probably many skeptics.
    The skeptics have reasons for putting down the games.
    Their reasons may be just as valid as mine.
    Their reasons are less convincing.

The following is not an ordinary building exercise. You are to write two letters using the information in this exercise. Your first letter is to C. J. McCoy, Editor-in-Chief of *The Gazette*, a smalltown newspaper. Using any information in the exercise that you think is relevant, compose a letter in which you apply for the position of reporter with *The Gazette*. You should establish your credentials, identify your strengths and career goals, and let the editor know just why he should hire you. Your second letter is to a close friend. Here, write an informal account of your experiences as a reporter for the college paper.

The Reporter

1. I have been working as a reporter for our college newspaper.
2. I have been doing this since September of last year.
3. The paper is called *The Inkwell*.
4. Most students refer to it as *The Stinkwell*.
5. Over 3,000 copies are distributed weekly.
6. The paper is free.
7. That is why most students read it.
8. They enjoy catching all the typographical errors.
9. I interviewed the college president.
10. I did this my first week on the job.
11. We chatted for an hour.
12. He was evasive.
13. My tape recorder wasn't turned on.
14. I discovered this later.
15. I hadn't bothered to take any notes.
16. Just as I was leaving he did tell me one thing.
17. He said that the bookstore manager had been fired for overcharging the students.
18. I wrote my story and turned it in.
19. It was put on the front page of the next issue.
20. Most of the work I do at the paper is tedious.
21. I run the printing press.
22. I help distribute the papers.
23. I keep track of our expenses.
24. Our advisor says that this is all useful experience.
25. I took a journalism course with Dr. Green.
26. He is an eccentric little guy.
27. He wears a bowler hat.
28. He wears a pin-striped suit.
29. He looks like some British lawyer.
30. He gave us some pretty absurd assignments.
31. We interviewed children at a kindergarten.
32. We wrote descriptions of traffic accidents.
33. I don't know if he taught me much about reporting.
34. He did help me become a better writer.
35. I was the only student in the class to get a final grade of A.
36. I'll be graduating this month with a B.A. in English.
37. I've managed to end up with an overall average of B −.
38. I've averaged B + in my English courses.
39. I've done this despite a lot of partying.

40. I really don't see how most of my courses related to journalism.
41. The exception may be the two advanced composition courses.
42. I took those with Dr. Crain.
43. I hope someday to become an investigative journalist.
44. In the meantime I'll try to pick up some experience.
45. I think I'll try a local rag like *The Gazette*.
46. They are advertising for a reporter.
47. I saw the ad in the want ads of *The Morning News*.
48. I have a pretty impressive-looking portfolio.
49. There are several sports articles in there.
50. There are interviews with teachers and students as well as the ones with the president and the kindergarten kids.
51. There is even a gossip column.
52. I've been writing that for the past four months.
53. I enjoyed covering sports.
54. I got to travel in a van with the cheerleaders.
55. The games were never very exciting.
57. We always lost.
58. I managed to make them sound more exciting than they actually were.
59. Our newspaper won a journalism award from the Board of Regents.
60. They mentioned my article on vandalism.
61. They said it was an example of good undergraduate journalism.
62. I don't know if that's a compliment or not.
63. I'm flat broke right now.
64. I hope to get a job soon.
65. If I don't get a job with *The Gazette,* I might just hitch-hike across the country to see my cousin.
66. If I do, I'll stop by to see you along the way.
67. I sure hope I get the job though.
68. I know I can be a good reporter if somebody will just give me the chance.

Paragraphs and Essays

The First Step to the Cemetery

KENNETH BERNARD

[1] The prevailing vision of the good life in America has for some time included early retirement. Numerous voices speak in its behalf, from insurance companies to unions to government agencies. Quit while

you're ahead, still healthy and young enough to enjoy a generous spread of the sunset years. Not only should you enjoy the fruit of your labors in this most bountiful of countries, say the many voices, but you should also give the young folk their chance to move up by exiting gracefully. There are, you are told, numerous benefits—tax, medical, recreational, psychological. It is not only foolish to overlook the opportunity; it is downright un-American. So why not do it? Why not? Because it will probably be the worst decision you have ever made. Here's why.

[2] To begin, it is an immediate, and usually irrevocable, step into second-class citizenship. Once retired, you are one with blacks, Hispanics, the handicapped, homosexuals, jailbirds, the insane, the retarded, children and women: America's Third World hordes. America doesn't like old people, and retired people are old people, whether they are 45, 55 or 65. Old people clutter up the landscape. Their families don't want them. Their communities don't want them. They are a nightmare vision of everyone's future. They are of interest mainly to doctors and hospitals, real-estate brokers and travel agents—but not as people, rather as bodies from whom some final payments can still be exacted.

[3] In America you are primarily valued not for your good deeds or your good character. You are valued for the money you command. The more money you have, the better you are treated by everyone from your local cop to your congressman. If you doubt this, go to any store or social agency. Go, for example, to any urban clinic and see what it is like to be old, sick and poor. There is a living hell. You get neither kindness nor respect nor service. To voluntarily take a step toward that condition you have to be either blind or mad. For as your ability to command money decreases, so too does your stature as a human being. To doctors, you are less important than the forms they must process to get money for their services. To landlords, you are a barrier to high rents. Small wonder that retirees band together in colonies, in clubs, homes, and hospitals. They want to belong, and they can do so only with their own kind. Everywhere else, their money will be taken, but they will be shut out.

[4] What are these colonies like? To be sure, just as there are decent people who respect old people, so too there are homes, hospitals and communities that are genuinely humanitarian, that perform genuine functions. But how many? Our public knowledge of old-age homes is that they are less clean and only slightly less efficient than slaughterhouses, dismal halfway houses to the grave: turnover is profit.

[5] In some societies where people live to be very old, it is observable that they, whatever their age, have useful, needed work to perform. In America, activities for old people are manufactured. People get degrees in how to occupy old people with busy work. But this has nothing to do with life; it is all meaningless filler. These people are out of it. Al-

though everyone knows it, everyone lies about it and society conspires to keep them there. It is a not so genteel form of genocide. The old people know it, too; and knowing it (and often being very gracious), they cooperate: they begin to die in spirit and then bodily. And no amount of shuffleboard, creative writing, canasta or sightseeing can hide the unpleasant truth. Society's message is: spend money, but stay out of the way, and make no demands.

[6] Old people are besieged by indifference, loneliness and uselessness. They are also physically assaulted by toughs and criminals. They are, understandably, fearful. Often they are imprisoned in their own homes. Yes, the perpetrators are few in number, but the assaults could not take place without a climate of sentiment, a cast of mind, that allowed for them. Our society fears the natural extinction of life so much that it behaves grotesquely. After all, with luck we will all grow old someday. Thus the mistreatment of the old is a form of self-mutilation. Nevertheless, the cruelty persists.

[7] Faced with such barbarism, why join the legions of the doomed and damned? All your life you maintain a certain schedule. You break that routine once or twice a year. You go on this way 30 or 40 years. Your heart, your bowels, your mind keep time with it. And then you stop. You leave your pleasures, your sorrows, your family, everything. You might as well run full speed into a brick wall. No body or mind was meant to stop like that. Things have to go wrong—your heart, your bowels, your mind. It is the first giant step to the cemetery. Why take it? What's the percentage? Why, indeed, do it younger and younger when people are living to be older and older? Would you invest money with the same logic? Does it make any sense? Perhaps it would if there were alternatives (for example, working less) but there aren't any alternatives for most of us. It's out, totally out, out all the way, and don't try to get back in.

[8] In our society, life is useful work and continuing income. Even what seems like a large retirement income is to be regarded with deep suspicion in this day of inflation. Life and respect are work and money. It shouldn't be so, but it is.

[9] There is something suicidal in retirement, just as there is something suicidal in society's callousness toward the old. So forget the young. You worked to get what you have. Keep it; enjoy it. They are young and strong; let them struggle. It isn't your problem; you shouldn't take the rap. Don't leave your job one minute before you have to—even if you hate it—unless you can't get out of bed. You have something to give. It isn't true that to be old is to be incompetent. Fight. Don't quit. Elect your own to legislative office. Band together: the old-age party, the life party. Don't let them convince you that the "golden years" await

you. It's a lie. No one should go down without a struggle. Kick. Scream. Be heard all the way to Washington. You have nothing to lose but your dignity and your life.

Drugs

GORE VIDAL

[1] It is possible to stop most drug addiction in the United States within a very short time. Simply make all drugs available and sell them at cost. Label each drug with a precise description of what effect—good and bad—the drug will have on the taker. This will require heroic honesty. Don't say that marijuana is addictive or dangerous when it is neither, as millions of people know—unlike "speed," which kills most unpleasantly, or heroin, which is addictive and difficult to kick.

[2] For the record, I have tried—once—almost every drug and liked none, disproving the popular Fu Manchu theory that a single whiff of opium will enslave the mind. Nevertheless many drugs are bad for certain people to take and they should be told why in a sensible way.

[3] Along with exhortation and warning, it might be good for our citizens to recall (or learn for the first time) that the United States was the creation of men who believed that each man has the right to do what he wants with his own life as long as he does not interfere with his neighbor's pursuit of happiness (that his neighbor's idea of happiness is persecuting others does confuse matters a bit).

[4] This is a startling notion to the current generation of Americans. They reflect a system of public education which has made the Bill of Rights, literally, unacceptable to a majority of high school graduates (see the annual Purdue reports) who now form the "silent majority"—a phrase which that underestimated wit Richard Nixon took from Homer who used it to describe the dead.

[5] Now one can hear the warning rumble begin: if everyone is allowed to take drugs everyone will and the GNP will decrease, the Commies will stop us from making everyone free, and we shall end up a race of Zombies, passively murmuring "groovie" to one another. Alarming thought. Yet it seems most unlikely that any reasonably sane person will become a drug addict if he knows in advance what addiction is going to be like.

[6] Is everyone reasonably sane? No. Some people will always become drug addicts just as some people will always become alcoholics, and it is just too bad. Every man, however, has the power (and should have the legal right) to kill himself if he chooses. But since most men

don't, they won't be mainliners either. Nevertheless, forbidding people things they like or think they might enjoy only makes them want those things all the more. This psychological insight is, for some mysterious reason, perennially denied our governors.

[7] It is a lucky thing for the American moralists that our country has always existed in a kind of time-vacuum: we have no public memory of anything that happened before last Tuesday. No one in Washington today recalls what happened during the years alcohol was forbidden to the people by a Congress that thought it had a divine mission to stamp out Demon Rum—launching, in the process, the greatest crime wave in the country's history, causing thousands of deaths from bad alcohol, and creating a general (and persisting) contempt among the citizenry for the laws of the United States.

[8] The same thing is happening today. But the government has learned nothing from past attempts at prohibition, not to mention repression.

[9] Last year when the supply of Mexican marijuana was slightly curtailed by the Feds, the pushers got the kids hooked on heroin and deaths increased dramatically, particularly in New York. Whose fault? Evil men like the Mafiosi? Permissive Dr. Spock? Wild-eyed Dr. Leary? No.

[10] The Government of the United States was responsible for those deaths. The bureaucratic machine has a vested interest in playing cops and robbers. Both the Bureau of Narcotics and the Mafia want strong laws against the sale and use of drugs because if drugs are sold at cost there would be no money in it for anyone.

[11] If there was no money in it for the Mafia, there would be no friendly playground pushers, and addicts would not commit crimes to pay for the next fix. Finally, if there was no money in it, the Bureau of Narcotics would wither away, something they are not about to do without a struggle.

[12] Will anything sensible be done? Of course not. The American people are as devoted to the idea of sin and its punishment as they are to making money—and fighting drugs is nearly as big a business as pushing them. Since the combination of sin and money is irresistible (particularly to the professional politician), the situation will only grow worse.

Video-Mania

JANICE WATERS

[1] Video games have become increasingly popular in both arcades and the average American home. People of all ages and from all walks

of life are enjoying hours of entertainment by feeding their time and quarters into these flashing, beeping machines. Many skeptics as well as prospective arcade owners have asked what it is that gives Pac Man, Centipede, and a multitude of other popular games their magnetic appeal to millions of players. As a video player myself, I believe there are many answers to that question, but three are outstanding: the rising cost of entertainment, the rapid advancements made in computer and space technology, and the psychological effect the games have on their players.

[2] Before a full-scale attack is launched against young video players for "throwing away" their quarters, one should first consider the rising costs of more traditional forms of entertainment. For instance, eighteen holes of miniature golf or ten frames of bowling will cost the player at least two dollars, and one movie costs four bucks. For just two dollars, a video player can get at least eight games, and the better he gets, the longer he can play. Compare that record with the game of miniature golf, where the better one becomes, the shorter amount of time he gets to play.

[3] Not only are the games less expensive than other forms of entertainment, but they are also more in tune with the important issues of the day. Even those people who have never been interested in science are beginning to appreciate how much science influences our lives today. Commercial shuttles and colonies in space are exciting realities which thirty years ago would have been considered impossible dreams. Computers and solar power are no longer scientific fancies when ordinary families can afford to use them. And with the rapid advancements made in electronics and computer technology, business may be conducted faster than ever. Video games, which are the products of advanced technology and uncontrolled imagination, have brought today's youth closer than ever to the exciting world of science by involving them in realistic battles and sophisticated new concepts in computer science. The new home video games have superior graphics and a wider variety of games than ever before. In fact, there are even cartridges which teach gamers how to program computers. It is exciting to be involved with the most up-to-date ideas of the day, and video games help provide people with the opportunity to be involved.

[4] Besides the fact that they help people to get involved in technology, video games also provide an outlet for the emotions and the ego. If a man gets frustrated with his boss, for example, he can go to the arcade after work to destroy enemy cruisers rather than drown his anxieties in liquor. Also, for those who feel they are not capable of excelling at anything, the games provide challenges which are easily mastered with patience and practice. It gives a person a good feeling to know that he has broken his own record or that of someone else.

[5] I know the reasons for the popularity of video games that I have

set down are reasonable because I enjoy playing these games. I realize that there are probably many skeptics whose reasons for putting down the games are just as valid as my reasons for defending them, but their reasons are quite simply less convincing.

Reporter (first version)

EMILY BONIN

[1] Dear Mr. McCoy:

[2] In response to your recent advertisement in *The Morning News,* I would like to be considered for the position of reporter with *The Gazette.*

[3] From September of last year to the present, I have been working as a reporter for our college newspaper, *The Inkwell.* My portfolio includes several sports articles, profiles of teachers and students, and an exclusive interview with the college president. My award-winning article on campus vandalism was cited by the Board of Regents as a prime example of high-quality undergraduate journalism.

[4] Because our staff is small I have had the opportunity to gain much useful experience in areas other than reporting. For instance, I have run the printing press, helped distribute the papers, and served as business manager.

[5] I have studied journalism under Dr. Green and advanced composition under Dr. Crain. My overall grade average is B−, with a B+ average in my English courses. I will be graduating this month with a B.A. in English and will be available for employment immediately.

[6] Enclosed is my portfolio and a copy of my résumé. I can be reached at the above address until the end of the month. Thank you for considering my application.

[7]   Sincerely,

[8]   Emily Bonin

Reporter (second version)

LINDA MAXWELL

[1] Hi!

[2] Jill, you won't believe this, but I'm a professional now—well, almost. No more Dairy Queen for me. I'm a **reporter.** That's right, like

Brenda Starr. It's just the college newspaper, *The Inkwell,* but it's a start, right? In fact, most students call it *The Stinkwell.* They only read it because it's free and they get a kick out of catching all the typographical errors.

[3] I interviewed the college president my first week on the job. It wasn't exactly investigative journalism. I didn't have much to ask him and he didn't have a lot to say. Not that it mattered, really, since I had forgotten to turn on the tape recorder in the first place. As I was shuffling out of his office he did feed me a tidbit about the bookstore manager being fired for overcharging students. I think he felt sorry for me and thought he'd do me a favor by giving me the scoop. As it turned out, my story was on the front page of the next issue.

[4] Did I ever tell you about Dr. Green? I took a journalism course with him. He's an eccentric little guy who wears a bowler hat and a pin-striped suit—like some funny British lawyer. He gave us some pretty absurd assignments, like interviewing children at a kindergarten and writing descriptions of traffic accidents. Still, I pulled an A in the course.

[5] I'll be out of here in a month: a B.A. with no place to go. Somehow, despite all the partying, I've managed to get a B – GPA. Not bad for a chronic good off.

[6] I'm trying for a job with a local rag, *The Gazette.* I have big ambitions, but I guess I better start on the bottom rung. This newspaper, I assure you, *is* the bottom rung.

[7] I'm flat broke now, so I hope to find some sort of job soon. If not, I'll hitch across the country and stop by to see you. Wish me luck!

[8]   Linda

Writing Suggestions

The following statements may be either defended or attacked in an argument essay:

1. College is wasted on the young.
2. America doesn't like old people.
3. The production and sale of cigarettes should be made illegal.
4. Participation in sports helps develop good character.
5. Americans have become overly dependent on machines.
6. Both parents should assume equal responsibility in raising a child.
7. America is a racist society.
8. Dieting makes you fat.
9. Romantic love is a poor basis for marriage.

10. All forms of government welfare should be abolished.
11. Americans should be required by law to vote.
12. A college education is a guarantee of a good job.
13. All government and military personnel should have the right to strike.
14. Convicted rapists should be punished by castration.
15. College students should have complete freedom to choose their own courses.

Index